THE CENTURIONS

THE CENTURIONS

profiles of the 21 batsmen
who have scored a hundred 100s
– from Grace to Amiss

Patrick Murphy

J M Dent & Sons Ltd
London Melbourne

First published 1983
First published in paperback, with revisions, 1986
© Patrick Murphy 1983

All rights reserved. No part of this publication may
be reproduced, stored in a retrieval system, or transmitted,
in any form or by any means, electronic, mechanical, photocopying,
recording or otherwise, without the prior permission of
J. M. Dent & Sons Ltd.

This book is set in Lasercomp Baskerville by the Alden Press
Printed and bound in Great Britain by
Biddles Ltd, Guildford and King's Lynn
for J. M. Dent & Sons Ltd
Aldine House, 33 Welbeck Street, London W1M 8LX

British Library Cataloguing in Publication Data

Murphy, Patrick, *1947*–
    The centurions: profiles of the 21 batsmen
    who have scored a hundred 100s, from
    Grace to Amiss.——[Rev. ed.]
    1. Cricket——Batting——History   2. Cricket
    players——Biography
    I. Title
    796.35'826'0922   GV927.5.B3

    ISBN 0-460-02475-2

Contents

Acknowledgments *vi*
Introduction *1*

1 **W.G.Grace** *9*
2 **Tom Hayward** *20*
3 **Sir Jack Hobbs** *27*
4 **Philip Mead** *39*
5 **Patsy Hendren** *47*
6 **Frank Woolley** *57*
7 **Herbert Sutcliffe** *67*
8 **Ernest Tyldesley** *75*
9 **Walter Hammond** *82*
10 **Andrew Sandham** *93*
11 **Sir Donald Bradman** *100*
12 **Les Ames** *113*
13 **Sir Leonard Hutton** *121*
14 **Denis Compton** *132*
15 **Tom Graveney** *142*
16 **Colin Cowdrey** *153*
17 **Geoffrey Boycott** *162*
18 **John Edrich** *175*
19 **Glen Turner** *183*
20 **Zaheer Abbas** *193*
21 **Dennis Amiss** *197*

Bibliography *211*
Statistical Appendix *213*
Index *273*

Acknowledgments

A book of this nature cries out for co-operation from not only the survivors among the appropriate batsmen; flesh on the bones is more important than cuttings from newspapers. I would like to thank all the players – both past and present – who gladly assisted me in compiling this book. So many were touchingly kind. Sir Donald Bradman replied by return post to a series of questions I put to him; Percy Fender, blind and frail, received me warmly in his Horsham home; Len Hopwood surmounted the tragedy of losing his brilliant son in his prime to give me his memories of Ernest Tyldesley. And there were many other examples of ready co-operation; men like Alec Bedser, John Edrich, Colin Cowdrey and Alf Gover took time out from their active business lives to answer my questions with courtesy and interest.

Others from the world of cricket were invaluable with introductions to certain players and background information. My special thanks to Bob Willis, A.C.Smith, Leslie Deakins, Jim Cumbes and Cyril Goodway from Warwickshire; to Bert Avery, Gloucestershire's genial scorer; to Ken Turner, the Northants secretary; to Jack Simmons of Lancashire and to Don Oslear, that fine umpire.

My friends in the media were equally helpful with introductions, advice, encouragement and a glass of something cheering when necessary. Special thanks to Don Mosey, Jack Bannister, Alan Lee, Brian Scovell, David Frith, Alan Hughes, Ken Kelly, Peter West, Richard Maddock, Gerald Howat and John Arlott.

AUTHOR'S NOTE

The chapters are arranged in order of achievement, running from Grace in 1895, through to Amiss in 1986. There is one exception – although Edrich preceded Boycott by a matter of a month in the summer of 1977, I feel that Boycott's eminence entitled him to precedence. Knowing John Edrich as I do, I feel sure he would be the last person to cavil at my decision.

Introduction

In 1895, W.G.Grace became the first man to score a hundred centuries in first-class cricket. He was forty-seven years old, and in the eyes of his adoring contemporaries, a phenomenon – only in recent years had the wickets started to play more easily after decades when the bowlers had enjoyed supremacy. The nearest challenger to his dominance was Arthur Shrewsbury, who had scored less than half of Grace's tally of centuries at that stage. The achievement was duly lionised in the hallowed pages of *Wisden* the following year and, amid the eulogies, A.G.Steel ventured to suggest that the feat of scoring a hundred hundreds would never be emulated. The cerebral Mr Steel was an imaginative and successful captain of Cambridge University and England but forecasting cannot be numbered among his many cricketing qualities. Perhaps his statement can be seen both in the context of typically Victorian self-confidence and in the genuine belief that W.G.Grace was a genius. Indeed he was, yet, since 1895, no less that twenty other batsmen have scored a century of centuries.

They have varied in styles, abilities and temperaments, from masterful players like Hobbs, Cowdrey and Hammond to the patient men who knew their own limitations and played accordingly – batsmen such as Mead, Sutcliffe, Boycott and Edrich. Genius is acknowledged in the presence of Bradman, Woolley and Compton. Some were better bad-wicket players than others, some were more unobtrusive, some gloried in offside play. What do they have in common? Surely there can be little similarity between the technique and style of Grace and the way Glenn Turner played fast bowling in the 1980s?

I believe all the twenty-one batsmen have certain consistent strains running through their careers. To score a hundred hundreds, you need to play at least fifteen years: consistency and stamina are vital, luck too.

1

You need the mental strength to come to terms with middle age, slowing reactions and an awareness of what are the 'business shots', the ones that can be played with the minimum of risk and the maximum of effectiveness on all wickets. An ability to adapt is essential – to be ahead of bowling trends. Colin Cowdrey put it succinctly: 'Cricket is evolutionary and it's up to the batsman to build on what he's got and prepare for the future when things might not work out. The proudest thing for me in my career was that I kept surviving.' Survival – a mundane aim, but laudable enough, especially during the period of the 1970s when intimidatory, short-pitched fast bowling was cowing techniques less accomplished than that of Colin Cowdrey.

Cowdrey adapted impressively during the last few years of his career and to the end he played fast bowling more comfortably than anyone. The same applied to Jack Hobbs forty years earlier. At the age of fifty-one, he played the fiery Learie Constantine better than any others in the land – this the batsman who had taken on and mastered a daunting array of bowling talent since 1905. W.G.Grace blocked the shooters as a young man on treacherous wickets, took on the lob bowlers in later years, then mastered the fast bowlers with illegal actions in the 1880s. Don Bradman had to meet the threat of Bodyline in 1932–3, Walter Hammond learned to accumulate on the legside after his majestic cover-driving was starved by niggardly, accurate bowlers. Glenn Turner could hardly get the ball past the inner ring of fielders during his formative years in English county cricket, yet the demands of the limited-overs game plus the desire to enjoy life at the crease led to a consistent stream of thrilling assaults in the latter years of his career.

So the qualities of these twenty-one batsmen are listed – and in many ways, the technique of batting is hardly different today that it was in the glorious twilight of Grace's career at the turn of the century. The ball is propelled in a different area of the batting crease than in previous eras, and its speed is now depressingly uniform, yet batting at the highest level remains orthodox in its principles. Watching Geoffrey Boycott inexorably moving towards another cherished century, his demonstration that batting is a 'sideways-on' art might now seem quaintly old-fashioned to the modern cricketing iconoclasts bred on audacious slogging in limited-overs matches – yet Boycott's method would strike a chord in the men who batted year after year, decade after decade, to reach immortality.

Yet the nagging doubt persists – can these twenty-one batsmen truly be called 'great'? Praise in an age of hyperbole is a debased currency and it is therefore necessary to examine sceptically the claims to greatness of these players. I believe a batsman can only be called 'great' if, for a consistent period, he has dominated a variety of bowlers to the extent that they often cannot bowl at him. Of course, bowlers will have their say and the great batsman will go through lean periods of form and self-examination, yet the litmus paper test must be the ability credited to W.G.Grace by an admiring old sweat of a county bowler: 'I puts the ball where I likes, and 'e puts it where 'e likes.'

On that basis, only eight of the twenty-one can be classified as 'great': Grace, Hobbs, Woolley, Hammond, Bradman, Hutton, Compton and (in his later years) Turner. On their day, their mastery would be so complete that they would garner runs at great speed with the bowlers all but helpless. The other thirteen can be classified as top-class, orthodox, 'percentage' players, admirable, vital to the side yet lacking that crucial ingredient of masterful, consistent brilliance. The type of quality possessed by Ranjitsinjhi, May, J.T.Tyldesley, Vivian Richards, Sobers, Barry Richards and Kanhai . . . men who all scored over sixty centuries, yet for various reasons, never followed the road signposted by Grace.

The story of the centurions is in itself the story of modern cricket. The year 1864 is one of those dates etched in the cranium of any cricket student: the year when bowlers were at last allowed to deliver from over the arm, the year when the remarkable *Wisden Cricketer's Almanack* was first published and when W.G.Grace made his debut in important cricket. The flame of batting eminence has passed down the decades from the crafty old doctor to the Warwickshire batsman, Dennis Amiss, a model of loyalty and consistency for country and club. From Grace to Amiss; from lob bowling to helmets; from the days when the county ground that staged a Test then picked the England team to the time when Dennis Lillee could kick the Pakistan captain up the backside and escape serious punishment. From three-day Tests to one lasting ten days in 1939, through to a Sunday Test Match, these twenty-one batsmen have witnessed the most drastic changes in cricket – socially and economically as well as in the play itself. They span the years from the time of Grace – when games like Smokers v Non-Smokers would be designated first-class status – to the age of Kerry Packer, of night cricket, coloured clothing and stumps being kicked down by disaffected bowlers; from the time when amateurs of the calibre of C.B.Fry and F.S.Jackson would refuse to play for England in Australia for business reasons to the age of limited-overs cricket and the swamping of the English domestic game by overseas players.

The periods in which the twenty-one batsmen played reflect the continuing difficulty of maintaining a balance between bat and ball. In the halcyon years of Grace (1865–90), the bowlers held sway; pitches were often prepared by turning sheep out on them to graze and a number of very fast bowlers were frighteningly erratic on countless dangerous wickets. Grace was approaching the end of his career before a batsman could look forward to a pleasant day in the middle if his captain won the toss. The staggering mastery of Grace on these shocking surfaces was vociferously acknowledged one day in 1868, when he blocked four shooters in a row in the first over. The crowd at Lord's that day rose as one and cheered him loudly.

The phrase 'batsman's paradise' was not used until the turn of the century. By that time, the wickets were truer and faster, the motor was still in its infancy and the heavy roller (whether hand or horse-drawn) moved slowly up and down the square, compressing the substance and binding it together. In the 1900 edition of *Wisden*, Lord Harris bemoaned the new age of batting prosperity; 'I am afraid that not only lengthy scores, but the want of liveliness on these artificial wickets will tend to make the game dull and reduce its popularity.' Not for the first or last time, the autocratic nobleman proved less than sagacious in his assessment – by common consent, the period 1890–1914 was the golden age of cricket. The influence of the amateur, the excellent wickets, the need for bowling variety and great public expectations ushered in a time of thrilling deeds. When *Wisden* remarked with characteristic asperity that C.B.Fry's 258 not out in 1911 was achieved 'with considerable caution', one can only wonder just what was expected of him when his innings lasted just 315 minutes. In those days, batsmen had many opportunities to score quickly; with spin bowlers often opening the attack alongside fast bowlers, the over-rate was always high enough to cause Leonard Hutton apoplexy, and the line of attack was usually of a full length at, or just outside, the off-stump. Wilfred Rhodes always maintained that he bowled with at least two men in the deep and he harvested hundreds of wickets from catches off lofted drives. The dominant theme was one of challenge and the amateurs, with their livelihoods not depending on the game, were far from being the only group pledged to play attractively – the professional batsmen of those days such as J.T.Tyldesley, George Gunn, Woolley, Hobbs and Denton were far removed in attitude from their successors after the Great War.

In the period between the Wars, the wickets became loaded in favour of the batsmen; as they got slower and slower, batsmen developed back-foot excellence to combat fast, short-pitched deliveries. The growing dominance of the bat was recognised in 1930 when it was decreed that play in the England–Australia series would be increased from three to four days and to a finish in the final Test if there had been no previous positive result. That same series saw the flowering of Don Bradman's acquisitive genius and for the rest of that decade, bowlers were the artisans.

It remained thus for a brief period after the Second World War. There were hardly any fast bowlers around in English cricket – they were either aged or fledgling – and the best bowlers were the spinners. Their presence made the game more attractive and batsmen of the calibre of Compton, Edrich, Hutton, Bradman, Weekes, Worrell and Walcott enjoyed themselves hugely. Seam bowlers and off-spinners were soon in the ascendant in England and it lasted through the 1950s to the present day. Batsmen had to learn to lunge forward against a seaming ball that stayed shiny much longer because of modern fertilisers and lush outfields. As the short-leg fielders became more and more prehensile, the batsmen opted for security rather than invention. Wickets became less and less reliable and by the 1980s, sardonic county batsmen were assuring me; 'The reason we don't hook any more is not because the bowling is too quick – it's because the ball is likely to come through on your ankles and get you lbw.' The mastery of overseas players only served to underline the inferiority complex of English batsmen in recent years, at their despair over an endless amount of slow, low wickets.

The dominance of overseas batsmen in recent years prompts the question – why have none of them (apart from Turner and Zaheer) got anywhere near the achievement of a hundred hundreds? Bradman was the only other non-English player to reach the target and he was simply a genius, a man who reached a century on every third visit to the crease. Zaheer has made it because he has played nearly a decade in English county cricket, totalling an average of forty first-class innings per season, while Turner played fifteen years for Worcestershire. Since 1968, when overseas players began to flood the English market, many non-English batsmen have turned in statistical feats of great consistency and it may be that the successors to Sobers, Kanhai and Lloyd will get near to the figure. Certainly it was only a lack of consistent first-class cricket over a period of time that kept several great overseas players out of the elite group of twenty-one men like Macartney, Harvey, Headley, Simpson,

Worrell, Weekes, Gavaskar and Greg Chappell could easily sit in the company of Sandham, Cowdrey and many others who scored a hundred hundreds. They simply did not play or have not played enough innings to get near: the great Gary Sobers made 86 hundreds, but that was buttressed by seven years of county cricket, while the superb Rohan Kanhai spent a decade with Warwickshire while playing his way to 83 centuries. In a normal overseas domestic season, a total of no more than about twenty innings would be available to a batsman – and the figure could be even less during a Test series. Thus Hazare, Hassett, Harvey, Hanif Mohammad, Pollock, Woodfull and Ponsford all have splendid records in terms of hundreds per innings but the lack of continuous cricket prevents them from climbing the upper slopes of statistical greatness.

In assessing the styles of batting since 1864, two major items of legislation have to be considered – the lbw law and the use of the new ball. First the lbw rule. In the Edwardian age, most top-class batsmen were too proud to use their pads when a bat would do the necessary defending – C.B.Fry said sniffily that it would be demeaning to a batsman's craft. The brilliant Victor Trumper batted 89 times for Australia between 1899 and 1912 and he was lbw just five times. His English equivalent, A.C.MacLaren, had 61 innings between 1894 and 1909, yet he was trapped lbw on just three occasions. For a thirty-year period, the supremacy of bat over ball worried cricket's administrators, reaching breaking point in the early 1930s when many batsmen had become masters at padding away deliveries pitching outside the off-stump, even though the ball might have broken in to hit the wicket. As a result, the inswinger, the off-break and the googly were all penalised. In 1935, the law was changed – a batsman could be given out if the ball pitched outside the off-stump and the obstructing leg was in line with the wickets. Most county captains agreed that the revision was long overdue and Herbert Sutcliffe's *cri de coeur* that he would never again score 2,000 runs in a season was dismissed as special pleading by the batsman who had perfected the art of 'padding up'. Yet the lbw law has only served to place the attack onto the legside; an undue emphasis has been placed on bowlers who can make the ball come into the bat rather than leave it and the inswingers have multiplied. As a result, batsmen became more solid and pragmatic, thrusting out the front leg to meet the ball pitching outside the line of wicket and wicket. Post-war batsmen therefore contented themselves with the maxim, 'if you play forward, you'll be unlucky to be lbw'. So the modern batsman is almost on the front foot before the ball is delivered and the clever bowler drops it a little shorter, to a length that would have been savaged by great cutters like J.T.Tyldesley, Andrew Sandham and Don Bradman. With most English wickets lacking pace and bounce, it is little wonder that current England batsmen look less than complete in their technique, in their ability to play back and forward with equal facility.

The availability of the new ball has also shifted the post-war pendulum towards the bowler. Not until 1907 was a second new ball an option – it was then made available after 200 runs had been scored – but from 1948 onwards, it was too readily gained. Don Bradman's Australian side had the benefit of a new ball every 55 overs in 1948 and Lindwall, Miller and Johnston profited accordingly – so much so that even a master like Hutton was dropped. Over the next thirty years, the new ball was made available from 65 to 100 overs and captains unashamedly based their strategy on keeping batsmen quiet with negative bowling until the new ball was due. Slow bowlers were forced out of the equation and to make things even easier for the seamer, wickets became greener and outfields that looked like bowling greens kept the shine on that much longer. The result was a drab uniformity of out-cricket and batsmanship of a cautious, one-dimensional nature. This in turn led to the birth of one-day cricket and the realisation that the public did not wish to sit and watch a technical exercise performed by 22 players. Since 1963, one-day cricket has kept several county clubs solvent, although the purists maintain that it is not the type of cricket that either breeds good batting or maintains the proper standards of the game.

The modern first-class cricketer often cites one-day cricket as the reason why great players like Hobbs, Grace and Hammond would not prosper today – a Pavlovian response culled from a few frames of flickering newsreels and the certainty that ground fielding is so much better now. I cannot believe that Bradman – with his amazing footwork, remarkable eye and speed between wickets – would do anything but prosper in limited-overs cricket. Patsy Hendren and Andrew Sandham – two of the greatest hookers – would relish today's short-pitched bowling. Jack Hobbs would still be his majestic self because he was a great player for thirty years on all wickets against all types of bowlers. The only concession to modern cricket I would advance on behalf of the batsmen who scored a hundred hundreds is that today their runs would perforce come at a slower rate. That would not stem from any lessening of their powers – more an acknowledgement that sophisticated captains regard twenty overs an hour as defeatist and tactically suicidal.

No amount of critical re-assessment can detract from the performances of these twenty-one batsmen. Like the goals of Greaves, the Wimbledon titles of Borg and the trophies of Nicklaus, their performances are writ large in the game's history. Perhaps undue attention is given to the scoring of a hundred; it is probably true to state that many matches have been placed in limbo due to the desire of captain or batsman to reach three figures. The history of cricket is littered with wonderful innings of less than a hundred, that in the circumstances, could truly be said to have won a match. It may be that the frequency of scoring a century is more admirable than the amount of hundreds scored by a batsman – in that case, Bradman and Hammond stand supreme:

	% of hundreds per completed innings
Bradman	39.7
Hammond	18.6

and, using that test, four other batsmen not among the others under consideration are also particularly impressive:

Hassett	20.3%
Hazare	18.2%
Sobers	16.7%
Ranjitsinjhi	16.4%

– better figures than Hobbs, Sutcliffe, Cowdrey, Woolley and Grace. Yet Hobbs and the others achieved something special. Philip Mead was one of the select band and he had his own idiosyncratic way of looking at the three-figure landmark. As he made the appropriate stroke to reach his century, Mead would mutter, 'Ah well, that's another bag of coal for the winter' – a reference to the talent money offered by Mead's county, Hampshire, for deeds of merit. According to the gospel of Philip Mead, twenty-one batsmen have done more for the coal industry than Arthur Scargill could ever achieve.

W.G.Grace

'I hate defensive strokes, you can only get
three off 'em.'

W.G.Grace was surely the greatest player the game has ever known, or ever will know. The reason is simple – he created modern cricket by his own example and force of personality. For almost forty years he played first-class cricket and he was the dominant force in thirty of them. Several batsmen have surpassed his total of 126 first-class centuries, but none of them – not Hobbs, nor Hammond, nor Hutton – has been so pre-eminent in his time as Doctor William Gilbert Grace.

When he entered first-class cricket in 1865, it was still a slightly shady pursuit with the best players intent on getting as much money as possible out of it. Cricket was a provincial game – the first tour to Australia had just taken place, but only because a proposed lecture tour by Charles Dickens had fallen through and the sponsors had to think of something to appease the Australians. By the time W.G.Grace played his last first-class game in 1908, it was the national sport – enlarged from a pleasant rural pastime into something binding counties together and spreading deep into the affections of normally unsentimental Englishmen. The Royal Family regularly asked about the Doctor's health, and his appearance at cricket matches sparked off waves of hysteria totally out of character with the undemonstrative times in which he lived. After Gladstone, he was the best-known Victorian Englishman and – *pace* the MP for Newark – surely the best-loved.

The breadth of his playing career ensured that he made runs against bowlers of all types on varying surfaces. In his early days, wickets were dangerous – one batsman was killed at Lord's in 1870 – yet Grace faced them with equanimity, turning in seasonal figures that are astonishing in their consistency and supremacy. In the same year that the Lord's wicket claimed the life of a batsman, Grace amazed hard-bitten professional bowlers by his bravery on a deadly Lord's pitch. For the

Gentlemen against the Players, he scored 66 against Tom Emmett and George Freeman, two Yorkshiremen who enjoyed legendary duels against him over the years. Freeman later recalled Grace's bravery: 'That day it was a marvel the Doctor was not maimed or killed outright. I often think of his pluck when I watch a modern batsman scared if a medium-paced ball hits him on the hand; he should have seen our expresses flying about W.G.'s ribs, shoulders and head in 1870.' Just a few figures underline his dominance. In the decade 1871 to 1880, he averaged 49 in first-class cricket with his nearest challenger on 26, having scored almost a third of Grace's runs. He also took a little matter of 1,174 wickets, more than anyone but Alfred Shaw. For eleven of the fourteen seasons between 1866 and 1879, he topped the batting averages. When he scored 2,739 runs at an average of 78.25 in 1871, the runner-up totalled 1,068 at 24.12.

From his early days he met and mastered wild, tearaway fast bowlers like 'Foghorn' Jackson and 'Tear 'Em' Tarrant; through the 1880s he dealt with men like Spofforth, Peate and Shaw, and a decade later with Richardson, Lockwood, Lohmann, Peel and Giffen, immortal bowlers on wickets that were still sporting. By 1900, Grace had scored 121 of his 126 centuries and only then were the wickets playing easier and truer. By now, at the age of 52, he was coming to terms with Rhodes, Hirst, Braund, Ernest Jones, Noble and the cunning googly bowler, Bosanquet. He was still good enough to score 74 on a fast wicket for the Gentlemen against the Players in 1906 at the age of 58 – this, in a season when there were no Test matches, was automatically the most important game of the year and not a place for the temperamentally unstable. Not that Grace ever showed such weakness, even if his beard was eventually streaked with grey and his back creaked as the ball was cut fiercely past him at point.

His cricketing longevity was remarkable and so was his influence on batting. Never before had one player embodied the principles of batsmanship that we now take for granted. He lacked the magical qualities of a Ranjitsinjhi, the controlled violence of a Jessop, the beauty of a Trumper or a Spooner. Grace had backbone – solid, sensible orthodoxy. From his early days, his mother and uncle had taught him the virtues of a straight bat – indeed his redoubtable mother had often been heard to scold him after rash shots in his formative years in county cricket – and he never forgot the basics. He simply played the right stokes to the right ball in a manner no other batsman had consistently achieved. His stance was upright, his backlift high and he brought the bat down on shooters astonishingly quickly; as James Shaw, the Nottinghamshire bowler once remarked, 'Oh yes, he blocks the shooters, but he blocks 'em to the boundary.' The faster the bowling, the happier he was – he had no time for subtle leg glances or pushes to the on-side for singles, he loved to smack the ball through the covers and straight drive it back past the bowler. 'Games aren't won by leaving the ball alone,' he would say in that curiously high-pitched voice of his, 'I hate defensive strokes, you can only get three off 'em.' He hit powerfully, an extension of a personality that was full of gusto and confidence. Pictures of him batting in the nets underline the fact that his left elbow remained high, despite advancing years and thickening waistline. For a heavy man, he was very nimble on his feet and he possessed the knack of all great batsmen to place the ball where there was no fielder. Perhaps this stemmed from his early days, when it was commonplace to bat against teams comprising eighteen or twenty-two players. When you have learned to slip the ball through such a cordon of fielders, the demands of first-class cricket must seem comparatively untaxing.

Like the man himself, his attitude to batting was simple and unvarnished. He was once asked, 'How do you stop a shooter?' He replied, 'why, you put your bat to the ball.' He played with his left leg very close to the bat, and when playing back in defence, his right foot moved near to the line of the ball. When going forward, the left shoulder pointed to the bowler – the lessons in the back garden of his home had been assimilated. His basic attitude was to play each ball on its merits – as James Shaw despaired, 'I put the ball where I likes and 'e puts it where 'e likes.'

C.B.Fry was not the kind of man or cricketer to be overawed by the achievements of others but he was dogmatic about the influence of W.G.Grace. Fry wrote of him, 'He revolutionised batting. He turned it from an accomplishment into a science. He turned the old one-stringed instrument into a many-chorded lyre. Where a great man has led, many can go afterwards, but the honour is his who found and cut the path. The theory of modern batting is, in all essentials, the result of W.G.'s thinking and working on the game.'

Contemporary pictures and rare film footage do not do him justice. Physically, he soon filled out from the young stripling to a massive, bearded man and that image remained in the public consciousness for the remaining years of his life. The beard satisfied the Victorian craving for authority and his innate self-confidence was tolerantly viewed as the characteristic of a born leader. In photographs of his batting, he looks a faintly comical figure to later generations accustomed to sleek, lissom sporting heroes: the bat looks too small in those massive hands, the great, grizzled beard gives him a homely, avuncular air and surely those enormous feet encased in brown boots could not carry the attack to the bowler? Yet he was no figure of fun to his admiring colleagues or suffering bowlers. As the legendary Yorkshireman, Tom Emmett, graphically put it, 'he should be made to play with a smaller bat.' It was Tom who bewailed loudly after yet another hammering by W.G. that 'it's Grace before meat, Grace after meat and Grace all the time'.

Grace's stamina was remarkable. Apart from his forty years in first-class cricket, he played countless other games in a season – it has been reliably estimated that his record in minor cricket totalled 25,000 runs (including ninety centuries) and more than 4,000 wickets. With joyous enthusiasm, he would dash off to grounds up and down the country to play cricket; he knew his railway timetables more intimately than his medical books. In 1876, he demonstrated both his stamina and batting mastery in one unforgettable August week. On the Saturday, he scored 344 for the MCC against Kent at Canterbury and the following day was spent in a cross-country train en route to Bristol. On the Monday, he made 177 not out against Nottinghamshire, then later in the week took 318 not out off the Yorkshire bowlers. A little matter of 839 runs, average 419.5, in an age when travel owed nothing to motorways and much to patience and good humour. Before August was over – he totalled 1,249 runs from ten first-class innings – he travelled from Bristol to Grimsby to score 400 against a team of twenty-two. The outfield was not closely mown and every run was physically completed by the inexhaustible Grace and his weary batting partners.

When he completed his hundredth century in 1895, the feat was embellished by two further examples of the legendary Grace stamina. It was a bitterly cold May day at Bristol and Gloucestershire was entertaining Somerset. The prospect of Grace's century proved more riveting to the public than the General Election which was taking place and as the snow-flakes whirled around W.G.'s beard, he hammered away a slow donkey-drop from Sammy Woods to the legside boundary. The crowd predictably roared itself hoarse, Grace raised his cap with as much false modesty as he felt he should display and Sammy Woods said to himself, 'Now we'll get the old devil out.' Not a bit of it – he scored 288 and both Woods and the wicket-keeper (A.P.Wickham, who was also a clergyman) always subsequently maintained that Grace allowed just five balls to pass his bat during the entire innings. All this he did at the age of forty-six, on a bitingly cold day, with the inevitable emotional pressure and the social responsibility of making a lunchtime speech amid the champagne that he willingly quaffed halfway through his innings.

When he was ninth out, caught at slip, he was still to have the last laugh of the day on Sammy Woods, a wholesome, ebullient character who loved the doctor like a brother. Over a celebratory dinner that night, Sam tried to forget that he had Grace plumb lbw when he had made three, and that he hammered a wicked shooter to the boundary when he entered the nineties. He was proud to have been involved in a day of cricket history and genuinely pleased for his old adversary. Yet Sam vowed to get his own back in a characteristic way – he would drink the old man under the table that night. It was not to be – Grace drank everything on offer and, at midnight, he cajoled the woozy Woods into a game of whist till two o'clock in the morning.

One further example of his remarkable physical powers occurred when Grace was over forty and had been fielding at Old Trafford for the best part of a day while Lancashire piled up more than 400 runs. A Gloucestershire fielder's throat was split open on a boundary fence after he had chased the ball and failed to stop in time. Grace took charge and held the open wound steady for fully thirty minutes until qualified medical help and equipment arrived. The lucky fielder was A.C.M. Croome, who later became cricket correspondent of the *The Times*. Years later he wrote, 'If his hand had slipped just once, I would not be here to tell the tale.'

His colossal strength not only enabled him to shine in other sports – he was a fine hurdler when young – but also propelled him into being the greatest all-rounder the game had known at that time. He just had to be in the action – whether diddling out 2,879 batsmen with his cunning slow-medium deliveries that cut into leg, or grabbing 871 catches in his massive hands. His stamina was not only productive in terms of performance but also in earning money. I doubt if any other sportsman has, pro rata, earned more than W.G.Grace; early on he realised how valuable he was to the game and he soon knew his price and how hard a bargain he could drive. He and his brother, E.M., were the backbone of the Gentlemen side in their prestigious tussles with the Players – when he threatened to pull out of the games along with his brother unless they were paid, W.G. soon had financial satisfaction. He was just too important to overlook and he knew it. Once he had qualified as a doctor, he made it clear to Gloucestershire that he would retire unless they could find him a locum to take over the practice during the summer. We can safely assume that W.G. had no intention of spurning the game he loved to distraction, but the Gloucestershire committee could not better him on brinkmanship. They found him a locum and in later years two filled the breach – both paid for by the committee. The generous expenses he picked up from his county and anyone else willing to hire his services were a mockery of his amateur status, yet at the same time, an acknowledgement of his unique place in cricket and public affection. In 1891, on his second visit to Australia, all his expenses were paid – including a locum for his practice – plus an extra £3,000.

During his great season of 1895, no less than three testimonials were opened for him. They were run by the MCC, Gloucestershire CCC, and the *Morning Telegraph* newspaper and they raised a total of £9,073 8s. 3d. Five years later, when Grace started the London County team, he was paid £600 a year, with munificent expenses. He always drove a hard financial bargain and it remains a mystery what this man of simple tastes did with his money. When he died in 1915, he left £7,278 10s. 1d. in his will, a tidy sum certainly but surprisingly low considering the vast amount he had earned for so many decades.

In defence of Grace, it must be said that he was not always acquisitive in his business dealings. He offered his services in innumerable benefit matches for the professional bowlers he had scourged up and down the land and he looked after the poor in his practice with devoted altruism. He knew how valuable he was to the game of cricket and so did the administrators. Legend has it that it was often possible to read the following notice outside a cricket ground; 'Admission threepence; if Dr W.G.Grace plays, admission sixpence.' Grace knew that people not remotely interested in cricket were interested in him. If someone had told him he was a 'superstar' he would blink at a phrase he did not understand – but he was assuredly the precursor of a public relations juggernaut that rolled in more sophisticated times and disrupted the private lives of cricketers such as Compton, Hobbs, Bradman, Lillee and Botham.

Grace enjoyed being a celebrity, but then it was more enjoyable to be one in his period. The devotion of the public, the respect of his Queen and the companionship of his playing colleagues touched his simple soul deeply. The homage the press paid him made his dealings with reporters that much easier – they contented themselves with recording faithfully his scores and eschewing more weighty considerations such as whether he was a cheat. The modern trend of erecting sporting heroes on a plinth of adjectival excess only to dash them to the ground within a year would have perplexed and angered the simple country doctor. As a personality he would have satisfied the hunger of the most demanding of sports editors but he would not have enjoyed the slow-motion replays and the scrutiny of his playing assets and behavioural defects on the field.

Opinion is divided on whether Grace cheated: his supporters tend to be those who played with him a long time, who grew to love his little idiosyncrasies and sense of fun. On the other hand, men of similar independence of mind were convinced that Grace bent the rules to suit himself. S.F.Barnes was a great bowler and a man who did not respect institutions unless they deserved that respect. He wrote, 'I once appealed for a catch at the wicket, being certain that he had played it, but the umpire said no. When Grace got to my end he said, "I played it, Barnes". I replied, "I know you did and so does everyone else but this chap", meaning the umpire, and that was the nearest I ever got to getting his wicket.' E.J.Smith – known to everyone as 'Tiger' – also had firm views about Grace's flexible attitude to the rules. 'Tiger' Smith began his career at about the same time that Grace was easing out of first-class cricket, but he played innumerable minor matches with him. Seventy years later, he would often tell me about the doctor's sharp practice: 'I kept out of his way because he could be a proper autocrat and I was just starting out and didn't want to upset him. But I often saw him stand his ground and refuse to go when given out. The umpires needed the money, they wanted to stay on the list and they knew that W.G. could get them struck off.'

H.D.G.Leveson-Gower, England captain and at one time chairman of the selectors, had a massive affection for the old man but he did concede that he occasionally bent the rules to suit his own powerful ego. Once, Leveson-Gower organised a match at Limpsfield and with many fine cricketers present, Grace captained his side. On this occasion, Grace won the toss and walked in to bat with Bobby Abel, that splendid little player who gave such great service to Surrey and, occasionally, England. They faced up to a young man who eventually played for his country and who, for a short period, was extremely fast – Neville Knox. Grace snicked a fast delivery from Knox to the wicket-keeper, and as the fielding side joyously celebrated, Grace stood his ground. As he rubbed his arm, he shouted: 'I didn't come here for nothing, nor did all these spectators! Play on!' After a batting exhibition that delighted the crowd, he was out and returned to sit beside Leveson-Gower in the pavilion. On being asked if he had touched the ball from Knox, he said: 'Of course – but I wasn't going. They didn't get my ashes that time, did they?'

Perhaps his gamesmanship was harmless enough but there was no doubt he liked his own way. His reaction to a controversial decision one day at the Oval epitomised his autocratic outbursts; one of the Gloucestershire batsmen was run out in less than sporting circumstances and W.G., who had watched the incident from the pavilion, bellowed out to the umpires: 'I can't have it, and I won't have it and I shan't have it!' The nearest Surrey fielder, who was leaning on the boundary fence, looked up at him and shouted: 'You've got to have it!', and indeed this was one argument that Grace lost, much to his chagrin.

Yet the bulk of his contemporaries put it down to a simple desire to be the artful dodger, without malice and with a twinkle in his eye. As one old sweat put it, 'I never knew the old 'un get up to sharp doings. No, he kept the ring of the law all right. But goodness me, the rum things he did do inside it!' Most of the umpires were old playing-cronies and they knew what to expect from him; they would smile indulgently as he appealed from point for lbw or rubbed his forearm solicitously after the ball had kissed his gloves on the way to the wicket-keeper. He loved to outwit someone who had pretensions to matching him in cunning. It happened one day to A.N.Hornby, that truculent captain of Lancashire and England. Hornby was fed up with W.G.'s habit of changing the field behind the batsman's back and telegraphing the kind of delivery the bowler should send down to gull the unsuspecting batsman. Hornby tried to get his own back: he told Johnny Briggs where to deliver the ball and as Grace stood there, waiting for it, Hornby signalled first slip to tip-toe over to leg-slip. Briggs was halfway through his run-up when Grace cackled: 'I can see what you're doin', I can see what you're doin'.' He loved a game within a game and his pleasure at such a success was harmless and childlike – reflecting a sense of fun that belonged to 'apple pie' beds and booby traps, rather than subtlety.

So many stories have attached themselves to him that some at least have the kernel of truth. The sheer multiplicity of Grace anecdotes is testimony to the fact that he was larger than life, that he was a character. As the most famous medical practitioner in England, it was inevitable that all the hoary old jokes about doctors should be visited on his broad back. There was the time when he allegedly reacted to a troublesome birth by remarking, 'The baby's dead, the mother's in a bad way, but I do believe I can save the father.' Or the advice given by him to a mother of twins, who thought they had measles: 'Put 'em in bed together and don't bother me unless they get up to 208 for two at lunch.' Whether or not he uttered such gems is irrelevant. He was such a character that he could have said them.

Grace may have lacked intellectual fibre, it may have taken him a long time to get his medical diploma, but I suspect he was a very good country doctor. He cared for his patients – hence the insistence on a locum – and he dealt out generous measures of jovial, hearty good sense as he did his rounds. In a working-class parish where money was scarce, W.G.Grace was more of a social worker than a harassed, money-conscious general practitioner. The landed gentry who craved his glittering services on the cricket field may have found him a hard man to barter with, but not so his patients. Invariably, he gave his services free to the poor.

His relentless hold on the affection of the public can be gauged by the fact that no cricketer has ever had more column inches written about him. One bibliography of cricket lists forty-five publications associated with him – yet there are only two under his own name. He was lucky that a journalist, Arthur Porritt, was on hand to assemble his random reminiscences into coherent form – Grace was never a forensic thinker about the game, he was instinctive and forgetful about his towering performances. Arthur Porritt wrote that Grace was 'singularly inarticulate' about his cricketing deeds but he loved him dearly: 'About Dr W.G.Grace there was something indefinable – like the simple faith of a child – which arrested and fascinated me. He was a big grown-up boy, just what a man who only lived when he was in the open air might be expected to be. A wonderful kindliness ran through his nature, mingling strangely with the arbitrary temper of a man who had been accustomed to be dominant over other men.'

Grace remained a schoolboy at heart, even in his last years. He loved boisterous, practical jokes, hated reading and when he transferred his attentions to bowls, displayed the same keenness as on the cricket field – he became the first President of the English Bowls Association. Like other childlike adults he could be petty, but he quickly recovered. As A.A.Thomson felicitously wrote, 'He never let the sun go down upon his wrath, though there were some colourful sunsets while it lasted.' He could be easily hurt. At Trent Bridge in 1899 he played his last Test after the crowd barracked him for failing to bend quickly enough at point to stop the fierce cutting of Noble and Hill. His batting skills were still relatively undimmed but this admission that 'it's the ground – it's too far away' was poignant. His break with Gloucestershire in 1900 hit him hard; he felt the committee was interfering in selection policy and, in turn, his autocratic ways had picked up a few enemies at the club over the years. As he left to join London County, his resignation letter was a typical blend of sentiment and defiance: 'I have the greatest affection for the county of my birth, but for the committee as a whole, the greatest contempt.'

He played good quality cricket for the next five seasons with London County, enjoying the comradeship and, with one eye on himself as a tourist attraction, the money that reflected his deserved fame. His glorious 74 in the Gentlemen v Players match at the age of 58 showed the younger generation a glimpse of his mettle and although he announced he would never play again, he continued in club cricket almost till the end of his life. His last game was one week after his 66th birthday. He scored 69 not out – the asterisk still meant a lot to him.

The Great War troubled him. He hated the idea of his fellow-cricketers being slaughtered in the mud of France, even though his patriotism had forced him to write a famous letter to the *Sportsman* magazine in 1914, which exhorted county cricketers to stop playing the game and to join the armed forces as quickly as possible. H.D.G. Leveson-Gower visited him at his Surrey home just before he died and found him in a melancholy mood; the loss of his cricketing friends saddened him and the Zeppelin raids over London rattled him. On being reminded that a man who tamed the fastest and fiercest of bowlers should not be concerned by a few Zeppelins, he said wearily, 'I could see those beggars. I can't see these.' In October 1915, he died after a heart attack in his garden, as he was tending his roses with the same delicacy that he would deliver healthy-lunged children into his Gloucestershire parish long, long ago. When he was buried, the cemetery chapel was packed with cricketers, mourning the loss of a man who had seemed immortal and ageless.

After the War, the administrators at Lord's wished to symbolise the national affection for him. The Grace Gates were duly erected and, fittingly, the simple inscription was the idea of F.S.Jackson, a man who had played for England alongside W.G. The words were, like the subject itself, simple and direct:

> To the Memory of
> William Gilbert Grace
> THE GREAT CRICKETER.

He was more than a great cricketer, he was an innovator, the right man in the right place at the right time. From his example, other batsmen learned how to play fast bowling, how to play forward correctly. Because he revolutionised the art of batting, he automatically did the same for bowling: to attempt to curb his mastery, bowlers had to devise new methods of attack, to vary flight and speed, and captains had to conceive new fielding positions. Grace acknowledged the influence of his elder brother, E.M., especially in the way he attacked fast bowling. He also believed his brother, G.F., would have been an even greater player if he had lived through his fever in 1880. Depite the links of heredity, he stood on his own and neither his brothers, nor anyone else, could match his output, influence or popularity. One single entry in *Wisden* confirms his remarkable effect on cricket. In the Births and Deaths section, only one woman is included – W.G.'s mother, the woman who reared five sons, three of whom played for England.

Statisticians examine his record minutely in these more cynical times and state that he played a long time to get his runs, that he only averaged 39 in first-class cricket. The first-class cricketer of the 1980s who has heard of W.G. Grace will state automatically that a man of that size and age, a batsman who stood with his left toe cocked off the ground, a player with such a high backlift, could not possibly adapt to the modern game and its physical demands. A cricketer – like any other sportsman – can only be judged by his performance at that time, on how he reacted to the contemporary tactical challenges. Grace showed his adaptability after the age of forty as his physical size began to resemble his national stature. He found he could not thrust out his left foot to the off-side in the manner of his pristine youth, so he learned to pull the ball to the on-side. His eye was still remarkable, his powers of hitting unimpaired and his confidence to play the shot as bullish as ever. He mastered the pull shot and in the process, set up the great seasons of his middle age. Seventy years after he first bowled at Grace, the great Wilfred Rhodes would still acknowledge what an effective hitter he was: 'He would take a good length ball from outside his off-side stump and bang it over mid-on's head like a cannon ball.' Grace was fifty years of age when he first encountered the subtleties of Rhodes, so we can assume that his ability to adapt took heavy toll of bowlers for many years. When modern county cricketers sneer at Grace from the lofty heights of a few hundred wickets at a mediocre cost, I prefer to believe the testimony of a shrewd Yorkshireman who was proved right 4,187 times at the bowling crease.

Tom Hayward

'He used to make my arm ache.' (C.J.Kortright)

Eighteen years after Sammy Woods tried to drink the old doctor under the table, the feat of a hundred hundreds was repeated by a man who was, in many ways, similar to the Great Cricketer. Like Grace, Tom Hayward had been a model of consistency over a long period of seasons, he based his success on an orthodox, unhurried style, he came from a cricketing family and, temperamentally, he could be as bloody-minded as W.G. when the mood suited him.

Hayward had cricket in his blood; the Hayward production line was almost as impressive as the one that rumbled out of Bristol in the 1840s. Tom was a nephew of Thomas Hayward, by common consent the best professional batsman in the country in the 1860s. Tom's father, Daniel, and his uncle had played for Surrey and by the time young Tom was born in 1871, the family had moved to Cambridge, with significant results. Hayward senior became groundsman at Parker's Piece, that famous area of ground in Cambridge that saw the dawning of the genius of Hobbs and Ranjitsinjhi and the imperturbable majesty of young Tom Hayward. Within a couple of years, Tom had shown that the family genes had issued forth another cricketer of class and he set out to mould his technique on the excellent wickets at Parker's Piece.

He first played for Surrey in 1893. He was bowled first ball by Joe Cresswell, the Warwickshire fast bowler. In the following match, he scored his first hundred for Surrey. He made an immediate impression with his sound, graceful method and clean driving and *Wisden* demurely remarked: 'We do not wish to seem over-sanguine, but we shall be greatly disappointed if he does not in the immediate future obtain a very high position.' So it proved. By 1896, he was playing for England – he did so thirty-five times – and, for twenty years in succession, he made 1,000 runs in a season. On two occasions he made over 3,000 runs and his total of 3,518 in 1906 remained a record until Compton and Edrich broke it in 1947 against vastly inferior bowling.

Like W.G.Grace, Tom Hayward was a wonderfully phlegmatic player of fast bowling. He was a typical product of the nineteenth-century school of batsmanship: upright, patient, a front-foot player who stroked the ball formidably hard once his eye was in. He would calmly take stock of the bowling and conditions when he arrived at the wicket and then gradually unfurl his shots. He could play all round the wicket, but his specialities were the cut and the off-drive. On the plumb Oval wickets at the turn of the century Hayward's off-driving was full of grandeur and power. Great slow bowlers like Blythe and Rhodes would wheel away for hours, pitching on or outside the off-stump, imprecating Hayward to loft an off-drive; yet all those hours of net practice under the tutelage of his father had taught him the value of a still head, the straight bat and the powerful follow-through. As he warmed to his task, Hayward's chocolate-brown Surrey cap would be pushed further back on his head – a sure sign to the bowlers that all was well with him and that he expected to be there for some time. On fifty-eight occasions at the Oval, that equanimity was reflected in a Hayward century.

It would be wrong to assume that the bulk of Hayward's 43,000 runs were accumulated with an inevitability that stemmed from perfect batting conditions. His innings for the Players against the Gentlemen in 1906 has rightly earned him a place in cricket history. He made just 54, but it came in an all-out total of 199 on a fiery wicket that had recently been watered and left to dry under hot sun. Earlier in the day, Arthur Fielder had taken all ten wickets to hustle out the Gentlemen for 167 and the amateur fast bowlers, Walter Brearley and Neville Knox, were determined to inflict the same punishment. Hayward was badly hit in the first over, but carried on batting valiantly against the bounce of Knox and Brearley. The other professional batsmen – Bowley, J.T. Tyldesley, Rhodes, Denton, John Gunn, Hayes and Lilley – cut a sorry figure as they backed away from the fast bowling onslaught that claimed all but one of the wickets. Only Hayward stood foursquare, taking innumerable blows on the chest and fingers, all the while getting in line with the ball. It was a classic innings from a classic batsman and cogent proof that the best innings do not always encompass three figures. No wonder C.J.Kortright, one of the fastest bowlers of all time, said of Hayward; 'He used to make my arm ache.' W.G.Grace, of course, was the acknowledged master of fast bowling over a longer period of time than Hayward (and on more dangerous wickets) but, in his day, no professional batsman was more at ease against them.

Yet Hayward was not just a masterful performer against the quick bowlers – and a conversation with P.G.H.Fender confirmed this in my view. A little matter of sixty-eight years had elapsed between an innings of Hayward's and my talk with Fender, but the memory of it was still fresh in his mind. The occasion was the match in August, 1914, between Surrey and Kent, Jack Hobbs's benefit game. On a rain-affected wicket, Hayward scored 91 out of 234 all out. Colin Blythe, that most beautiful of slow left-arm bowlers, took 9 for 97 and Fender, who batted for a time with Hayward said it was the best bad-wicket innings he ever saw. From a man who saw Jack Hobbs display his greatness regularly on difficult wickets, this is high praise indeed. Fender scored 48 in characteristic style in that Surrey innings and recalls, 'Mine was just biff-bang stuff but Hayward met everything in the middle of the bat. It was a master-piece' – a masterpiece at the age of forty-three, with his career just two weeks to run, against Blythe, Woolley and Fielder, not to mention a certain A.P.Freeman who was to cause some problems after the War.

For the last ten years of his time at Surrey, Hayward's name was overshadowed by that of Jack Hobbs. That must nevertheless have given him great pleasure, because Tom Hayward was largely instru-mental into bringing Hobbs to the first-class game. Like Hayward, Hobbs came from Cambridge and on one occasion at short notice he stepped into a local side scheduled to meet a Tom Hayward XI in Cambridge. Hayward bowled at the youngster, was immediately impressed and arranged a trial for him at the Oval. The rest can be told in a subsequent chapter, but it is clear that Jack Hobbs would have been lost to the game without Hayward's quiet encouragement. When Hobbs's father died in 1902 – three years before his son ever played for Surrey – Hayward arranged a charity match for the widow and her family. A year later, Hobbs was offered a contract by Surrey – and as soon as he could, Hayward went to see the Surrey secretary, C.W. Alcock, and arranged a £10 bonus for young Hobbs in view of his family's financial worries. Hobbs did not know about that for years afterwards, but it is a measure of the awe in which he held Hayward that, for several seasons, he could not bring himself to call his fellow-professional by his first name, even when he was capped by Surrey. He could not even invite him to his wedding; he was too shy in the presence of such a dominating person.

Eventually the relationship between Hobbs and Hayward blossomed and so did their opening partnerships. Hobbs always acknowledged the good fortune of being able to watch the best professional batsman in the country at the other end, to see how he coped with awkward wickets and testing bowlers. By the time their partnership had been severed by war in 1914, they had set a new record for century opening stands and, since then, only three other opening pairs have surpassed their total of forty. In 1907, they achieved something that has never been beaten: in the space of one week, they added more than a hundred for the first wicket no less than four times, 106 and 125 against Cambridge University and 147 and 105 against Middlesex. They were a handsome pair of openers, both defensively sound but with a rich array of strokes and a reluctance to be tied down. It would have given them infinite pleasure to succeed together in Tests, but they opened only once at Lord's in 1909 against Australia. They put on just 23 and 16 and Hayward, who played against the advice of his doctor, was dropped for good at the age of thirty-eight.

It is easy to see why the shy Hobbs would look up to Hayward in those days of the early twentieth century. Hayward was a typical product of the Victorian age, a provincial figure but proudly so, a man who belonged to a community and looked forward to returning there to bask in the glory of his worldwide deeds for his country. If he did not tour with England in the winter, he would come to Cambridge and enjoy the respectful welcome; his self-confidence ensured that Surrey County Cricket Club paid him enough to live comfortably. He was a proud professional and, in his own way, did much to raise the status of the breed. In previous decades, some professional cricketers had been notorious for their inability to hold their liquor or keep track of their money. Public-spirited captains like Yorkshire's Lord Hawke would try to invest their cash for them before it disappeared down their throats. A man of Tom Hayward's stature had no need for such paternalism, he knew the value of self-discipline and as senior professional at the Oval for the last decade before the war, he expected a similar code of conduct from the other pros. At away matches, every professional knew what time he must appear in the dining room and how he should dress, and Hayward cracked down very hard on any midnight skylarking in the hotels. It did not really matter who was the Surrey captain at any given time – Tom Hayward was the boss. With his tall, commanding bearing, rugged good looks and bushy moustache, he looked like an irascible yet kindly regimental sergeant-major.

Like W.G.Grace, Tom Hayward knew his own mind and his commercial worth and if the offer was not satisfactory to him, he would withhold his services. In 1896, he withdrew from the Oval Test against Australia because he wanted £20 appearance money, twice the going rate. The rubber depended on the Oval Test but Hayward would not budge, because he felt the amateurs were getting too much money when they were allegedly of independent means. Note the date – 1896. He was just twenty-five, in his first season as a Test player and only beginning to establish himself in the Surrey team. Hayward was no blind respecter of institutions, even if he became one himself by his batting eminence. A decade after his first brush with authority he again ruled himself out of a contest with Australia, refusing to go on the 1907–8 tour, because the terms were not right. He could be equally single-minded with his employers at the Oval: in 1898, both Hayward and J.T.Brown scored triple centuries in the same week and when Hayward heard that Yorkshire had given Brown a cash reward, he told the Surrey committee he would make do with single centuries in future. Furthermore, they could forget about him bowling the medium-pace off-breaks that had picked up 114 wickets in the previous season. Thereafter he bowled reluctantly, sparingly, and with a highly-developed sense of grievance.

He was a proud man who set himself high professional standards. After his wonderful season of 1906, he was unprepared for the dazzling quartet of googly bowlers (Vogler, Faulkner, Schwarz and White) that came over from South Africa in the following year. He was dogged by knee trouble and a thickening waistline and his difficulties against the googly bowlers were magnified by the success of his junior partner, Jack Hobbs. One day, Hobbs got himself out after a perfectly simple miscalculation against the ball that turned into him. Hayward, watching from the pavillion, laughed loudly: 'Ah, there's the master of the googly showing us how to play it.' Judging by the respect Hobbs had for Hayward, we can charitably assume that remark stemmed from frustration at his own poor performances, rather than from envy of Hobbs's mastery.

If he could never pick the googly, Hayward still had many more days in the sun ahead of him, days when the chocolate cap was pushed back with relish from the broad, sweating brow. Recurring knee trouble slowed his progress in the field and – mercifully – gave him a good excuse not to bowl, but he could still roll out the centuries. He scored more than 2,000 runs in 1911 and all the while he was advancing with measured tread towards the day when he could at least sit on the same statistical pedestal as W.G.Grace. It came on Friday, 27 June, 1913 against Lancashire at his beloved Oval. With his colleagues failing, he batted nearly five hours for 139 to achieve his hundredth hundred in first-class cricket. It was not one of his most fluent knocks; he was cut over the eye when his score was 16 and hit several times. As he acknowledged the cheers of the 5,000 spectators with his usual dignity, he did not know that in years to come, Jack Hobbs would always envy him for getting the appropriate hundred in front of his own supporters.

By 1913, mammoth scores were becoming commonplace and Hayward's feat was therefore received with more decorum than that of Grace in 1895. Nevertheless, the tributes were warm and deserved. A.C.MacLaren, a man who knew more than enough about the technique of batting, wrote: 'I doubt if any professional has been more careful in his living or more painstaking in his methods to attain success for the captains for whom and the sides for which he has played. Let me beg all young players today to note the use of the left shoulder, and how the left leg is brought across for Hayward's off-drive. Note, too, that he never gets back onto his wicket and then plays forward, as some have got into the way of doing.'

One satisfying season remained for Hayward before the golden age of cricket was blown away for ever by the Great War. In 1914, Surrey won a truncated championship and Hayward captained the side in a few matches in the absence of C.T.A.Wilkinson; he did so shrewdly and capably, which came as no surprise. Woe betide any of the players stepping out of line when the gleam was in his eye! In a fortnight in August – with war already declared and a sense of unreality hanging over cricket grounds – Hayward demonstrated his ageless mastery for the last time: 122 against Kent, 91 in the return match and 116 against Yorkshire, adding 290 with Hobbs for the first wicket against Drake, Booth, Hirst, Rhodes and Kilner. His last match was against Gloucestershire at the Oval: he scored just a single but had the satisfaction of catching the last man off Percy Fender's bowling as Surrey won by an innings. So Surrey's pre-war history was ended by the hands of one of its most illustrious players.

When cricket resumed in 1919, Hayward was forty-eight and clearly too old and unfit to play again. He spent several happy years at Oxford, coaching the undergraduates, taking their banter in genial fashion, and doing his best to avoid breaking into a sweat in the nets. He would bowl his off-breaks and steadfastly refuse to bat, despite the entreaties of his young pupils. Just once he relented, playing a couple of majestic off-drives and then walking out of the net. He would rarely talk about his batting deeds, but loved to sit watching the undergraduates learning their trade against the county sides. He would happily sit all day in the pavilion, still wearing his Surrey cap, his walrus moustache giving him a melancholy air that was belied by his pleasure at suddenly meeting an old friend.

His brother Dan was in charge of the rival pavilion at Cambridge and after his retirement from the Parks, he lived contentedly enough in his home town. It was there that he died in July 1939, at the age of sixty-eight, his life ending on the brink of the Second World War, just as his great playing career had been extinguished by the Great War of 1914. It was somehow appropriate that he died in his home town, in the place where he felt at ease throughout his life. It was even more fitting that he should live to see the whole of Jack Hobbs's wonderful career, to experience the glow of satisfaction that a jewel picked out by him from Parkers' Piece in 1901 should dazzle the world for the next thirty-three years. It is no mean effort to score a hundred hundreds, and usher onto the cricketing stage an even more impressive player. That must have been worth a tug or two on the chocolate cap.

3

Sir Jack Hobbs

'By his behaviour and ability, he earned respect
for himself and his profession' (G.O.Allen)

No one scored more hundreds or runs than Jack Hobbs, yet to profile him within such a context is dismissive. He certainly was no run machine; he often said the papers would do cricket a favour if they refrained from publishing the first-class averages, that he cared little for hundreds, but that his friends would be disappointed if he missed out. He made a habit of giving his wicket away as soon as he reached three figures (unless, of course, the circumstances of the game demanded extra commitment from him) and of his 197 centuries, no less than 51 of them were scores of between 100 and 110.

What was the secret of Jack Hobbs, that quality which still turns grizzled old cricketers misty-eyed at the very mention of his name? He was not a character in the Hendren or Compton mould, while others like Phil Mead were more impressively prolific, and he lacked the intimidating presence of W.G.Grace, the power of strokeplay of Hammond or Woolley and Bradman's rapacity. From the distance he looked ordinary enough on the field; of medium height, slim, wiry, thoughtful. No gestures, no flamboyance. Yet the public adored him, probably more for his sheer ordinariness than his wonderful batting achievements. He came from a poor home and he never forgot it; the experience moulded a quiet determination which was masked by his graceful behaviour. The small boys, the lad from the corner shop enjoying a free half-day, the office clerk spending a Saturday at that most unlovely ground, the Oval – they all could warm to Jack Hobbs, identify with him, wish him well and declare with passionate intensity that the day's light was dimmed whenever he was out. He was an ordinary, decent man of wonderful skills, yet on the same level as his worshippers.

Jack Hobbs brought batting to a level of perfection that has never been matched. Grace was a more creative batsman in that he moulded batting technique to the emerging game of first-class cricket, but it was Hobbs who refined the art. He was as sound as Hutton, as daring as Bradman and his temperament was the equal of Sutcliffe. He simply understood how to bat, he instinctively knew what to do with the bowled ball. He never had an hour's coaching in his life, he just watched, listened and put into practice the advice given by his father before he was ten – 'don't draw away'. Bill Bowes summed up the effortless mastery of the man thus: 'When he stood at the wicket before playing the shot, he looked a great player. All was ease, grace and confidence.'

During a thirty-year period in first-class cricket, he met and mastered every type of bowling – swervers, fast bowlers, cutters, seamers, top-spinners, leg-spinners, off-breaks and googlies. When he was over fifty, he was occasionally ruffled by short-pitched, intimidatory bowling, but that was a human frailty in a man whose batting seemed god-like for so many blissful years. His mastery of the basics enabled him to pass through three distinct phases of batting – before the 1914 War, he was a glorious dasher, revelling in the knowledge that he had all the shots, then for a decade afterwards he was simply 'the Master', a mature artist, while for the last few years of his career his beautiful technique enabled him to come to terms with physical stresses. One of the most revealing statistics about Hobbs is that he scored no less than 98 hundreds after his fortieth birthday in 1922. When he reached his century of centuries in May 1923 he had only batted once with Herbert Sutcliffe, a partnership that was to prove legendary – so he had done enough for any mortal before embarking on his most famous collaboration. Just one more fact to consider and it confirms what an attacking player Hobbs must have been – no one has bettered his total of 15 hundreds before lunch, 13 of them on the first day. Gilbert Jessop – a name synonymous with fast scoring – is next in line with 13.

It is one of the human touches of Hobbs's career that luck was on his side on several crucial occasions. Tyros like Grace and Bradman made their own luck by sheer willpower, battering down the door of opportunity, but Jack Hobbs could easily have been lost to the game before he was twenty. He was the first of twelve children living in a Cambridge back street; his father, a pro cricketer *manqué*, had to make do with groundsman's and net bowler's duties and when he died in 1902, the sensitive, eldest son felt his responsibilities keenly. At the age of twenty, he had to make a start on some sort of career. Enter Tom Hayward, as we have already seen. Without his kindness, encouragement and ability to put the right word into the right ears at certain times, Jack Hobbs's batting genius would have been smothered by the deadening hand of poverty. He was turned down by Essex – the club never answered a letter of recommendation from an old friend of his father – and Hayward's influence at the Oval remained his only hope. He was as good as his word and after satisfactory trials, he was taken on the staff. It seems incredible from a distance of eighty years, but Hobbs had to qualify by residence for two years before making his first-class debut for Surrey; he could not even return home to Cambridge in the winter, although he characteristically ensured his mother received a generous portion of his wage.

He was twenty-two years and five months old upon entering first-class cricket. At that age, Bradman had scored 334 in a Test, Hutton had improved on that with 364 and Compton had scored two hundreds for England. Hobbs had been content to bide his time, watching, taking stock and drinking everything in at the Oval. Perhaps he realised how lucky he was, how he managed to be in the right place when a vacancy occured. In his first organised cricket match, he made up the team when it was one short. Later he impressed Tom Hayward in a charity game but only played because the local side had ten men. On his debut for Surrey at Lord's while qualifying, he scored a splendid half-century against the Cross Arrows, yet would not have played but for Tom Richardson's injury. He fitted snugly into the Surrey first team as an opener by dint of ability but also because Bobby Abel's long tenure as Hayward's partner had come to an end. Then in 1907, his first England tour to Australia was secured because batsmen of the calibre of Fry, MacLaren, R.E.Foster, Warner, J.T.Tyldesley and Hayward could not, or would not go.

Even on his first-class debut – on Easter Monday, 1905 – the fates were kind. None of the four contenders for the place of Hayward's partner was available for a variety of reasons – in some cases, because it was early in the season and bitterly cold – and by another stroke of fortune, the Surrey captain, Lord Dalmeny, was absent. Tom Hayward was the stand-in skipper and he decided to take Hobbs in with him. A considerate action – he must have known how nervous his young protégé was.

The opposition on that day was the Gentlemen of England, captained by W.G.Grace – and by a happy coincidence the first three men to score a hundred hundreds took the field at the same time as the career of the Master began. At the end of Hobbs's career, the pattern repeated itself when, in 1934, he played with and against Walter Hammond and Don

Bradman, the two men who dominated the world's bowlers for the next decade.

As W.G. loomed at point, Hobbs made 18 and a polished 88, impressing both sets of players and showing he could not be rattled by Grace's little ways. In the second innings, he thought of a quick single to W.G.'s bowling, but the old man was too sharp – 'Thank you, youngster, just tip it back here and save my old legs.' He did so – but tapped other deliveries a little harder and scored his 88 in two hours. The following week, he scored 155 against Essex, the county that had rejected him. Did an anonymous clerk in the Essex office blush at the event?

After the Essex match, Hobbs was presented with his county cap by an admiring Lord Dalmeny. I wonder if a cap has ever been presented so early to a player? One can assume that the kindly Hayward was instrumental in accelerating that award; he knew his family needed the extra money and also that Surrey had unearthed a jewel of a batsman.

The story of the next ten years is familiar . . . a worrying loss of form for most of his first season, nearly 2,000 runs the following year, a splendid, mature England debut in Australia and fascinating battles with the South African googly bowlers in 1907 and on the 1909 tour. He began the second of his four great opening partnerships – with Wilfred Rhodes – in South Africa and their contrasting styles served England magnificently in Australia in 1911–12 and again in South Africa in 1913–14. Hobbs always said that Rhodes was the best runner of all his illustrious partners – just a nod was sufficient and they were home before the fielders could take stock. They were the first opening partners not to call, relying on intuition and trust, and in their happy collaboration only two run-outs occurred – on the admission of Rhodes, both his fault.

The performance of Hobbs on the difficult matting wickets in South Africa against the wonderful googly bowlers established his credentials as the world's best batsman, just five years since his debut before the quizzical eyes of W.G.Grace. Googly bowling was in its infancy – it had been discovered by B.J.T.Bosanquet at the turn of the century–but it had already won Test Matches for Bosanquet and for the South African quartet of Vogler, Faulkner, Schwarz and White. Many famous batsmen of the time were perplexed by the new form of attack; they would play the off-drive from the front foot and, to their horror, watch the ball dip in to the leg from basically a leg break action. Tom Hayward never fathomed its intricacies and R.E.Foster – classical batsman of the public-school style – wrote sniffily in *Wisden* that the googly would mean the demise of off-side play.

The matting wickets in South Africa made the googly even more formidable because of the extra bounce. Only Hobbs, with his deft footwork, swift reactions and instinctive awareness of the bad ball, prospered. He used the classic methods – pushing forward if he thought the ball could be smothered, and going back as far as possible to play off the pitch. His ability to spot the point of pitch was uncanny and somehow he could sense which ball was the googly. The South African quartet was never the same again and Hobbs, demonstrating how a great player can adapt to changing bowling methods, returned home with his captain, H.D.G.Leveson-Gower, paying him due homage: 'I have never seen better batting either in England or anywhere else.'

Challenge always brought out the best in Jack Hobbs. Gathering runs for the sake of it was never his forte, at any stage of his career. Mastering the South African spinners was a matter of unaffected pride to him and an innings of 69 not out at Edgbaston in 1909 against Australia also pleased him immensely. On a pitch badly affected by rain, Hobbs was lbw first ball. In England's second innings, the target was 105 on a difficult wicket. Fry and Hobbs – two men on a 'king pair' – knocked off the runs in even time, a wonderful effort in the circumstances. Now C.B.Fry was no blushing violet and he was entitled to be pleased with his 35 not out, yet even this engaging egotist was moved to write of his young partner: 'I have to say that this was as great an innings as I ever saw played by any batsman in any Test match, or any other match. His quickness with his bat and his skill in forcing the direction of his strokes made me feel like a fledgling.' In later years, Hobbs would diffidently acknowledge: 'I played really well – you know when you play well.'

The year 1914 was the peak of Hobbs's career. After 1919, he was more certain, more masterful, the complete player – but before the Great War, he was a dazzling improviser. During the 1914 season, A.C.MacLaren, the former England captain, recognised the genius of Hobbs by commissioning a film on his technique. MacLaren selected 98 shots illustrating ten strokes, and when they were reproduced in book form, MacLaren's euologistic words were in contrast to his usually stern pronouncements: 'He has never departed from sound methods, but has kept his natural free game pure throughout his career. I never recollect him being sent back to the pavillion, having played the wrong game for the occasion.'

One can only hazard a guess at the kind of entertainment Jack Hobbs would have given had not more important matters distracted mankind from 1914 to 1918. He always said he was twice the player before the

War – afterwards, he had to play more off the back foot. He was rising thirty-seven when first-class cricket resumed, approaching middle age in playing terms, and if he had to adapt to the ravages of times, he did so with typical grace, economy of movement and with little depreciation in aesthetic appeal. His post-War phase was even more glorious, his place in the public's heart more affectionately fixed than ever before. He entered a prodigious period of consistency – 35,017 runs in 15 years, 131 of his 197 hundreds and only once (in 1923) was his average less than 51. Before Bradman, he was the most consistent run-getter of all time, yet no one worried less about the sheer slog of carving out big scores. He was, quite simply, the Master, and the runs came automatically, the product of a wonderful technique, a keen, tactical intelligence and a serene temperament.

Hobbs often pointed out to his friends that the post-War bowlers were not quite as good as their predecessors, that the wickets were better, and that he was fortunate enough to play all his career under the old lbw rule, which had enabled him to play off-spinners on a turning wicket with his pads. Yet surely Hobbs, the man who dominated every type of bowling on all wickets over thirty years, would have solved the technical problems caused by the new lbw law? He batted according to the laws of his time, but he was so skilful at playing the ball coming into him, so strong on the legside, that just a little tinkering with that smooth engine would have sufficed.

His technique was solidly and elegantly based: relaxed, perfectly balanced, so that he could go back or forward in an instant. His footwork was so fast – even in his forties – that he could dictate the length of the ball. He gripped the bat firmly with his bottom hand, which helped him play all the shots. He manipulated the ball with consummate ease, almost checking the shot, so that it travelled slowly to the fielder, while he stole a single. Only Leonard Hutton, among the great batsmen, has approached this touch on the ball. Hobbs delighted in placing the ball into a space, then watching the fielding captain plug the gap, only to plunder the position where the fielder had been. His running between the wickets was safe, assured, graceful – and totally demoralising.

Hobbs liked to get off the mark as soon as he took strike; it was common knowledge around the county circuit and many plans were laid to try to run him out in the first over. Jack Mercer – splendid bowler for Glamorgan and Sussex and a close friend of Hobbs – devised a scheme with the aid of his Glamorgan captain, Maurice Turnbull. 'We were due to play Surrey in a week and so we practised and practised, running out batsmen in the middle. Come the day, I bowled the first ball, expecting Jack to stroke it slowly to cover point – he hit it like a bullet past square leg to the boundary. He grinned down the wicket at me, almost as if he knew what we'd been planning.'

F.R.Brown told me that the ambition of Hobbs early in his innings lay far beyond getting one off the mark. He told me; 'In my early days at Surrey, Jack was nudging fifty years of age, but he used to tell me that the time for easy runs was at the start of an innings, despite the new ball. He said the bowlers weren't loosened up at the start, and he would try to pick up as many fours as he could to disconcert them and knock them off their length. I can vouch for his effectiveness.' So can Bill Bowes: 'The first time I bowled at him, he went down on one knee and hit me past the left hand of square-leg. The ball had pitched seven or eight inches outside off-stump. My jaw dropped and George Macaulay at mid-on shouted reassuringly: "It's no good you peepin' – he'll do that three times an over when his eye's in." And he did. I had to think harder bowling at Jack Hobbs than against any other player.'

When necessary, he could launch blistering assaults on certain bowlers. This was usually in the interests of the side – perhaps the wicket was a difficult one and Hobbs would worry about the influence of the opposition's star bowler. His treatment of Charlie Parker is legendary among the old Gloucestershire players. With his left-arm spin Parker was a destroyer on the helpful Cheltenham wickets and Hobbs would often knock him out of the attack by driving him several times over cover. Parker, who always knew Hobbs had the mastery over him, would slouch away to third man, and refuse to bowl until Hobbs was out. Reg Sinfield – Parker's team-mate in the 1930s – recalls a game on a bad pitch, when Hobbs was dropped at slip early on off Sinfield's bowling. 'He said, "bad luck, Reg, I'll give you my wicket when I get a hundred." Charlie Parker heard that and moaned, "Oh God, that means he will get one." It was a devil of a wicket, an old-fashioned sticky one, and Jack smashed Charlie out of sight. I was bowling at him just after he got his hundred and he said, "look out Reg!" and put up a simple catch to the fielder. It was an amazing innings – Bradman wouldn't have made ten on that wicket'.

That parting shot from Sinfield was echoed by every contemporary of Hobbs I have interviewed. Les Ames confirmed the magnificence of the Hobbs/Sutcliffe partnership at Melbourne on the 1928–9 tour of Australia. England needed 332 to win and a thunderstorm soaked the wicket. The hot sun came out and Hobbs and Sutcliffe had to face a typical Melbourne sticky wicket – the worst of its type in Australia. Hobbs had his cap knocked off and he and his great partner were beaten and bruised many times. They somehow survived, added 105 before Hobbs was lbw for 49, and Sutcliffe steered England to a great three-wicket victory. Les Ames watched that stand and recalls: 'It was an absolute pig of a wicket, we should've been out for less than a hundred. I have never seen such an exhibition of bad-wicket batting.'

Hobbs was aged forty-six at the time. Effortlessly he adjusted his technique to suit the tactical situation, his physical powers and the needs of his side. Two years before the classic Melbourne performance, he and Sutcliffe had wrested back the Ashes with an historic stand of 172 on an Oval wicket soaked by overnight rain and rendered spiteful by warm sunshine. Clearly Arthur Richardson's off-breaks from round the wicket to a six-man legtrap should have been more productive; Arthur Mailey and Clarrie Grimmett also did not do themselves justice. Yet the conditions were foul – Sutcliffe was hit in the face by one ball that popped – and England had a bare 22 runs lead on the first innings, with the Ashes depending on the result. Jim Laker would have posed a much sterner test and Hobbs later agreed that someone like Parkin, Astill or Macaulay would have been unplayable. Having made such allowances, it was nevertheless a *tour de force*; both men made famous hundreds, the wicket dried out and England won by 289 runs.

For Hobbs, the joy of batting was never far from the surface, despite the occasional crisis that he would steel himself to surmount. His wry remark to Sutcliffe on the morning of their classic Oval partnership ('I think the rain has done us') typified a humour that was always gentle, occasionally ingenuous. He was no show-off, but he loved to see the expression on the face of his old friends as he played some dazzling shot or other. Once Arthur Mailey managed to get Hobbs on a dry, dusty wicket that was ideal for his expansive leg-spin. Mailey bowled him a leg-break that pitched on middle and leg and turned a long way towards the off. Hobbs stroked him in front of square leg for four and smiled at Mailey: 'Poor old Arthur, they always put you on when it won't turn!' Alf Gover remembers his playful genius – and again the victim was the misanthropic Charlie Parker. Gover came in last man on another spiteful turner and watched Hobbs manipulate the strike against Goddard and Parker in masterly style. With the bowlers distractedly trying to get at Gover, the *coup de grace* arrived. Gover recalls: 'Charlie bowled at Jack with four men very close in on the offside. He was bowling away from the bat on a turning wicket and he wanted to keep

Jack down that end. Off the last ball of the over, Jack leaned back and calmly placed the ball past slip for a precious single. Jack chuckled, "What about that, Charlie?" and Charlie, snatching his cap, could only sniff – "Bloody marvellous!" From a man like Parker that was quite a compliment.'

Gover still talks about another stroke by Hobbs that lingers in his memory, fifty-four years after the event. Hobbs captained an all-professional Surrey side against Northants and, with Sandham ill, he took Gover in first with him. Gover – a career batting average of nine ahead of him – asked Hobbs to look after the dangerous Austin Matthews, a lively fast-medium bowler who later played for England. Hobbs did so and one particular delivery from Matthews convinced the young Gover of his partner's genius: 'Jack thought it was an inswinger and leaned into it; but it moved away off the seam. Matthews had one hand up in the air, thinking he had got through his defence – but Jack rocked back and cut it wide of cover for four.'

The amateurs of his time regarded Hobbs with a mixture of affection and respect. R.E.S.Wyatt, who led him in his last Test in 1930, recalls how helpful and charming he was to the nervous young captain. Percy Fender, Hobbs's captain at Surrey for many years, said he was a marvellous bridge between the skipper and the other professionals – 'he would talk to them and make sure we were all on the same wavelength in the team.' G.O.Allen first met him in 1921 when he was at Cambridge; Hobbs asked him if he was nervous before a game and when Allen confirmed that he was, Hobbs replied: 'So am I, and I wouldn't have it any other way.' Allen recalls: 'He was so charming to me, who was just a young student. He did so much for the professional players over the years. By his behaviour and ability he earned respect for himself and his profession.'

That was important to Hobbs. He was happy to leave the duties of captaincy to Herbert Strudwick if the amateur captain was unavailable, but he always insisted on the highest standards from his fellow-professionals. Alf Gover received early notice of this when he first came into the Surrey side; he had had some bad luck with his bowling and was loudly bemoaning this state of affairs in the dressing-room, interspersed with a few colourful adjectives. Hobbs said quietly, 'Alfred, come over here' and proceeded to lecture him about his responsibilities as a Surrey cricketer on and off the field. Thereafter, Gover never swore in the dressing-room and for several years, could not bring himself to call Jack anything other than 'Sir'.

His standing in the eyes of the public was Olympian during the 1920s. When he passed Grace's total of centuries at Taunton in 1925, he was bewildered by the battery of cameras and reporters. He found it hard to come to terms with being a public figure, yet accepted it with his usual shy grace. Much of the ballyhoo distressed him, but some of it was a great source of amusement. For instance, when he equalled Grace's total of 126 centuries, Percy Fender brought him out some ginger ale in a champagne glass. By gratefully taking the toast Hobbs unwittingly stirred up a hornet's nest among the temperance bodies. Indignant letters to *The Times* spluttered that a national hero had let them down and thereby encouraged the working classes to quaff even more alcohol. It was a farcical claim, especially against such an abstemious man, but it made Hobbs chuckle in his retirement.

In the last few seasons of his wonderful career, his powers inevitably declined, but not to a demeaning extent. He was rattled by some short-pitched bowling by 'Hopper' Read of Essex – F.R.Brown remembers him saying to Read, 'If you bowl properly, I'll play properly' – and more seriously, by Bill Bowes of Yorkshire. Bowes is frank about his intentions: 'I knew I couldn't bowl him, so I wanted to get him hitting in the air.' Hobbs protested in an uncharacteristically public way: after the first bouncer, he walked down the pitch to the bowler's end and patted a spot. At the goading of George Macaulay, Bowes bowled another bouncer – 'I saw Jack coming up to my end again and I said "not there, Jack", and, pointing to a place in my run-up, I said "up there". Jack said, "sorry Bill", and proceeded to walk past the wicket and pat a spot. He was rattled but although he was fifty years of age, he was still a great player.' Hobbs did not resume his innings after lunch – he was said to have sunstroke.

If his feathers were ruffled by that assault, he showed his greatness against fast bowling in the following summer of 1933. Learie Constantine and Manny Martindale were in England with the touring West Indian team, determined to show that anything Larwood and Voce could do under Jardine, they could return with interest. When the West Indies came to the Oval to play Surrey, W.H.Ferguson, the tourists' scorer told Hobbs he would not get many runs, because Martindale had pronounced he was finished. Hobbs smiled at the barb, looked out of the dressing-room and surprisingly forecast, 'I think I'll get a hundred today, that looks a good wicket.' He made 221 in six-and-a-half hours and, afterwards, Martindale came into the Surrey dressing-room and said, 'Mistah Hobbs, yous a great player.' It was Hobbs's first game of the season and he was stiff for a week. He was, after all, fifty-one.

One season remained and an innings against Maurice Tate accelerated his retirement. He made 79 against Sussex in cool, unhurried fashion, but it took him more than four hours and, in frustration, he ran himself out for the second time that season. When he returned to the dressing-room, he said: 'That's it, I'm finished – I just can't move my feet any more.' His last innings in first-class cricket was neatly appropriate – he scored 18, the same score that opened his account in 1905.

His prestige at his retirement was deservedly massive and nothing in the remaining thirty years of his life altered his reputation one jot. In 1953, the Master's Club was formed at the instigation of John Arlott and they would meet annually on Hobbs's birthday – old cricketing and business friends, supplemented by a few of the young breed. They were happy, mellow meetings illuminated by the man's modest pride in the company around him. After his death, the Master's Club continued to convene and there seems no reason why it should ever lapse. Like the batting of Jack Hobbs, it should defy the march of *anno domini*.

He was proud to be the first professional games player to be honoured with a knighthood in 1953, although initially he tried to refuse it, in case his friends would think he had changed. His knighthood marked the full circle of the social revolution that turned the professional cricketer from little more than a serf into a man to be respected. He always wanted to remain a professional cricketer and the sports shop he founded in 1920 gave him precious financial independence and clarity of mind. In his quiet way, Jack Hobbs moulded events to his satisfaction; in 1924, he at first refused to accompany England to Australia because he wished to have his wife with him. At first the MCC refused permission – only amateurs had previously been accorded such a privilege – and there was a worrying impasse for a month. Hobbs began to make plans for a private tour with his wife to South Africa, but finally Lord's relented. Mr and Mrs Hobbs went to Australia and the partnership of Hobbs and Sutcliffe prospered – but the great man had shown the principled side to his nature.

His fellow-professionals revered him. Jack Mercer told me in all sincerity that he had tried to model his life on the way that Hobbs lived. He admired his human touches – 'whenever he went in the nets before the game, he would encourage youngsters to bowl at him. He always made sure at least one of them clean-bowled him, he knew what it would mean.' When I visited John Langridge he showed me the prize possession from his career – a signed photograph of Langridge catching Hobbs at slip from the 1933 season. Alf Gover chuckles at Hobbs's impish sense of humour – the 'apple pie' beds, the times he'd shout 'he's out' and the next batsman would be on his way to the middle before he realised it was Jack's little joke. F.R.Brown remembers Jack setting up the dour Jardine to demonstrate some textbook cover drives in the dressing-room, only to see the light bulb come crashing down on his distinguished Harlequin cap.

He set new standards of sportsmanship and decency. There is an evocative photograph from the 1920s showing Hobbs just after being dismissed by a googly from G.T.S.Stevens for 87. In later years, Stevens would say, 'Jack waved and shouted, "Well bowled Mr Stevens, I never picked that one." ' This to an amateur eighteen years his junior. Stevens felt as if he had been knighted and that night proudly worked out his average against Hobbs: it was 1 for 257.

John Arlott says Hobbs never grumbled about umpires. 'In all his career, Jack reckoned he had the wrong end of a decision just once. When I pressed him for details, he said: "No, he was a dammed good umpire" and he wouldn't discuss it further.'

The statistical roll-call from his career is awesome. He shared in a stand of a hundred for the first wicket on no less than 166 occasions (15 of them in Tests) – with Sandham 66 times, with Hayward 40, and 26 with Sutcliffe. He never 'bagged a pair' – much to his pleasure. He missed five seasons through war and illness and would have amassed thousands more runs if he had so wished. Cricket can only be grateful his genius lasted so long and flowered so luxuriantly.

4

Philip Mead

'Hard enough for four is hard enough'

In the spring of 1903, two optimistic young cricketers presented themselves at the Oval, eager to impress the authorities of Surrey County Cricket Club. One was Jack Hobbs, the other a sixteen-year-old slow left-arm bowler from Battersea, a few miles from the Oval. Within the space of twenty-four hours, Hobbs had been clean bowled twice in trial matched by the sturdy teenager – for 37 and 13. It was a minor hiccup in the serene progress of Hobbs towards greatness but for Charles Philip Mead, it was the only highlight of his time at the Oval. Despite scoring a hundred in a London schools match at the age of ten, the Surrey club saw his future in slow bowling – mediocre slow bowling as it turned out, and at the end of the 1903 season he was not retained at the Oval.

Imagine the slaughter over the next thirty years if Mead had stayed at the Oval! Think of him coming in after Hobbs and Hayward, or Hobbs and Sandham of later vintage! Instead Philip Mead joined Hampshire in 1904 and launched a career that established him as one of the most prolific batsmen of all time. Only Hobbs, Hendren and Hammond have bettered his total of 153 centuries and just three batsmen – Hobbs, Woolley and Hendren – have surpassed his 55,061 runs. He holds one record that will surely never be approached; his total of 48,892 runs and 138 centuries is, in both cases, more than any man has ever scored for one team. He scored 1,000 runs in a season on 27 occasions – only Grace and Woolley with 28 have done better – twice he made 3,000 runs in a season and nine times 2,000 runs. No wonder an admiring Herbert Sutcliffe wrote, 'I wonder if there has been another player in the game who understood more of the science of batsmanship than Mead?'

He certainly had the respect of his opponents, but Mead never really struck a responsive chord with the spectators – partly because he was a dour, solemn character, partly because of his pragmatic batting methods. He was tallish, with shoulders sloping like a bottle; with wide hips, a pear-shape body and strong bowed legs, he rolled out to bat with the intention of staying there all day. On his arrival at the crease, he went through the same ritual before every ball: he would look towards the square leg umpire, tug the peak of his cap four times in his direction, then ground his bat in the blockhole and tap away four times. After that, he would take four shuffling steps into position. Only then was he ready to face the bowler. He did that before every delivery in thirty-one years of first-class cricket, during his 1,340 innings. He wore out countless peaks on his caps and no matter how often the bowler tried to hustle him out of his routine, Mead would never allow him to deliver until he was ready.

The 'Mead Shuffle' would be copied by generations of Hampshire schoolboys in back gardens and parks but otherwise he never caught their imagination. He was 'the unbowlable', lacking the romantic hitting prowess of Woolley, the courtly mastery of Hobbs, the impishness of Hendren. Mead's left-hand batting was chockful of commonsense – he would nudge, tickle, glide and accumulate. Occasionally he would lean forward and punch an off-drive – he seemed to have longer arms than normal – and rarely would he loft the ball. He would often aver, 'hard enough for four is hard enough.'

Mead may have looked sluggish on his feet but, in fact, he got into position remarkably quickly. When he moved he was well-balanced and he was in position to play the ball with time to spare. Les Ames stood behind the stumps for Kent on many occasions when Mead's footwork and positional skills were too much for 'Tich' Freeman's leg-spin. Ames recalls, 'No one played "Tich" better. Players like Hammond and Hendren might murder "Tich" on occasions, but he would also get them out. Not so with Phil – he seemed to play everything round to leg and he always spotted the googly. He got into position smartly and often played him a yard down the wicket, invariably right in the middle of the bat.'

He played straight and after a time, in the words of R.E.S.Wyatt, 'his bat seemed twice the normal size'. Indeed, the waggish Cecil Parkin once suggested that Mead's bat should be taken to a carpenter for a close shave. With his imperturbable calm, he was a superb player of fast bowling, a point confirmed by G.O.Allen, one of the fastest bowlers of the 1920s: 'He was dogged, extremely correct and a very good, proficient player. He was never hurried out of his rhythm, kept his head still and watched the line of the ball. He may not have caught the eye, but the players in the middle knew just how good he was.'

Bill Bowes is fascinating on Mead's positional skills. Maurice Leyland had told him what a good 'leaver' Mead was and when Bill first met him, he asked if he would demonstrate it during the forthcoming match. 'After he'd scored thirty-odd, he started on at me – I was throwing up my arms as the ball missed his off-stump by a couple of inches. I couldn't believe it, I wish I'd never said a word.' In fact, Mead had a very fine record against the excellent Yorkshire attacks over the years and Bill Bowes offers this technical assessment of him.

> He was never out of position for the shot. If you beat his bat, his pad was always there as a second line of defence – remember this was before the change in the LBW law. He didn't hit the ball strongly off the front foot, and I would try to get him playing forward. Having said that, he could quickly recognise a half volley and lean into it just a little harder. He didn't hook, but liked to nudge it square and backward. Phil would always hit the bad ball for four and push singles off good deliveries so easily that you would be amazed that he had reached fifty or a hundred so comparatively quickly. He had this knack of playing the ball slowly enough to a fielder to steal a single, then as the field was brought in to stop the ones, he'd chip over their heads for two.

Alf Gover confirms that Mead hit the ball harder than many realised – 'the first time I played against him, I was in my usual position at short leg. Phil said, "I wouldn't stand too close if I were you, young fellow," but I stood my ground. Soon the ball went like a rocket past my ear off a short-pitched delivery and he grinned wickedly at me.'

Yet his reputation as a slow scorer never left him. His physical bulk gave the impression of solidity and he never thought of playing to the crowd to gain affection. When Mead was chosen to tour Australia ahead of Woolley in 1928, Gerry Weighall, the former Kent player, described the Hampshire man as a 'leaden-footed carthorse'. On closer examination of Mead's career the description was grossly unfair, even though admittedly he lacked the charm of Woolley's batting. Most of Mead's hundreds were scored at a rate of 40/45 runs an hour in the days when captains did not deliberately slow down the play. Assessed on the modern method of runs per balls faced, Mead would appear positively skittish. G.O.Allen recalls a double hundred by Mead that appeared in impressively fast time and was compiled with certainty of strokeplay – it was in 1929, for the MCC team that had toured Australia, and he scored 233 in five hours against Lord Hawke's XI, a side containing bowlers of the calibre of Allen, Jupp, Haig and Rhodes. With Hendren as partner, Mead added 272 in 150 minutes.

In 1911 – the year he came second in the national averages with 2,562 runs – Mead scored 401 runs in two days in a total of six hours and ten minutes. Against Warwickshire, he made 207 not out and the next day, against Sussex, he made 194. The total runs included 66 boundaries and his rate of scoring was more than 65 runs an hour. Yes, Mead was a stodgy performer! No less an authority than R.W.V.Robins believed this to be so. Once when Mead's dourness had driven the mercurial leg-spinner to distraction, he moaned: 'Mead, you've been in since ten past twelve and you've just stonewalled!' In vain did Mead protest that his score was 218 and that he had taken less than five hours in the process.

The England selectors usually preferred the more elegant and dashing Woolley to Mead, and one can hardly quibble at that. Yet it must be observed that Mead's Test average was 49.37 compared to Woolley's 36.07. The England selectors gave him an extended run just once – in his first series, in Australia in 1911–12 – and he failed, scoring just 105 runs at an average of 21. In 1921, when Gregory and MacDonald were frightening many England batsmen, one of the best players of fast bowling had to wait until the last two Tests to shore up the batting. He did not fail – 47 and 182 not out – and both Tests were drawn. He played just once more against Australia, in the first Test at Brisbane in 1928. He scored 8 and 73 – out lbw to Clarrie Grimmett both times – and when Percy Chapman decided to play an extra bowler for the rest of the series, Mead shuffled away and devoted more time to following horse racing. No doubt Gerry Weighall felt justice had been done. His Test average against Australia was nevertheless 51.87.

His treatment at the hands of the selectors served to deepen his already morose nature. He would carp a little about those lucky enough to play for more favoured counties and he seems to have had a point. He simply decided to keep churning out the runs, gaining immense pleasure from frustrating bowlers. He did not believe in net practice before a season started, or even during the season, rightly surmising that he got enough match practice. He would say to the other Hampshire batsmen: 'you lead in May and I shall catch you in June'. He once scored a century in the first county match of the season and roundly declared that he had not timed one shot. When asked the last time he had a bat in his hand, he replied: 'last Scarborough Festival'.

He lacked a sense of humour and could not see the funny side of a remark addressed to him by an Australian during the 1928-9 tour – 'Ah, Mead, how good to see you, I recall watching your father play in 1911.' He lacked the ability to laugh at himself and he had a strongly-developed sense of injustice. Once at Bournemouth he batted most of the morning against Surrey without attempting to play many shots. He played almost as stodgily as his reputation suggested and when he was tackled about it by the Surrey players at lunchtime, he pointed to their captain, P.G.H.Fender, 'That b_____ let me down in South Africa last winter. I bowled at him in the nets for three quarters of an hour. When it was my turn to bat, he couldn't be found to bowl at me. Well, he can bowl all day now.'

He was not amused when the ebullient Lionel Tennyson decided to pull his leg about his alleged slow scoring. Now Tennyson deeply respected his batsman's ability and soundness and knew that the jibes pricked him deeply. One day, as Mead proceeded in his usual, unhurried way to the inevitable century, Tennyson arranged to have a telegram sent out to the middle. The captain and the other professionals watched with glee as Mead looked quizzically at the messenger, opened the envelope and read the missive: 'Mead – get on or get out – Tennyson.'

Mead's solemn nature left him bereft of intimate companions in the Hampshire dressing-room, He and Jack Newman were fairly close through their passion for horse racing and they would dolefully share hard-luck stories, but the charges of selfishness were regularly laid at Mead's door. The talent money system used by Hampshire meant that scores of 49 and 99 were not only frustrating, but cost him money. The desire for 'another bag of coal for the winter' meant he was an unreliable judge of a run at certain periods of his innings – and invariably he would be the one to survive muddles that originated with him. In his last season in the Hampshire side, it was common knowledge that his team-mates were vying with each other to run him out at every opportunity. They failed – he was not run out once in 1936. Philip Mead often had the last word – with colleagues as well as opposition fast bowlers.

Bill Bowes recalls an incident which suggested that all was not well between Mead and his team-mates. Hampshire had been caught on a vile sticky wicket and Yorkshire's Hedley Verity was running through the side. Mead, a great defensive player on bad wickets, was combating

Verity with immense skill and application. Finally, he accepted the single that Verity had been offering to get him away from the strike, and as he ran to the other end, he said, 'Don't think I don't know what you're up to – but it's time the youngsters learned how to bat.' Yet it was his job to take Verity and save the game.

Did he have a batting weakness? R.E.S.Wyatt, one of the shrewdest of cricket judges, thought he could be worried by in-swingers to a leg-side field. Reg Sinfield agrees and remembers bowling the best three consecutive balls of his career to dismiss Mead. 'I always kept a mental note of the way the top batsmen played,' he explained, 'and Phil would get off the mark most of the time by tickling one round the corner. When he came in, I asked for no less than four short-legs, even though my off-spin would be leg-breaks to the left-hander. My captain, Bev Lyon, thought I was mad but I got my own way. First ball, he was plumb lbw and given "not out", the next one was dropped at the wicket and the third time, the keeper managed to hang onto the catch! Phil wasn't best pleased.'

He never was, if it meant going back to the pavilion, his cigarettes and the racing page. They could always wait for the interval, when he could reflect on how many bags of coal lay within his compass that day. Percy Fender, his *bête noire*, winkled him out one day with a typically creative piece of captaincy. Mead was making his inexorable progress towards lunch with twenty or so runs against his name. Fender suddenly realised that Mead had never seen Bob Gregory bowl his slow leg-spin that hardly ever turned. 'I put Bob on for the last over before lunch and told him to pitch them up. Mead had no idea what was in store, so I placed three fielders round the corner on the legside with exaggerated care. Mead kept shuffling into his stance, and looking around at the leg-trap and I could see his mind ticking over. For the first three balls, he pushed out suspiciously and each time after playing the stroke, he would look round at the three legside fielders. The fourth delivery didn't turn at all, it came straight on a little quicker, Mead played for the turn, the ball got an outside edge and slip caught it.' A tactical coup for Fender but at the same time it was a tribute to the respect he had for Mead that he realised something unorthodox was needed to prise him out before he settled in to his post-prandial, prolific groove.

In his last season, he predictably scored his 1,000 runs, including two hundreds. Hampshire, recognising his gargantuan feats for them, paid his salary for another year and opened a subscription for him. Just before the Second World War, he played Minor Counties cricket for Suffolk – averaging 76 and 71 – and coached at Framlingham College. Alec Bedser played against him for Surrey Seconds in 1939 and remembers Mead scoring 132 in about three hours. 'He didn't run around much, he seemed to hit the ball hard with no apparent effort. His eyes were going a little, but he hit everything in the middle of the bat.'

Tragically, he went blind after running a sports shop in Southampton and a pub near Bournemouth. He went to live with his daughter at Bournemouth and often turned up at Dean Park, where he was a shy, modest visitor to the Hampshire dressing-room. John Arlott says he had mellowed over the years and was an agreeable companion: 'He would never criticise the modern players. He thought he would have had trouble with the inswingers and negative field placings of the modern game' – perhaps he remembered his occasional problems with Sinfield and being outwitted by Fender. Although completely blind, Mead would sit happily discussing cricket, able to tell whether someone was playing well by the sound of his bat – 'he's not middlin' 'em is he?' he would chuckle. How appropriate – an innings by Mead had its own distinct sound, one of solidity as the ball met the middle of a staunch, unyielding bat.

He died in 1958, a few days after his seventy-first birthday. He had faced his blindness as calmly as the thunderbolts of 'Tibby' Cotter when he made his impressive debut – 41 not out – for Hampshire against the Australians in 1905. His death brought a re-assessment of his worth, an acknowledgement that you cannot be a stodgy player and score 55,000 runs (all of them in three-day games), and the fervent wish that more players with his defence and sheer competence would soon appear on the horizon. Hardly any did, and it would have been instructive to step into a time machine, whisk Philip Mead into the 1970s and watch him cope with the aggression and intimidation of Thomson, Lillee, Holding, Roberts, Imran Khan and Croft.

Alec Kennedy, his old team-mate, used to say that only Jack Hobbs rivalled Mead's ability to score a run off every ball, if he so wished. Kennedy paid tribute to Mead's ability on turning wickets: 'He almost seemed to prefer batting when the ball was doing something.' Philip Mead preferred batting full stop; or rather he preferred making runs, no less than 1,609 of them in a six-week period in 1921, or in 1927, a matter of 1,257 in fourteen innings. He was twice top of the national batting averages, second three times and third on four occasions.

Unwittingly, Mead's immovability led to the blossoming of one of the greatest medium-pace bowlers of all time. On 26 July, 1922, Hampshire was making slow progress against Sussex at Eastbourne. Philip Mead was batting in his detached style and Maurice Tate was bored and frustrated. His career as an off-spinner was stagnating, and he was making few runs to boot. As he ran up to bowl to the stolid Mead for the umpteenth time, he suddenly decided to bowl the fastest delivery of his life out of sheer frustration. It pitched on his leg-stump and whipped across at great speed to hit the top of the off-stump. Tate, sufficiently encouraged by the dismissal, took to the nets, perfected his style and within two years, he was a great bowler.

Towards the end of his life, Mead confessed he had been greatly surprised by the quality and speed of that delivery. When asked if he had said anything to Tate as he passed him en route to the pavilion, Mead chuckled and revealed the attitude of the run machine: 'Say anything? Not me, I never encouraged bowlers!' No, no one could ever suggest that of Philip Mead.

5

Patsy Hendren

'One day he will be given out, smile before wicket'
(Neville Cardus)

The batting record of Patsy Hendren is a towering monument to his ageless skills, but it tells only part of the story of this most lovable of men. If he had been a mediocre player who passed through first-class cricket for a couple of seasons, he would nevertheless have left warm memories of a man who believed in entertainment, in free expression of personality.

A look at his achievements first. Only Jack Hobbs has beaten his 170 centuries and just Hobbs and Frank Woolley have passed his total of 57,611 runs. In the list of double centurions, his total of 22 is third to Bradman and Hammond. He was the most prolific scorer of runs in the 1920s – 28,711 – and only Hammond has scored more in any decade. After a traumatic start, his Test career blossomed and in 51 Tests, he averaged 47 with seven hundreds. He made more centuries at Lords – 74 – than anyone.

He was a thrilling batsman, incapable of ever being dull, a compact parcel of energy. With a marvellous eye, supple wrists and dazzling footwork, he whacked the ball rather than steered it. He had all the shots, none more dazzling than the pull and the hook. G.O.Allen, his Middlesex colleague for many years, considers him one of the greatest players of slow bowling in the game's history. A complete craftsman with no real flaw, he may have lacked that intangible spark of genius but, for all that, he was one of the finest batsmen in the period between the two wars.

Patsy would be the last person to cavil, but I have always believed it unfair that his prodigious batting talents have been somewhat obscured by the laudable desire to pay tribute to his charming, spirited nature. On the other hand, it may be said that the batting style mirrors the man's character, and if you think about Bradman, about Hammond,

Compton, Hutton, Boycott, or many other high-class players, the point is apposite. It was Patsy's generosity of spirit, his sense of fun and of honourable challenge that beguiled spectators and opponents alike and made him one of the most popular cricketers in the game's history. Those who witnessed his final match for Middlesex in 1937 still talk about the moment when 10,000 emotional spectators sang, 'For He's A Jolly Good Fellow' as soon as he had reached his century. Ian Peebles, a team-mate for Middlesex and England, wrote, 'He had a talent for attracting the instant and lasting affection of all sections of society to a greater degree than any other sportsman or games player in my experience.' Joe Hardstaff, that fine Nottinghamshire batsman, told me: 'Happiness exuded from Patsy, he would walk into a room and immediately everyone would feel happier for his presence.'

Note the name 'Patsy'. He was christened Elias after being born in Chiswick of Irish parents, but no name was ever more unlikely for that sturdy india-rubber frame, for the owner of that long upper lip, mobile mouth, jolly round face and twinkling eyes. He looked Irish and so his team-mates called him 'Pat', his intimates 'Murphy'. Jack Hearne, his partner in so many productive stands, dubbed him 'Spud', while to the crowd he was ever 'Patsy'. No one could ever think of him as 'Hendren' in the way they would view Bradman, Hammond, Sutcliffe with a proper mixture of awe and respect. No sensible person ever held Patsy in awe. As Neville Cardus put it so evocatively, 'His smile says Patsy – one day he will be given out, smile before wicket.' Even *Wisden* relaxed its magisterial guard to pronounce in its obituary of Patsy Hendren that 'no game in which he was engaged could be described as dull.'

No doubt Patsy was responsible for some fairly effervescent games in the back street of Chiswick when he was a lad at the turn of the century. His origins were as humble as could be imagined: one of six children of Irish parents, both of whom were dead by the time he was fourteen. Lamp posts and trees were the wickets for Patsy, yet he managed to develop a batting potential that ran in the family – his brother, Dennis, played for Middlesex without ever rivalling Patsy's ability. At the age of fifteen, Patsy was playing for Turnham Green, watched benignly by an old bearded man who knew a little about the game. 'That's right, young 'un', he would say, 'hit 'em like that and you'll play for England.' The bluff character with the beard was W.G.Grace, now living in the capital and playing occasionally for London County. At about the same time, J.T. Hearne, the great Middlesex bowler, brought a side over to play the local team and Patsy made a good impression by batting capably through four overs against Tom Richardson, not the great Richardson of old, it is true, but still a lively proposition on the uncertain Chiswick Park wicket.

Also playing that day was G.W.Beldam, the Middlesex all-rounder and cricket photographer. He managed to arrange an interview at Lord's with the captain, Gregor MacGregor, who told Patsy: 'you must eat more pudding if you want to become a cricketer.' Perhaps the Cambridge graduate, England wicket-keeper, Scottish rugby international and successful businessman did not realise that puddings were fairly scarce in the Hendren home. Patsy did not take it to heart, was greatly encouraged and in 1905 he was on the Lord's staff, selling scorecards and bowling in the nets for hours against wealthy MCC members.

He had enjoyed no formal coaching, a fact that did not escape the attention of Pelham Warner. The England captain was one of those kindly amateurs who believed in picking out young talent, nurturing and encouraging it through a period of years, in the belief that it would eventually flourish. He was often proved correct – the careers of Harry Lee and Jack Hearne bear witness – and in the case of Patsy Hendren, his support eventually triumphed. It was Patsy's fielding that impressed Warner in those early days at Lord's; almost to the end of his career, Patsy remained a wonderful fielder, either in the outfield or in the slips. Warner felt that anyone who could field so decisively had cricket in his blood. So Patsy made his Middlesex debut in 1907, batting number eight, and for the eight seasons until the War the encouragement of Warner was not rewarded by any consistency. When war broke out, he was nearly twenty-six; he had played 131 championship matches and scored just over 5,000 runs, for an average of nearly 30. Was the legendary Warner talent-spotting on the decline?

The first season after the War marked the start of Patsy's advance towards batting maturity: he averaged 61 for 1,655 runs, then 2,520 at 61 the following year, and in 1920–1 he travelled with the England team to Australia. The next phase of his career had begun and in common with the previous stages, he met with adversity right away. Although he scored three fifties in his first three Tests in Australia, he was never very impressive, even though prolific in the State games. Back home in England, the pattern was more pronounced – he made 2,000 runs in the 1921 season, yet just seventeen runs in four innings for England. Gregory and MacDonald were just too much for him and he was still very nervous on the big occasions. At Trent Bridge he was bowled second ball by a vicious break-back, he ran out Donald Knight in the second innings and at Lord's he was bowled third ball. The cynics had a field day about 'Warner's pet', that he only played for England because he was a Middlesex man.

He had to live with the jibes about his Test Match temperament for several seasons as he piled up massive scores for Middlesex in delightful style. He began to assert himself in 1924-5 against Australia, averaging 39, then in 1926 he scored his first Test hundred against them. Another followed on Jardine's tour of 1928-9 and thereafter he was more or less a fixture in a very strong England batting line-up. On the 1929-30 England tour of the West Indies, he not only established himself as the number one folk hero, but he broke all records for an overseas season – 1,765 runs, average 126 (including four double hundreds) and in Tests he averaged 115 for 693 runs. His handling of the fast bowlers on that tour was, in the opinion of George Gunn and Wilfred Rhodes, the finest they had seen – he hooked and pulled Constantine with thrilling control. He patented one stroke that was pure Patsy; to a short ball outside his off stump, he would draw back from the wicket and slash out with his arms fully extended. Half cut, half square drive, the ball would travel at blistering speed between point and cover. On the hard, fast West Indian wickets, it was a productive shot and the crowds – accustomed to expressive batting – adored him. His antics kept them constantly amused. One of his favourite tricks in the West Indies was to creep in close on the legside as the bowler was running in; the spectators would shout: 'Watch dat man; Watch dat Patsy!', the batsman would be alerted and Patsy would make a great show of feigned petulance that he had been rumbled. For the rest of his days in cricket, Patsy would tell the tale with inspired mimicry.

F.R.Brown confirmed to me the quality of Patsy's mimicry, especially of the West Indian accent – 'he'd say "hello dere, man" to anyone in the dressing room.' One day, Patsy saw the chance to outwit his great West Indian friend, Learie Constantine, and he enlisted Freddie Brown's help. 'We were both playing for the MCC and Patsy asked me to bowl a googly on middle and leg for Constantine. He was sure that Learie would try to lap it and, sure enough, he did. Patsy caught him at deep square leg and as the ball was going towards him in the air, he was chuckling. He caught it and said to Learie: "dere you are, man, dere you are". Even Learie had to laugh at the quality of the accent.'

He was no less popular in Australia. The Hill at Sydney, never the subtlest or friendliest area, took Patsy to their heart. They enjoyed his dazzling out-fielding, the way he caught the ball in baseball fashion in front of his head, the good-natured reaction to an apple being thrown at him (take a bite and bowl it back at them) and his habit of jumping the fence and swigging a beer at the fall of a wicket. Once a barracker on the Hill called him an 'ugly little b——' and Patsy, recognising that at least two-thirds of the description was accurate, nevertheless decided to seek revenge. He told the barracker he would be over to see him at the fall of a wicket; eventually he started to climb over the fence in search of the loud-mouthed drunk and the Hill cheered Patsy to the echo as his taunter fled.

Patsy's humour was good-natured, uncomplicated and, above all, he knew when to stop. Japes would come to him spontaneously, as R.E.S.Wyatt once discovered in a friendly match in South Africa. Patsy was playing for the opposition scratch side and Ian Peebles was partnering Wyatt, a man who always saw the serious side of cricket, whether or not the game was of first-class status. No one could ever accuse Patsy of that frame of mind and when Peebles played forward and missed, Patsy – fielding at mid-on-shouted: 'come on, he's missed it!' Peebles, assuming the wicket-keeper had fumbled the ball for byes, raced up the pitch to find Wyatt still in his ground. It suddenly dawned on both men that mimicry of the Wyatt voice had just been added to the copious Hendren comic repertoire.

R.W.V.Robins fell victim to a similar trick in a championship match one damp afternoon at Derby. Patsy always admired the way Robins played the spinners – he would get down the pitch, trust his luck and play them defensively on the walk if he could not drive. If he missed the 'walking shot', he would carry on to the pavilion, leaving the formality of a stumping. This particular day, Tommy Mitchell was plying his leg-spin and Robins, playing the 'walking shot', missed and kept walking. Patsy, his partner, shouted, 'get back, he's missed it!'; Robins spun round and did a spectacular crash-dive into his crease. As he collected the vestiges of his dignity, and deplored his muddy shirt, he looked up to see the bails on the ground and the wicket-keeper in idle chatter with his slips. Stumped Hendren, bowled Hendren.

During one match at Trent Bridge, Jack Hearne was up till dawn playing cards and drinking. He and Patsy were the not out batsmen overnight and Hearne was in a dreadful state when play resumed. He implored Patsy to look after him, to keep him away from Larwood until he had sorted himself out. Patsy was typically solicitous, led him onto the pitch and escorted him out to the wicket, all the while enquiring after the health of his colleague, who was too occupied moaning about the bright glare of the sun. Patsy said when they reached the middle, 'I reckon we're a little early, Jack, we're the only ones out here,' and in his befuddled state, Hearne believed him and sat down. It was only when he heard the cries in the distance that it dawned on him – Patsy had edged him forty yards away from the umpires and fielders and he was sitting on a spot halfway to the boundary.

He would delight in foxing both spectators and players about the true destination of the ball. One of his favourite tricks was to chase after the ball, stop, seem to pick it up and stand there. As the batsmen hesitated over another run, they could not be sure whether the ball was twenty yards past Patsy or in his hand. Once he gulled Surrey's Alan Peach when fielding at long on; he caught Peach's straight drive one-handed, put it straight into his pocket and looked around for the ball. Peach assumed he had hit a six and as it was the end of the over, Patsy walked towards the middle. When he reached Peach, he said, 'What are you doing here, Alan?' and when Peach replied that he had hit a six, Patsy produced the ball and said; 'No you didn't, I caught you.' Even the umpires were unsure. Joe Hulme, a Middlesex team-mate, also fell victim to Patsy's spontaneous humour when Errol Holmes swept a ball to long leg at the Oval. Hulme lost it in the background of the gasometers and Patsy shouted, 'there it is, Joe'. Hulme, an athletic man, flung himself full length, only to discover that he had frightened a low-flying blackbird. The ball had already hit the fence before he started to dive.

Alf Gover remembers running up to bowl at Patsy one day, all fire and brimstone and rumbling effort – only to collapse with laughter, because Patsy was sticking his tongue out at him. Gover is the source of another story that is classic Patsy. In 1928 Gover was a young, enthusiastic quick bowler, anxious to make a name for himself and unworried about how many batsmen he frightened out in the process. He was playing at Lord's for the first time and met Patsy in the dressing-room. Patsy eyed him up and down and said, 'Are you fast?' On receiving the expected affirmation from the cocky young Gover, Patsy said, 'well go easy on me, young feller – I'm getting on and you might hit me.' Gover had no qualms about 'going easy' on this rotund little man and when Patsy came in, he had three balls to face from Gover. He hooked the first one for four, crashed the next to the third man boundary and the next was hooked for six. Says Gover, 'I thought he had just been lucky until Jack Hobbs asked me what I was playing at when the over ended. When I told Jack what Patsy had said, he burst out laughing and told me Patsy was the best hooker in the world. For the rest of his career, Patsy would ask me for a short one to get him off the mark!'

Patsy's fondness for the hook brought him injury just once. In 1931 he was badly hit on the head by Harold Larwood and many on the field thought he was dead. Joe Hardstaff was at cover point and recalls, 'His back legs were twitching as he lay motionless on the ground. He was carried off the field and we were all terribly upset.' Patsy was taken unconscious to hospital, but was back on the field within three weeks. Even then he turned that frightening event into comic advantage two years later when he wore the first protective helmet against the West Indians, Constantine and Martindale. It had three peaks, the brain-child of his wife, and Patsy said he was wearing it because at his age (44) he did not want to be badly injured by the fast bowlers. That season, he scored more than 3,000 runs with eleven centuries. As Alf Gover had discovered, the old boy could be a supreme bluffer.

Patsy never experienced that perceptible deterioration in powers that so perturbed Jack Hobbs. In his last season, at the age of fifty, he scored over 1,800 runs and he was still perfectly capable of delighting the crowd on a batting as well as comic level. When he was asked why he had decided to retire, he replied: 'While you can still say why, rather than when.' It had given him immense pleasure to play O'Reilly so capably when he encountered the great Australian leg-spinner for the first time in 1934; although O'Reilly dismissed him four times in the Test series, Patsy scored three hundreds against him, including one for England – at the age of forty-five.

Near the end of his career, he was delighted to play alongside two youngsters who shared his view that cricket was a game of fun. Bill Edrich and Denis Compton joined the Lord's staff at the same time and they idolised Patsy; they could not believe that the great man would want to spend so much time in their naive company, but they were wrong. He never turned them away, quite the reverse. He would often say, 'Now, lads, come and sit over here for a minute and I'll tell you about Joe Small in the West Indies back in '29.' Bill Edrich told me that he learned more about cricket from Patsy in his early days than from anyone since. He recalls the game against Somerset in 1937, when Patsy showed him how to play that splendid left-arm spinner, Jack White. 'Watch my feet,' Patsy told him,' you need to get far enough down the wicket to play the half volley, don't be afraid to get close to the ball.' Both men got hundreds that day. Denis Compton remembers Patsy's advice one day when he came in to face two fairly quick bowlers – 'I hope you've got your box on today, son?' Above all, Patsy was always there, never too busy to impart a few technical tips to the two youngsters; when rain stopped play, it was a consolation to know that soon Patsy would come over and say, 'right lads, let's have a little chat'.

He was even more generous with his time when he retired from first-class cricket. He coached at Harrow, then with Sussex, and from 1952 to 1960, he was the Middlesex scorer. Patsy was no Bill Frindall at that job, he was never particularly good at sums, and he could easily be distracted by the presence of some old playing chums in the scorers' box. Current players from other counties would seek him out, a fact that touched him. He always loved the young – from his blissfully happy marriage there were no children – and they gravitated to a simple, lovable man, a man without conceit about his tremendous record. The players from that Middlesex era in the 1950s speak with unaffected love of him, remarking on his one idiosyncrasy – he was very particular about who drove him to the various county fixtures. Edrich and Compton, his two pre-war protégés, were on Patsy's blacklist, they were just too fast behind the wheel. He preferred speed over a distance of 22 yards.

Eventually, the duties of scorer became too much for him and he retired in 1960. One night, his wife was woken by what seemed like a large sob by her husband. A qualified nurse, she deduced he had suffered a stroke. He died in a London hospital in October 1962, aged seventy-three. Earlier that year, his brother, Dennis, also passed away.

At his death, Sir Jack Hobbs said that Patsy 'was as good a player as anyone' and if that was a typically kind remark, it was Hobbs's own way of making the cricket world realise that there was far more to Patsy Hendren than his delightful personality. Les Ames considers him a wonderful player of slow bowling – 'I used to look forward to his duels with "Tich" Freeman. Patsy went further down the wicket to him than anyone I can remember.' F.R.Brown, another fine leg-spinner, said everyone relished the challenge of bowling at Patsy – 'I could never see him coming down the wicket, but as my arm would be coming over, he'd be two yards down the pitch. If you beat him, he'd grin and say "well bowled"; he always had a smile for you and I consider him one of the most endearing men I've met anywhere.' Bill Bowes remembers a wonderful exhibition by Hendren on a drying pitch against Wilfred Rhodes at Bradford in 1929. 'It was an education to see him get down the pitch to the greatest bowler I've seen and flat-bat him through the covers. Twice he hit Wilfred into the football ground and then we thought we'd got him when he slipped – but as he fell forward, he managed to kill the ball. Wilfred took his sweater, he'd had enough of this man.' Hendren that day, batting at number four, got 86 not out in a total of 154.

He was a bad starter, and, like Denis Compton, an unpredictable runner. (A soccer player of professional status, too, he played for England in a Victory international in 1919; he was very quick on his feet and on the turn, but he sometimes forgot that his partners lacked his dynamism.) He could never learn to open his account in the leisurely manner of a Hobbs, languidly playing the ball to cover and trotting home. Patsy wore his nervous heart on his sleeve and his first run was completed with open delight, hugging the bat in his arms as if someone was going to take it away from him. Perhaps that was part of Patsy's appeal; he was fallible, human, he knew what failure was like, and the deprivations stemming from grinding poverty.

He had no idiosyncrasies in batting, other than a backside that jutted out defiantly in his low stance. He had great strength of wrist and arm, which helped him control the blade and give power to the easy circular sweep of his bat. When playing forward, he compensated for his lack of height by getting a great distance to the pitch of the ball, with arms that were thrust out to their full extent. Those powerful wrists would allow him to clip a short-length ball through the covers without lofting it and for the hook shot, he would pick the length of the ball quickly, his excellent footwork would get him into the right position – back and into the wicket – and he would play the shot down with a horizontal bat. He could usually play the hook in front of square, the hallmark of a top-class player.

He played against Grace and Trumper and his career in the game lasted more than fifty years. His mentor, Sir Pelham Warner, survived him for just one year. He lived to see the end of Compton's career and the start of Geoffrey Boycott's. Patsy proved he had the character to supplement his innate skill and he remained an inspiration to the young. He was not the ideal senior professional, because he lacked the necessary steel to admonish. To Patsy, life was about making people laugh, keeping the ball down in the hook shot, wondering which of the youngsters could take a joke and leading a good Christian life. Jim Sims, hardly a po-faced character himself, summed up Patsy's common touch: 'Wherever he went he was recognised by all manner of people. The cockney would say, "Wotcher Patsy", and the ordinary person would smile at him. At the end of a train journey the engine driver and his mate would lean out of the cab and nod. Patsy would go to them and give them a couple of half crowns, thanking them for getting him back home.'

A devout Roman Catholic, he would never spurn fund-raising activities at his local church. He was methodical and precise in his habits and in clear, beautiful legible style, would answer every letter he received. Once he had a letter from a French monastery; some Irish trainee priests were asking him for details of cricket gear, the best value, etc, etc. By return post, Patsy sent them all the equipment they needed, free of charge.

He never forgot the favours afforded him when he was a pallid little orphan in need of a few puddings. No one ever starved at Patsy Hendren's cricketing table – players, umpires, spectators, they all got second helpings.

6

Frank Woolley

'To see a hundred by Woolley would keep you going
for years' (Bill Bowes)

No batsman has hit the ball harder or further for a longer period of time
than Frank Woolley. In the opinion of many good judges, he was the
greatest left-hander the game has seen, even if Mead was statistically
more impressive, Leyland had a better Test record and Sobers proved
his greatness in a later period. Woolley batted with a grace, power and
individuality that charmed the critics and brought grudging admiration
from his opponents. Neville Cardus waxed more lyrically about Woolley
than any other player ('When he was out, it seemed as if the sun had
set'), but hard-headed Yorkshiremen like Bill Bowes were equally
impressed: 'To see a hundred by Woolley would keep you going for
years.'

Patsy Hendren, not surprisingly, had *le mot juste* for Woolley: 'here
comes the lion-tamer', he would say as he made his angular, stiff-legged
way to the crease. At six feet three inches, Woolley justified the
soubriquet 'Stalky' that his colleagues bestowed on him, but once he had
taken guard, the harsh edges disappeared from his style. It was almost
impossible to bowl a good length to a man so tall: he could transform
anything into a half volley or long hop without major adjustment of feet
or body. He hit like a golfer – a wide swing allowed him to time his shot
to the appropriate length and away the ball would soar. He stroked,
rather than hit the ball, playing with an ease that was positively
tranquil. The contrast between the sweating, straining fast bowler and
the dismissive air with which Woolley would deal with the deliveries was
remarkable. Yet he seemed the soul of courtesy as he stroked twenty runs
in an over. Somehow the game did not have any harsh or combative
overtones when Woolley batted; unassertively, inscrutably, he would
annihilate great bowlers with the kind of detachment a butler uses when
he passes the sherry.

There were no airs and graces about Frank Woolley, no overt concessions to the crowd. He lacked the common touch of Hendren, indeed he never once dreamed of playing to the gallery. He knew the spectators were happy enough with him as a cricketer – and so were most of his opponents in those more chivalrous, unsophisticated days. At Canterbury in 1930, Woolley toyed with the Australians with his usual languid radiance, quickly reaching his half-century and taking a liking to Alan Fairfax's medium pace in the meantime. Fairfax, perturbed that the ball kept disappearing over the long-on and midwicket boundaries, asked his colleague, Vic Richardson, if he ought to keep bowling at Woolley's off-stump. Richardson replied with relish: 'All right, it's bloody marvellous, we're enjoying it!'

His method was simplicity itself: he would stand as upright as possible at the crease with hands high on the long-handle bat and feet slightly apart. He would pick up his bat with a long, easy sweep and it would come firmly down, close to the line of the off-stump. As Bill Bowes remembers with a shudder, 'He was always in a position to hit you off front foot or back.' R.E.S.Wyatt studied his method many times when they batted together: 'He was so perfectly poised. He could assume rapidly another position while retaining his initial balance. Even when bowled, he looked graceful. He played with such ease that I cannot remember seeing him in a defensive position – and there was no point in bowling short at him, he would swat it away, half-pull, half-hook. His straight driving was absolutely devastating: I have never seen anyone hit the ball harder back over the bowler's head.'

Les Ames, who partnered Woolley in so many thrilling assaults for Kent, says Woolley's elegant dominance stemmed from steely determination. 'He simply would not be dictated to. He often used to say to me, "this chap's bowling too well, we've got to get after him," and he led the attack.' Ames, vastly experienced and not the kind of man to live in the past, nominates Ian Botham as the only man who could today be compared to Woolley in attitude and power of strokes, but feels that, as yet, Botham could not play the kind of innings he saw at Bradford in 1931 against Yorkshire. 'We had been put in on a wet wicket and Hedley Verity looked unplayable. I came in and Frank said to me, "I don't know who this new bowler is, but he's good – I'll take him." He did so, and he pulverised Verity.' Woolley made 188 out of 296 for 4 on a dreadful wicket. It took him $3\frac{1}{2}$ hours and included seven sixes – five off Verity. One of the other two sixes came off the bowling of Bill Bowes, a shot he will never forget. 'It was the last ball before lunch,' Bowes told me, 'and when I saw coming down the pitch at me, I pitched it short. He hit it on the up and it sailed over the pavillion at long on. Up and up it went, it was like a pea in the distance, right out of the ground. He hit me further than anyone ever managed, and I was pretty quick in those days, I can tell you. . . '

That Bradford innings was typical of the flavour of Woolley's batting: it had a wonderful, quixotic gallantry about it, especially when he was tilting at the fast bowlers. An innings by Woolley never seemed to last very long – few of the good things in life do – and that ephemeral quality added to the attraction of the man. English spectators, accustomed to mundane feats, would hug themselves with glee when Woolley was at the crease: he played the same way all his life, whatever his score. He was out 35 times in the nineties and he made nought 89 times. On his retirement, he wrote, 'It was never a question of the nervous nineties, I was out many times forcing the game. We were never allowed to play for our averages in the Kent side or take half an hour to get the necessary ten runs.' That unselfish attitude, and the precarious nature of his batting should be borne in mind when the statistically-minded consider his career record.

Very well, let us examine his statistical achievements. A career average of 40.77 and one of 36.07 in Tests does not look terribly impressive in the context of an age of batting cornucopia. Yet any man who consciously took the risks that he did would be more than happy with a run-tally of 58,959 (second only to Hobbs), a total of 145 centuries (sixth in the list), a little matter of 1,000 runs in 28 seasons (a shared record with Grace). Let us not forget his other cricketing qualities – the greatest number of catches by a fielder (1,015) and more than 2,000 wickets with slow left-arm bowling that, in the opinion of the Kent wicket-keeper, Fred Huish, was superior to that of the brilliant Colin Blythe. Of course, Woolley played a long time to build up such impressive figures, but by any standards, he was one of the greatest all-round cricketers the game has known. And entertainment, not statistical prowess, was his abiding aim.

Scores of batsmen have more impressive Test records, but I wonder how many of them could have played the type of innings he played at Lord's in June, 1921? Twice Woolley led England from parlous starts to some sort of respectability but it was the manner of his counter-attacks against Gregory and MacDonald that was so thrilling and legendary. On a fiery wicket, against great bowlers backed up by brilliant fielding, Woolley scored 95 and 93 out of 187 and 283; he was stumped in the first innings, going for his shots with the last man in, and his dismissal in the second innings was a freak, Hendry miraculously catching a pull from a long-hop. That was the way Woolley played his cricket; runs for the side were more important than the prestige of Test centuries. In his retirement, Woolley modestly reasoned that both innings were worthy of 150 in normal circumstances and cricket history has accorded them a deserved status.

It always seemed appropriate that Woolley played for Kent. The tents, the bunting, the animated atmosphere of those intimate grounds in the hop county seemed to strike a chord in him. He came into the Kent side when their reputation for dynamic, attractive cricket was deservedly high and for the next thirty-two years, Woolley did nothing to dim its lustre. Genius has no geographical limitations and one can only speculate how much encouragement he would have received if he had wandered down to the county ground at Derby, Leicester or Edgbaston in those days. Would he have been able to bowl in the nets with an England cricketer when he was just twelve years of age? That was the happy introduction of Frank Woolley to Kent cricket. Born and reared in Tonbridge he just picked up the game along with his brothers, one of whom later played for Gloucestershire and Northants. One day he happened to be standing at a net on the Angel cricket ground, watching a slow left-hander practising. Asked if he bowled, Woolley confirmed that he was of the same style and was asked to join in. The youngster was sufficiently impressive to be told to keep in touch with officials at the county ground. He needed no second bidding and he remained deeply grateful to his partner in that first net practice – Colin Blythe.

Blythe's acumen was rewarded by encouraging words from the Kent manager, Tom Pawley, and Woolley developed his bowling and batting under Blythe's benevolent tutelage. In 1906, when he was nineteen, Woolley made his debut for Kent – ironically Blythe was injured – and his experiences in that game would have been enough to daunt lesser men.

On a hot, sunny June day, Woolley walked onto the turf at Old Trafford, unaware that the next six hours' play would stay forever in his memory. Despite his ability as a slip fielder, he was initially posted at third man, to face the dazzling square-cutting of one of the shot's greatest exponents. J.T.Tyldesley. Soon, Tyldesley launched into a low, skimming square cut that was nevertheless catchable. It hit Woolley on the breastbone, the batsman ran three and the crowd laughed. He was moved to mid-on and a few minutes later, dropped Tyldesley off a skier. It hit Woolley on the back of the neck. He never heard the cry of 'no-ball', so, as far as he was concerned, that was a dropped catch. He was moved to mid-off and two overs later, he chased another skier from Tyldesley. He misjudged it, the ball hit his boot and Old Trafford hooted once more with derision at this gangling youth with no co-ordination. When he bowled his left-arm spin, Tyldesley climbed into him – he took 1 for 103 in 26 overs. At close of play, Lancashire were all out 531, Tyldesley 295. The following day, Woolley, batting at number eight, was clean bowled third ball for nought. Could it possibly get worse? Happily, he recovered his nerve and made a blistering 64 in the second innings. Soon he was scoring a hundred against Hampshire in ninety minutes – at Tonbridge, his home town.

His talent was remarkable and his gaucheness and naivety were also a source of wonder and amusement. When he first played against Surrey, he had only heard of Tom Hayward among the opposition, but had no idea where he batted and what he looked like. Midway through the Surrey innings, at the fall of a wicket, he said, 'When does Tom Hayward come in?' and was mortified to be told, 'He was the second man you bowled out.'

Woolley adorned that pre-war Kent side, but he was just one of many magnificent players. Kent won the championship in 1906, 1909, 1910 and 1913 and the influence of the amateur batsman confirmed his initial impression that the only way to bat was by attacking the bowlers. Subsequently, Woolley always felt that the quality of cricket before 1914 was much higher than afterwards, that men like Hammond would need to be at the very peak of form to get in the England side. Woolley managed that in 1909 for the first time and he remained in it until 1926 – an unbroken run of 52 consecutive Test appearances. His bowling was keeping pace with his thrilling batting – he performed the 'double' three times before he was 27 – and in the 1912 Oval Test against Australia, his match analysis was 10 for 49.

His most spectacular pre-war innings was in Hobart, Tasmania on the 1911–12 tour of Australia. He scored 303 not out, including two sixes and 47 fours and owed it all to Sydney Barnes. Woolley had been complaining to Barnes that he never seemed to be batting higher than number seven on the trip and here he was in Hobart, down to bat at number eight. Barnes told him, 'As soon as our innings starts, get your pads on. Phil Mead's due in first wicket down, but I'll take care of that. Walk into bat as soon as one of the openers is out.' Woolley did as he was told, and the captain Frank Foster did not know anything about the switch till he noticed Woolley thrashing the Tasmanian bowlers out of sight. The whereabouts of Mead have never been ascertained: perhaps the racing page had proved even more engrossing than usual.

It seems ironic that a man of Woolley's consummate batting ability should be turned down by the Army during the Great War because of poor eyesight. Cricket lovers can only be grateful to that unknown medical officer, otherwise Woolley might have suffered the same fate as his great friend and mentor, Colin Blythe – killed in France in 1917.

After the War, Woolley still had twenty years' first-class cricket left in him and his example ensured that Kent remained popular visitors on any ground. His attitude to batting never changed as his captain, Lord Cornwallis, once discovered. Woolley was decimating the Nottinghamshire attack with his familiar abandon and the skipper suggested to him that he should consolidate his innings just a little. He was told in no uncertain terms, 'I can only play one game, Captain Cornwallis' – he proceeded to hit the next four balls to the boundary, and was caught off the fifth.

Only one way of playing indeed – and a thrilling one it was. At Dover in 1937, he showed the Gloucestershire bowlers his way of playing. Kent needed 217 to win in 95 minutes and Woolley, going in first, set the tempo of the attack: he made 44 out of 68 in 25 minutes and Kent won with 24 minutes to spare.

Jack Mercer tells a lovely story that illustrates Woolley's supreme confidence: 'When we played Kent at Cardiff, I got Frank caught with a late inswinger, which pleased me greatly. In the return game at Maidstone, I tried him again with a slowish inswinger. He hit it straight back at me, I got a hand to it, yet it still went for six. Frank called to me that he'd been waiting to do that since Cardiff!'

Les Ames maintains that Woolley was the greatest entertainer of his age, apart from Bradman. 'Just look at the crowds he used to draw. The Kent match was invariably the choice of a beneficiary, because of Frank. Wherever we played, we got the best gates, due to his batting and influence on the rest of us. He could score so quickly that our bowlers had had extra time to bowl the opposition out.' W.H.V.Levett – 'Hopper' Levett – was sent in as night-watchman ahead of Woolley for simple economic reasons. 'In those days, the gate was vitally important and Frank was such a great attraction that he would put thousands on the crowd. County treasurers couldn't afford to have him dismissed late in the day.'

Woolley suffered two major disappointments in his post-war career, and they both concerned Australia. In 1928, English batting was at a peak of efficiency, depth and variety that has not been emulated since. Woolley scored 3,352 runs, including twelve hundreds, yet was not selected for the winter tour to Australia. Maurice Leyland – thirteen years his junior – was picked ahead of him, a justified choice as it proved, but the selection of Mead was bitterly criticised. He was the same age as Woolley, but lacked his bowling and fielding ability. The furore only served to confirm the affection that Kentish supporters felt for their languid hero, but Woolley kept a dignified silence on the matter.

In 1934, Woolley was unwisely recalled for the Fifth Test at the age of forty-seven. The captain, R.E.S.Wyatt, felt he might demoralise O'Reilly but he made 4 and 0. Worse was to come – Les Ames ricked his back and Woolley had to keep wicket in the second innings. He let through 37 byes, extras was third top scorer in the innings and England lost by 562, a disastrous end to Woolley's Test career. Why a man of his age with no previous experience kept wicket is beyond my comprehension and it was a sad experience for Woolley, one that he did not deserve.

He did deserve the accolades that came his way on his retirement in 1938. It was fitting that he should captain the Players in their match against the Gentlemen at Lord's. An abstemious, reserved man, he had done much to raise the status of the professional in his time. Woolley was respected by all cricketers, except for one man – Douglas Jardine. Woolley never forgot the autocratic way he was treated by Jardine, when he captained England against New Zealand at Lord's in 1931. It was bad enough to send a great slip fielder down to third man and fine leg without any explanation, but worse to come. As the bowler ran up, Jardine stopped him imperiously and shouted, 'Go to B, Woolley' – the 'B' referring to the numbered sections of the grandstand. Still Jardine was not satisfied and one ball later halted play again and called out: 'I said B, Woolley, not C!' It was unforgivable behaviour towards a great cricketer and Woolley felt he had been made to look inferior in front of a large crowd.

Woolley bore life's misfortunes with quiet stoicism – including the loss of his son on active service during the Second World War and when his house at Cliftonville was blown up. And only one thing used to rattle him as a player; he could never work out why he had been dismissed. Many old players have confirmed to me that Woolley would stand at his crease after he had been bowled, waiting in vain for a call of 'no-ball'. Bill Bowes told me; 'Whenever he was out, he would keep looking over

his shoulder on the way back, in case the umpire had changed his mind.'
Les Ames remembers when he hit a ball straight to cover, who took it
beautifully, but Woolley patted away at the pitch, getting ready for the
next delivery, under the impression it had been a bump ball. F.R.Brown
told me that he once refused to go when he had bowled him out of the
rough created by Alf Gover's footholds. Woolley asserted that the
wicket-keeper had padded the ball onto the stumps and Frank Chester,
that great umpire, had to tell Woolley to leave.

Perhaps a remark made by Woolley on another occasion to an
umpire gives some clue to his attitude to being dismissed. It was 1923
and Kent were playing Warwickshire at Dover; the young medium-
pacer, R.E.S.Wyatt, had dimissed Woolley in the first innings and then
got him out again, for the second time in the match. He was given out at
once and Woolley stared down the wicket incredulously before depart-
ing. Afterwards Woolley told the unpire, 'I wasn't disputing your
decision. I just couldn't believe that such an awful bowler could get me
out twice!' Perhaps he was so confident of his ability, so sure in his
touch that he convinced himself that he alone could get himself out, not
any bowler.

Certainly the Australians were aware of Woolley's non-walking
reputation. During the great innings of 93 in the 1921 Lord's Test, Nigel
Haig walked out to join the valiant Woolley. On arriving at the wicket,
he heard the following conversation between Woolley and the rumbus-
tious Australian captain, Warwick Armstrong. . . .

ARMSTRONG: 'Nobody but a bloody Pom would have stood there!'

WOOLLEY: 'Nobody but an Australian would have appealed in the
first place.'

Flashpoints in Test matches are not the exclusive preserve of the 'action
replay' era!

One more personal criticism of Woolley, and then an end to it: he was
spectacularly mean. All of his contemporaries have told me this and, in
most cases, they brought the subject up. It was common knowledge
along the county grapevine that Woolley would permit himself an
occasional drink as long as it was bought for him. No one I interviewed
could recall him returning the favour. The scurrilous joke among the
professionals during the 1930s was that he did once buy a drink on an
Australian tour – a tonic water to share with his wife. The preoccupa-
tion with money shines through a revealing interview with David Frith
in the *Cricketer* magazine in 1976. Just two years before his death, he was
complaining that his abilities were not sufficiently rewarded in talent

money, compared with others in the Kent side. He told Kent's president, Lord Harris, that an American had informed him he would earn far more by playing baseball and that he was tempted to give up cricket. Lord Harris promised Woolley a testimonial if he would continue in cricket, vowing, 'You'll get more than W.G. did.' Soon afterwards, Lord Harris died and the fund for Woolley raised £900. Judging by the tenor of his remarks to David Frith, he felt he should have made immeasurably more money out of his career. That must have preyed on his mind in the 1950s when he was reduced to working at Butlin's Holiday Camp at Clacton, coaching guests and organising nets. At his death in 1978, another fund had been opened among Kent supporters to help pay for his medical fees, but it had about as much success as the one organised forty years previously.

It seemed a pity that money matters preyed on his mind, because he played like a millionaire. Even in the nets, he hit the ball with devastating power, as Doug Wright confirms; 'I would never bowl at him, because I couldn't get my length. I spent all the time dodging a ball that clattered straight back at me. You could tell by the look on his face that he didn't think much of the bowlers.' Godfrey Evans, who was on the Kent staff for the last two years of Woolley's career, feels that only Ted Dexter hit the ball with comparable power, and Les Ames points out that he was different from the majority of great players because he consistently hit the ball in the air. 'He would back himself to clear the fielders. As I was next man in, I was always expecting to walk out at any time, but my word, he was rich entertainment.'

Ames considers his main weakness was against slow-bowling – he lacked the patience: 'He wouldn't dance down the wicket to them, but play them from the crease.' This view was supported by P.G.H.Fender, who often ensnared him with his leg-spin: 'I always made sure my mid-on, Miles Howell, dropped back a little for him. If I dropped one short, he would hit it in the air and I had him caught once or twice by Howell. I remember also getting him with a faster, stiff-arm leg-break which bowled him.'

He was a magnificent player of fast bowling and Ames says: 'He would have a field day against the modern fast bowlers who pitch it too short.' R.E.S.Wyatt agrees: 'His bat was all middle against the quick bowlers, he had so much time to spare.' Perhaps the need for quick singles would perturb Woolley if he came back today; he was a poor runner between the wickets, with an irritating habit of turning after the first run and then stopping dead in his tracks after of couple of yards and watching the ball. Les Ames would always do the calling in their productive stands, to their mutual satisfaction, although when Woolley batted in his usual fashion, quick singles were never really necessary.

Woolley believed that it was a disadvantage to be a left-hander. He felt he had trouble coping with the bowler's rough which affected his cover driving and that he was vulnerable outside his off stump because most right-arm bowlers could move the ball away from the left-hander's bat. He also thought the pre-1935 LBW law favoured right-handers; they could pad away with impunity to certain deliveries, whereas the left-hander was often more vulnerable.

The very idea of Frank Woolley complaining about having to use his bat is risible. No other great batsman seemed to relish more the impact of bat on ball; to shoulder arms would be an affront to his dignity. Perhaps he felt those dreadful umpires would spoil his fun if he let the ball hit his pads. Frank Woolley may have taken a slightly curmudgeonly view of life but on the cricket field he spent his talents with the prodigality of a sailor on shore leave.

In his last years, Woolley was still a remarkably handsome man: erect, bright-eyes, with an impressive head of full silver hair, he looked like one of those urbane Hollywood actors who played dignified old English gentlemen. He loved to sit quietly with his old colleagues at the Canterbury ground, and Doug Wright recalls his incredulity at the modern field-setting: 'But Doug, they've got no man out straight,' he would say, 'why aren't they hitting them over the top?' How was Woolley to know that the game had become so esoteric, so competitive? Or was he still judging cricket in the best way – simply, sensibly and without jargon?

7

Herbert Sutcliffe

'Ah, Mr Warner, I love a dog-fight!'

Herbert Sutcliffe's career is a marvellous testimony to the eminence that can be achieved by intelligence, application, soundness and, above all, a good temperament. His technical equipment was far inferior to that of Hobbs, Woolley, Hendren or Hammond, yet for a decade he was as indispensable to the England side as anyone.

He was a natural opener, the kind of man for whom Alec Bedser craved during his tenure as chairman of the England selectors in the 1970s. He may have lacked elegance, variety of strokes and flair, but he knew his limitations, his value to the side and he had the confidence to force the pace if his captain demanded. Above all, Sutcliffe possessed the most remarkable self-confidence, to a degree only approached by W.G.Grace. His *sangfroid* made Ian Botham look like a tremulous teenager in comparison. On the field, Sutcliffe's demeanour graphically revealed his attitude: the bowlers were mere hewers of wood and drawers of water, there for his pleasure, indulgence and interest. If they managed to shave his stumps with a good delivery, that was due to an aberration on his part, not any merit by the bowler.

Once Alf Gover beat Sutcliffe seven times in two overs with classic break-backs and late movement off the seam. At the end of the second over, with Gover convinced the dismissal was only a matter of time, Sutcliffe leaned on his bat, crossed his legs and said, 'Well bowled, Alfred, I shall get a hundred now, I've got it out of my system.' He did, too. Bill Voce experienced the same reaction at Bramall Lane, Sheffield, after beating Sutcliffe five times in one magnificent over. At its end, Voce stood in the middle of the wicket and his frustrated cry was also tinged with admiration: 'Look at that b——, standing there as if he's just hit me for six sixes!'

One day, Middlesex played Yorkshire and G.O.Allen bowled fast and well right from the start. Early on, he bowled a superb outswinger at Sutcliffe, the ball deviated after a loud snick and the appeal for a wicket-keeper's catch seemed a formality. Frank Chester, the umpire, rushed down to Sutcliffe's end, saw the mark of the new ball on the off-stump and said, 'I thought so, it hit the stump – not out.' But it was the attitude of Sutcliffe that astonished Allen: 'There he stood, leaning on his bat, looking around him, totally unperturbed as the rest of us chattered about my misfortune and Frank Chester's brilliant decision. To Herbert, the next ball was important, he could do nothing about the previous one.'

Sutcliffe demonstrated that unflappable quality to eleven incredulous Australians, two umpires and his batting partner at Sydney, in December 1932. The situation was pure Sutcliffe; he had already survived one over in which he played and missed at seven deliveries and he scratched his way to 49 without ever looking comfortable. He then played a delivery from Bill O'Reilly hard onto his stumps without removing a bail. R.E.S.Wyatt, his partner at the other end, takes up the story: 'I've never seen a ball played so hard onto the wicket without dislodging a bail. Everyone gathered round the stumps, some of the Australians were blowing hard at the bails in amusement, some came up from the deep field to observe the phenomenon and Bill O'Reilly stood there, cursing his luck. Herbert stood apart from it all, waiting for the fuss to die down, so he could get back to work.' When the fielders had exhausted their vocabulary, Sutcliffe went on to make 194, his highest Test score.

Sutcliffe's self-confidence was so colossal, his temperament so serene, his batting methods so effective that he must have been an immense morale-booster to any side as he walked out to bat. Jack Hobbs had four marvellous opening partners during his career, yet Sutcliffe was the only one on whom he sometimes seemed to rely. Just occasionally, the great man would appear fallible and Sutcliffe's tenacious presence would be vastly reassuring. After he retired, Hobbs would tell an affectionate story about the first time they opened against Australia. It was at Sydney in 1924 and Hobbs, in his usual custom, took the first over from Kelleway, a bowler with the ability to move the ball away late. In that over, Hobbs gave a masterly demonstration of how to leave a ball swinging late – he was into position early, dropping his wrists at the right instant and although Hobbs knew exactly what he was doing, he must have looked a little unsafe. At the end of that over, Sutcliffe came down the pitch and said to the Master: 'Best to leave the new ball alone, Jack.' As Hobbs later said affectionately, 'I knew we'd found the right opener for England.' How true – the fledgling Sutcliffe helped add 157 and 110 in that match, scoring a hundred on his debut against Australia.

It seemed that Sutcliffe could never countenance the possibility of being dismissed, an act of positive thinking that must have been of incalculable benefit to him. As Bill O'Reilly wrote, 'He would look down the pitch and sniff at you as if you were the bloke sent out to pick up bones.' At the Oval in 1926, Sutcliffe first shared in that wonderful partnership with Hobbs on a spiteful wicket, then, as the wicket eased, he carried the innings to give England an impregnable position. In the last over of the day, with his score on 161, he was bowled off his pads by Arthur Mailey and strode off, smacking his pads with his bat in disgust. It was not enough that he had played one of the great Test innings of all time; in his eyes Homer had nodded.

Neville Cardus gleaned a fascinating insight into the diamond-hard mind of Sutcliffe one morning at Leeds. Maurice Tate, one of the greatest of medium pace bowlers, dismissed Sutcliffe with an unplayable delivery and, later in the pavilion, Cardus commiserated. 'What do you mean, bad luck?' was the Sutcliffe riposte, 'I could have played it, but a man in the pavilion moved.' As Cardus wrote, 'He was more than indignant; he was outraged. I had blotted the Sutcliffe family escutcheon.'

Lest anyone assume that Sutcliffe was a hoarder of runs for their own sake, a collector of not-outs to boost his average, I must come to his defence. None of his contemporaries I interviewed demurred from the statement of Norman Yardley: 'He was a thorough team man, dedicated to his side. If quick runs were needed, Herbert would do his absolute best to get them, even though foreign to his nature. No one could ever accuse Herbert of selfishness.' Both Yardley and Bill Bowes remember vividly the treatment he handed out to Kenneth Farnes at Scarborough in 1932; Farnes was rash enough to feed Sutcliffe's favourite hook shot, and even with two deep fine legs, he hooked him time after time for six. He advanced from 100 to 194 in forty minutes and that night Farnes broke down and cried in front of Bowes, convinced that Sutcliffe had finished him as a bowler. Fortunately, he recovered his self-respect, vowed never to bowl short again at Sutcliffe and played fifteen times for England.

That knock at Scarborough was no isolated instance: in that same 1932 season, he hit eight sixes in his 132 against Gloucestershire and the bowling of Parker, Goddard, Sinfield and Hammond. The following year there was another splendid performance – 113 against Northants, including ten sixes, on a treacherous wicket. Northants had been bowled out for 27 before lunch and Sutcliffe decided to attack the dangerous off-spin of V.W.C.Jupp. He scored his 113 out of 181 in two hours and eight of his sixes came off Jupp's bowling, five of them in two overs.

R.E.S.Wyatt has fond memories of Sutcliffe's unselfishness. On the 1927–8 tour of South Africa, he opened with Sutcliffe against Eastern Province and in the second innings needed about 180 to win. Wyatt had entered the nineties, while his partner was in the seventies and Sutcliffe said to Wyatt, 'look here, you've got a chance to get a hundred, we need about twelve to win. Take the strike.' Wyatt, on his first England tour and anxious to make the Test side, needed no second bidding and gratefully reached his century. 'That was typical of Herbert. Other great players would have tried to catch me up, to put me in my place. He was never the kind of man to thrust himself to the forefront and, what's more, he never avoided the nasty stuff, like some other big names.'

In his twenty-two years in first-class cricket, Sutcliffe scored 50,138 runs with 149 centuries. He never knew a period of prolonged failure at any stage and he passed 2,000 runs in a season on fourteen consecutive occasions. Three times he scored 3,000 runs in a season. He took part in 145 stands of more than a hundred for the first wicket, 69 of them with Percy Holmes and 26 with Jack Hobbs. His Test record is unsurpassed by an Englishman and only bettered by Don Bradman and George Headley (in his case by a decimal point) – his average is 60.73 in all Tests and 66.85 against Australia, in his day the ultimate furnace of temperament. With a Test average fully eight runs above his overall first-class average, Sutcliffe was the Test Match batsman *par excellence*.

Despite his wonderful record, he was always second best to his famous partners in the affection of the public. Jack Hobbs held a unique position in the cricket world before he ever opened with Sutcliffe, and nothing subsequently dimmed that lustre. Percy Holmes only played seven times for England, yet his brilliant batting regularly overshadowed the calm, measured contributions of Sutcliffe. Both men loved to talk cricket, and a friendship that began in a Leeds train as they noticed each other's cricket bags continued for the rest of their lives. Sutcliffe always acknowledged the jaunty contributions of Holmes, his senior by eight years, and would never miss the opportunity to commiserate over his scanty number of England caps. He felt Holmes's positive strokeplay was an ideal complement to his efforts and treasured Holmes's remark as they unpadded following their record stand of 555 at Leyton in 1932: 'By heck, Herbert, if my back hadn't been givin' me trouble, we'd have brayed 'em!'

Even after Holmes's retirement, Sutcliffe was happy to share the spotlight with Leonard Hutton. Sir Leonard has confirmed to me that Sutcliffe was the best opener he ever partnered, that his example and advice were unsurpassed, and that he never pulled rank on him. For his part, Sutcliffe was uncharacteristically lavish in his praise of the young Hutton: 'I am only setting up these records for Hutton to break them', he once said.

Perhaps underneath the refined arrogance on the field, Sutcliffe knew deep down that he was not a truly great player, that he had achieved statistical greatness by a massive effort of character, tenacity and iron will. If Hobbs was the elegant willow, Sutcliffe was oak through and through; a handsome, strong man, his batting was not handsome or graceful. He had just a handful of shots – the hook, the pull, the off-drive and a back-foot force through gully or point that invariably got him off the mark. All of these strokes were sensibly and ruggedly played; the hook was accomplished with a bent right arm as he swept across the flight of the ball, so that it ended up as a hoick, rather than a hook in the style of a Hendren. He would hook in the air – hence the many sixes – and this often led to his dismissal. Another productive shot was an awkward shovelling flick down to fine leg and his off-drive was a sturdy 'smack' with the wrists turning on impact. In his stance, the bat face would point towards cover; on the pick-up, it would face towards gully, but he brought it down straight. He often looked stiff and awkward, occasionally out of position and unbalanced as the ball deviated suddenly, but he was a late adjuster with the art of playing defensive shots with a loose bottom hand. Thus on a turning wicket, he would look vulnerable – but he would battle it out. His relish of a bad-wicket innings was never more evident than in his remark to Sir Pelham Warner after his historic 161 against Australia in 1926: 'Ah, Mr Warner, I love a dog-fight!'

Sutcliffe thought through an innings, he saw it in stages. He admitted his habit of hooking in the air worried him initially, but he would calculate that for every failure with that shot, he had ten successes – 'and an average of eighty will do for me'. He would not hook until he had scored 40 if both fine-leg and square leg were in position. Only after a couple of hours could he back himself to bisect the two fielders. If there was either a fine leg or square leg, then he would hook right from the start of his innings.

His running between the wickets was superb, and helped offset the times when he was becalmed. A push, a glide, a nod to his partner and the scoreboard would keep ticking over. He was a master at pushing the ball into an open space, he seemed to be able to remember exactly where the fielders had been stationed.

Transcending all other qualities was his extraordinary strength of mind. He was more ruthless than Hobbs or Holmes, he would reason that he should cash in if it was his lucky day, because the next time he might have no control over events. Was he a lucky batsman? Perhaps he was, in that he was fortunate enough to be blessed with the gift of mental clarity, the realisation that the previous ball cannot send you back to the pavilion. He grasped this axiom in his second season in first-class cricket, in 1920. He battled through the Yorkshire innings against Essex at Southend, to carry his bat for a century that, in his own admission, was a fortunate affair. That fine new-ball bowler, J.W.H.T.Douglas, made the ball swing and dip prodigiously, but somehow Sutcliffe hung on, being dropped three times, while more experienced colleagues floundered. That night, he dined with Douglas and a few friends and although they talked much about his bad luck, Sutcliffe sensed that the fighting instinct that was never far from the surface of Douglas's cricket had encountered a worthy adversary. Four years later, Sutcliffe scored 255 not out against Douglas; he had learned to make his own luck.

A self-made cricketer, he was also a self-made businessman. Sutcliffe soon grasped the value of his cricketing prestige and wasted no time in capitalising on it. He started up a sports shop in Leeds in partnership with that rubicund character, George Macauley, and when Sutcliffe realised that his partner was not fully involved, he severed the partnership with all the ruthlessness that epitomised his batting. Thereafter, Sutcliffe's business career matched his cricketing deeds in efficiency and his time in the dressing-room was always constructively spent, as Norman Yardley recalls: 'If he was not out at lunch, he would have a quick wash, lay out his kit and then produce his briefcase. He would write a few letters, then look at his watch and with five minutes left, put away his briefcase, don his pads and be ready to bat again. Mentally, it seemed no problem at all to divorce business from cricket and vice-versa.' Once he gave Alf Gover a tip that served Gover well in his own business career: 'I came across him at the Oval, doing his accounts during a halt for rain. He said to me, "Just doing my accounts, Alfred. If ever you work for yourself, do your own ledgers, because then you'll know where the money is going." When I started at the cricket school in Wandsworth, I remembered his advice.' Gover also recalled an instructive remark when he stayed at Sutcliffe's house one weekend. Sutcliffe showed him around the house with proper pride, pointing out the double garage doors, a cherished momento of a tour here, an antique desk there. He took him out into the garden and reeled off the types of vegetable and fruit display and then said: 'I might as well make commercial use of the ground, Alfred.'

From the top of his immaculately-cut, dark hair to the pure whiteness of his boots, Sutcliffe looked a cricketer. He was of the new breed of cricket professional, a man who knew his commercial worth and was proudly conscious of his standing in his local community and beyond the shires of Yorkshire. He had been commissioned in the Sherwood Foresters in the 1914–18 War and had observed the gentlemanly order of social matters. His accent was a whimsical contrast to the broad, flat vowels of Roy Kilner, Percy Holmes, Emmott Robinson and the other doughty members of that great Yorkshire side. He used eau de cologne in the dressing room after a shower, read the financial pages of the newspapers avidly and wrote every word of his autobiography, in an age when such a chore was invariably handed over to journalistic 'ghosts'. Somehow, Sutcliffe seemed *with* the Yorkshire side, not *of* it: on away trips, he would stay in a hotel while the others made do with boarding houses. Yet he was a proud professional and when Lord Hawke asked him to become Yorkshire's first professional captain in 1927, Sutcliffe refused, while stating that he would serve loyally under whoever was appointed. He was fanatical about raising the status of the cricket professional – he would tell youngsters just coming into the side, 'You may not make the grade, but make sure your manners and bearing are better than those of the amateurs. Try in every way to be better than them, remember you are representing Yorkshire, not just yourself.' Bill Bowes was given a Sutcliffe wigging during his first away match for Yorkshire; he went into the dining room at tea-time and prepared to tuck into the fare with all the eagerness of a young, strong fast bowler who had worked hard in the previous two hours. Sutcliffe leaned over to him and whispered, 'Bill, you don't look right – go and put your blazer on.' Bowes never went to tea again without his uniform.

Hitler's War ended his career when he was forty-four just as the Kaiser's War had delayed his entry into first-class cricket until his twenty-fifth year. He was still a considerable force, averaging 54 in his final season, still a neat, immaculate figure with his cricketing faculties as sharp as his business antennae. His gloomy forecast that the 1935 revision of the lbw law would reduce his effectiveness was not borne out by his runs in the subsequent four seasons – 1,532 in 1936, then 2,162 the following year, 1,790 in 1938 and 1,416 in his last season. He did not seem to appreciate that the new law was in itself a great compliment to his defensive prowess, his mastery at using the pads as the last line of defence. No batsman did more to force that revision through than Herbert Sutcliffe.

It seems incredible that such a wonderful opener did not accompany G.O.Allen on his gallant tour to Australia in 1936–7, a tour that saw the estimable Hedley Verity open the England innings in one Test. Perhaps it was thought that Sutcliffe's powers of concentration were on the wane, that the new lbw law would affect him. No one who saw him batting calmly and resourcefully for Yorkshire against the 1938 Australians could doubt that this man was still a great 'big-match' performer.

He lived a long and happy old age and died in a nursing home at the age of 83, shortly after demonstrating to at least one elderly female inmate that his powers of stamina and decisiveness had not been solely confined to the cricket pitch. His son, Billy, captained Yorkshire in the 1950s – one of his middle names was 'Hobbs' – but the burden of being the son of the great Sutcliffe was too great. Herbert had long been accustomed to the standing ovations he received on every Yorkshire ground where he attended play and he would acknowledge the tributes with his usual patrician dignity. He remained a stickler for the old virtues, informing John Hampshire in all sincerity that his erratic, attractive batting would improve if he attended church regularly, and telling Barry Wood in 1972 that his England career would flourish if he would only get his hair cut. Wood was not sure whether to be flattered by the letter from the great man or amazed at the advice.

Bill Bowes was terribly fond of Sutcliffe and admired the stoical way he bore the pain of acute arthritis in his last years. 'He was a very great man. I never knew him guilty of a shabby or underhand act.'

In his immaculate suits, he looked like a sleek, confident civil servant, the absolute master of his portfolio. At the crease, he batted like a canny Yorkshire businessman, declaring a dividend when he was good and ready and eking out his rations in the meantime. At his death, another famous self-made Yorkshireman was ploughing the same furrow. Who said there was no continuity in cricket?

8

Ernest Tyldesley

'His batting was like the man himself: modest yet
firm of character, civilised in its call for action.'
(Neville Cardus)

If you gathered a group of cricket enthusiasts round a table, gave them
all a scrap of paper and a pen and asked them to write down the names
of the men who scored a hundred centuries, the results would be
instructive. They would whip through many of the great names: Grace,
Hammond, Boycott, Hutton – they would be no problem. Some would
look smug at remembering Mead, Hayward and Sandham and the
younger element would probably winkle out Turner, Edrich and
Cowdrey from the recesses of their minds. One name would remain
elusive to the majority: George Ernest Tyldesley. His name would be
greeted by either an irritated 'oh yes, Tyldesley' or an aggressive, 'who?'

He was the eighth batsman to reach a hundred hundreds and only
W.G.Grace took longer and was older at the time of achievement. He
scored more runs and centuries for Lancashire than anyone else in its
history – more than Washbrook, Paynter, MacLaren, Hallows and his
brother, J.T.Tyldesley. His Test average was ten points better than his
first-class average, an unchanging sign of class.

Ernest Tyldesley was one of the finest professional batsmen of the
inter-war period, and surely one of the unluckiest. Like Andrew
Sandham and Percy Holmes, he lived in the wrong period; with such a
plethora of batting talent available to the England selectors, Tyldesley
had to make do with whatever came his way, and retain his sense of
proportion when thanked for his pains and bundled back to county
cricket.

He was also unlucky to be the brother of a batting genius.
J.T.Tyldesley – Johnny Tyldesley – was one of the most brilliant
players of the period before 1914, and no one who saw him bat for an
hour ever forgot him. Audacious, dynamic and resourceful, he deservedly stands in the pantheon of great English players. At the height of his

powers, Johnny told all those who cared to listen that he had a kid brother at home who would turn out to be the better player. At the time only Trumper, and the young Hobbs, could match the genius of J.T.T., never mind a boy sixteen years his junior. His words were dismissed as simple fraternal duty.

When Ernest made his Lancashire debut in 1909, he was twenty and still very much in the shadow of his brother. The pair added 43 in Ernest's first match – against Warwickshire – and although he made 61, he looked a mundane player with none of his brother's panache. The following year, he made just 302 runs in twenty innings, in 1911 a total of 500 with an average of 25.21, and in 1912 a slight improvement to 561 at 25.50. At last – in 1913 – he broke through the mediocrity and made 1,316 runs at 30.61, but even then he was overshadowed by J.T.T. When Ernest scored a fine 110 against Surrey, his brother's magnificent 210 harvested all the newspaper eulogies.

In a perverse way, the Great War helped Ernest's career. When first-class cricket resumed in 1919, he was just thirty years of age, but his brother was forty-five, with his halcyon days behind him. Army training had toughened up the slight physique, and consequently his offside play developed a new power. Before the War, he had been almost exclusively an on-side player. Batting now at number three – his brother's old position – he methodically began to silence those snide whispers of nepotism. Len Hopwood, who played with Ernest for many years in the Lancashire side, remembered the criticisms of his technique as he tried to come out of the shadow of his great brother: 'They used to say that Ernest's back swing started in the direction of point, rather than in line with the middle stump. Ernest would reply: "It's not where it starts, it's where it finishes that matters." How right he was – the bat was straight enough at the crucial moment.' Hopwood had a great opportunity to watch Tyldesley's technique during one memorable week in 1934, when the pair added 273 against Glamorgan and then 316 against Gloucestershire. Hopwood used to scoff at the suggestion that Tyldesley's technique was faulty: 'During those partnerships I studied him closely, and believe me, no bat ever looked straighter, or broader or more punishing.'

Just as the batting of Frank Woolley epitomised the county where he lived and its way of playing cricket, so did Ernest Tyldesley in the post-war Lancashire team. By the *force majeure* of geography Lancashire had to play on wetter wickets, slower outfields and on more taxing surfaces than Woolley faced for at least half the season. The tactical need for Lancashire was a sensible, solid platform leading to a big enough total to allow brilliant bowlers like MacDonald, Parkin and Dick Tyldesley the chance to get the opposition out twice. It worked; between 1926 and 1934, Lancashire won the county championship five times.

They did so at a cost, being valued more in the north than in the south, where strong amateur influence still dictated tactics at certain stages of the season. If Harry Makepeace's dictum that there should be 'no fours before loonch' was a deliberate exaggeration of Lancashire's attitude to batting, nevertheless they had a workmanlike batting line-up, accustomed to posting 300 for 2 at close of play and then praying for rain. With the lbw law still favouring batsmen who used their pads, Lancashire's batsmen did not ignore the first principles of their technique – bat and pad close together and if the ball pitched outside the off-stump, get the bat out of the way and shove the pad across. Anyone bowled by an off-spinner would face a severe inquest in the Lancashire dressing-room.

Little wonder that Lancashire batsmen of that era were judged a pretty dour lot – Ernest Tyldesley suffered in the generalisation. It was unfair to an elegant, unruffled player who excelled in the off-drive, the cut, the hook and the flick off his legs. His leg glance was beautiful; leaning forward, perfectly balanced, he would flick the ball round delicately off his pads. He never seemed brutal in his treatment of bowlers, he would answer their technical questions with the practised grace of a classics master in a tutorial. Even when he hooked – that lip-smacking shot, that excursion into the 'macho' world of a Botham – it was with deference to the bowler, an acknowledgement that unfortunately he had been forced into taking drastic measures and I-sincerely-hope-I-haven't-knocked-your-ball-out-of-shape, sir. Bill Hitch, Surrey's hale fellow of a fast bowler, felt the draught of Tyldesley's hooking once at the Oval. Lancashire started the day with four wickets in hand, a hundred runs in arrears and a long tail to keep Tyldesley company. Hitch began the morning with four slips and a gully observing his tremendous pace. Within half an hour, three of the slips had been moved to defensive positions on the legside to combat Tyldesley's hooking. He made 236 in five hours and the game was easily saved.

G.O.Allen had good reason to remember the underrated talents of Ernest Tyldesley. In 1929, Allen bowled fast and straight to take 10 for 40 for Middlesex against Lancashire, who were bowled out for 241. Allen clean bowled eight men – including Tyldesley, but not before he had made 102 against six men who bowled for England at some stage. Allen recalls, 'That was a typically sound, stubborn innings by Ernest. Adversity brought out the best in him and he made many high-class hundreds without getting the praise he deserved.'

Underrated, yes. Inconsistent, no. In 1926, he made twelve fifties in thirteen consecutive innings, including a run of ten in ten, a feat only equalled by that master of consistency, Don Bradman. That year, he scored 2,826 runs, and in 1928 amassed 3,024 runs. It was not enough to force his way into the England side for any length of time when all the household names were available.

Ernest Tyldesley's treatment by the selectors was in keeping with some of the eccentric decisions made during the 1920s by that august body of men. In 1921, a season of lightning fast wickets and a 'scorched earth' bowling policy by the Australians, Tyldesley was picked for the First Test at Trent Bridge. He was out first ball, chopping a very fast ball from Gregory onto his stumps. In the second innings, Gregory bowled him again for seven – he mishooked a short one onto his forehead and it fell on his stumps. Tyldesley was dropped. The selectors tried to persuade C.B.Fry – a mere stripling at forty-nine – to return, but that wise man would have none of it. Instead they brought in men of the calibre of Alf Dipper, a one-paced journeyman with Gloucestershire, Wally Hardinge, a reliable county player and no more than that, and Andy Ducat, an attractive run-getter on the Oval billiard tables whose main cricketing claim to fame would be that he died while batting at Lord's in 1942. Worse was to follow for the professional pride of Tyldesley: among the new caps was one A.J.Evans (Winchester, Oxford University, Hampshire and Kent), who was selected on the strength of an innings of 69 not out for the MCC against the Australians earlier in the tour. Evans contented himself with just eight innings in that season – 217 runs – and never has an England cap been gained so easily in a modern home series.

As the selectors ran out of options, Tyldesley was at last recalled for the Fourth Test on his home ground, Old Trafford. In his only innings, he made 78 not out on a damp pitch; in the opinion of many Australian players, it was easily the best innings against them on the tour and the most dazzling postwar one for England until Hammond's dominance in 1928–9. After that, he had to be retained for the final Test, and although not reproducing the splendour of Old Trafford, he made a solid 39.

His reward was a single Test against South Africa in 1924 and one appearance when the Australians came again in 1926. He made 81 against them – and was immediately dropped. He managed to scrape a place on the boat to Australia for the 1928–9 tour (3,000 runs was a reasonable recommendation, even though not enough for Frank Woolley), yet he managed just one Test, taking the injured Sutcliffe's place and scoring 31 and 21. Thereafter the way was barred by Hammond.

That tour was a frustrating one for Tyldesley; he never really forced his way into contention by weight of runs, a great disappointment to him after an excellent tour of South Africa in the previous winter. On the matting wickets, he had mastered Nupen's devastating off-cutters with aplomb. The ball that turned in on him held few terrors and the extra bounce of the matting meant his slightly crooked pick-up was not punished by balls keeping low. He topped the batting averages in the Tests – 520 runs at 65 – and the South Africans thought him the best player they had seen there since Jack Hobbs nearly twenty years before.

The Test at Melbourne in 1929 ended Tyldesley's Test career. He could not be dismissed as a failure – 990 runs at an average of 55 with three hundreds. In comparison, his brother only averaged 30 in his 31 Tests. Ernest had done his best, but Hammond was a great player; moreover, Tyldesley's fielding (a safe catcher but a slow mover) could never be counted as an asset.

He returned to county cricket and continued to pile up charming centuries, including one of 256 not out that took just six hours at the age of forty-one. When he reached his hundredth hundred in 1934, it must have come as a surprise to many cricket experts outside Lancashire. The post-war Tyldesley had always been consistent, dedicated, a pretty batsman – but surely not of the elite? He certainly batted like a master in 1934, limbering up early with 239 against Glamorgan in just over six hours. On 7 July he scored 122 in three-and-a-half hours against Northants to register his century of centuries. The venue seemed somehow appropriate – Peterborough. That cathedral city is hardly noted for its cricketing history and while Boycott chose a Test Match for his achievement, Hayward the Oval, and Woolley and Compton picked Lord's, Ernest Tyldesley reached his ambition on a fustian ground that is no longer on the first-class list. No matter; he had long been used to counting his blessings. His only regret was that his brother had not lived to see it: he had died in 1930.

The innings at Peterborough was just one of many splendid performances in 1934 by Tyldesley – now aged forty-five. He made eight hundreds, including one against the Australians (off-driving

Grimmett and Fleetwood-Smith with controlled precision) and altogether made 2,487 runs at 57.83, to finish third in the national averages. Just to complete a marvellous season, Lancashire won the championship. With Tyldesley playing so fluently, it came as a surprise when he announced his retirement; the persuasive tongues of Lancashire cricket were mobilised and Tyldesley stood up at the celebration dinner and announced he would play on for as long as he was needed.

He made a couple of appearances in the 1936 season as an amateur before finishing for good. For the rest of his life, he kept in close contact with the club, serving on the committee and behaving with the grace and good manners that characterised his batting. G.O.Allen speaks with affection of many happy yarning hours in Ernest's company at Old Trafford – no doubt a certain match at Lord's in 1929 exercised their memories on occasions. Les Ames recalls what a splendid team man he was on the Australian tour, swallowing hard his disappointment at his form, volunteering to bowl in the nets and offering to do twelfth man duties when more selfish team-mates longed for the beach. R.E.S. Wyatt, who toured with him in South Africa, said he was the best senior professional he ever met on an England trip. 'His good fellowship had nothing to do with his excellent form with the bat. Ernest was as sound as a bell from first to last. A thorough gentleman.' Bill Bowes said he was one of the few cricketers who smiled and said 'Hello' during a Roses match – 'a Lancastrian who smiled at us during those three days was an exceptional person.' Len Hopwood remembers Tyldesley's great influence on a Lancashire side that contained more than one stormy petrel: 'He had no time for selfish cricketers and was a great advocate of side before self. He would come down like a ton of bricks on anyone exhibiting such signs. He was kindly and considerate and never one to give a snap judgement. "You've got to wait and see" was his reaction to a rash suggestion.' Hopwood recalls one occasion when Tyldesley strayed from his customary dignified attitude to the game – it came after Gloucestershire had contrived to beat Lancashire for the first time for many seasons. Alf Dipper, the man who played against Australia in 1921, was so overcome at the victory that he threw his cap into the air in jubilation, an act of demonstrativeness of which Tyldesley thoroughly disapproved. The sequel came shortly afterwards at Lord's when Middlesex – or more particularly R.W.V.Robins – annoyed Lancashire with some provocative and questionable tactics. Tyldesley's sense of propriety was so outraged that he announced to his team-mates: 'If we win this match, I'll do a Dipper and throw my blooming cap into the air.' When Lancashire turned probable defeat into a splendid victory, ten pairs of eyes focused on Tyldesley as the last Middlesex wicket fell: he shouted 'hurrah' and threw his cap into the air. Says Hopwood: 'We just couldn't believe it – the most unassuming and dignified player in the game giving a performance like that, and at Lord's of all places.'

Among the premier batsmen of his time, he was perhaps a little too diffident. He had long ago cured himself of the cross-bat tendency that caused his brother to wince, but he was always a nervous starter. He seemed dogged by myopia and self-consciousness; he would thrust forward indiscriminately until he had gauged the state of the wicket. Then the strokes would flow, the strokes that he had watched men like MacLaren, Spooner and his brother play while learning his trade. Yet with Ernest, those strokes lacked the 'hauteur' of the Edwardian age: 'toujours la politesse', the 'parfit gentle knight' rather than the D'Artagnan of his brother. That lack of a dominant strain must count against him when assessing his standing in the highest company, but there could be no quibbles about this style. R.C.Robertson-Glasgow bowled against him many times for Oxford and Somerset, and he admired Tyldesley greatly: 'On him were the sure signs of mastery – extreme lateness of stroke and the easy answer to each question of the ball.'

Neville Cardus saw most of Tyldesley's great innings. He wrote, 'His batting was like the man himself: modest yet firm of character, civilised in its call for action. He never exceeded the privileges of class and manners.' If he had played for another county and batted in a less utilitarian environment, he might have been a coruscating batsman. He remained proudly and emphatically a Lancastrian with a quiet, dry wit. Len Hopwood visited him towards the end of his life and was shocked to see him suffering cruelly from rheumatoid arthritis; the two old friends talked fondly about their days together for over an hour and not once did Ernest mention any of his own performances. As Hopwood stood up to leave, Ernest smiled bravely and whispered, 'We had some fun, didn't we Hoppy?'

Hopwood did not see him again but will never forget his unselfishness, even on his death-bed. George Duckworth was the last of his team-mates to see him before he died in 1962. After he had made the ritual enquiry about his health, Ernest replied: 'Well Ducky, I've seen the man about me eyes and one of 'em's goin': this chest o' mine is giving me soom trouble; and ah keep gettin' soom pain in me back. Mind you – there's nothin' the matter wi' me!' Ernest Tyldesley never believed in making a fuss about anything.

9

Walter Hammond

'Whenever I saw him bat, I felt sorry for the ball'
(Leonard Hutton)

Walter Hammond was a rare first edition in the library of cricketers. The genuine article. His deeds gain 27 separate mentions in *Wisden*, yet Hammond could not be appreciated from the scorebook alone. In the opinion of his contemporaries, he was on a different plane – majestic, assured, poised, a devastating amalgam of the physical and mental attributes that make up a great batsman. He was not a flamboyant batsman, he introduced no novelty of technique; he simply personified the classics of the game to the highest possible degree. The left leg was never far from the bat when he played forward, the footwork was that of a born dancer and he dismissed the ball from his presence. His very name radiated authority. The popular press found it easier to dub him 'Wally', and so did the bulk of his team-mates but that was tantamount to calling Churchill 'Winnie' or de Gaulle 'Charlie'. Walter Hammond. The emperor of batting.

Len Hutton, who played several Tests with Hammond, summed up his majesty neatly: 'Whenever I saw him bat, I felt sorry for the ball.' When he joined his Gloucestershire team-mates in the nets, the spin bowlers would deliver to him, then rush to the side of the net as the ball crashed past them like howitzers. At Lord's in 1938, he gave the Australians one chance during his prodigious innings of 240 – Chipperfield got a hand to a sharp caught and bowled chance, yet the ball rebounded yards back into play from the pavilion rails. Chipperfield retired from the match with a broken finger.

Hammond's control was so awesome that bowlers in county cricket measured success by the number of times they passed his bat or caused him to play defensively, rather than in dismissals. Charlie Elliott – Test umpire, England selector – recalls fielding to him in the 1930s when he made three hundreds in four innings against Derbyshire: 'If you didn't get him in the first ten minutes, he would just do as he liked.' Doug Wright, magnificent leg-spinner for Kent and a colleague of Hammond in the England side, told me: 'It was a pleasure to bowl at him. If you managed a maiden at him, it made your season and when he hit me vast distances, I felt like applauding. He was the best cricketer I ever saw.'

Note that – the best cricketer. He was not just a wonderful batsman, he was a high-class medium-pace bowler with an action straight out of the Tate/Bedser gallery. His slip fielding was superb; he never seemed to hurry yet he would take the sizzling edge with time to spare. F.R.Brown swears he never saw Hammond take a catch one-handed or dirty his flannels: those dancing feet always got him into position. Charlie Parker, devastating Gloucestershire slow bowler when the wicket favoured him, owed much to the predatory catching of Hammond at slip. 'Caught Hammond, bowled Parker' became as familiar a sight in the newspapers as 'caught Tunnicliffe bowled Rhodes' of earlier vintage . . . no less than 229 times in fact.

His aloofness on and off the field accentuated the feeling of cricketing divinity. Everything he did had the air of a thoroughbred: striding to the wicket, blue handkerchief peeping from his pocket, his entry into the fray was, in the eyes of many, worth the admission price alone. It is remarkable that all his contemporaries I interviewed would eventually say the same thing: 'You should have seen him walk out to bat.' He brought the same detached superiority to his beautiful bowling action with its curving run-up and thrilling delivery, and to his fielding. His physique was perfect; just over medium height, broad-shouldered, deep-chested, with massive forearms and an ease and grace of movement that marked him out as a natural games player. He seemed to excel at every athletic pursuit: in his youth Southampton's manager begged him to take up soccer as a career and the handicap system could never deny him in the games the England cricketers would play on the ships that took them to Australia, West Indies and South Africa.

Although small boys would forget their scorebooks and charts when he batted, his record deserves scrutiny. He made 167 hundreds, scored just over 50,000 runs, took 732 wickets and held 819 catches. It would have been even more impressive but for a combination of bad luck, illness, war and administrative dogmatism, which together robbed him of seven full seasons.

In his early years, only his talent came easy to him. He spent some time in Malta – his father was in the Army – until he was shipped over to Cirencester Grammar School in the Cotswolds. His father was killed in the Great War and the schooldays were solitary ones for Hammond, who had learned to look after himself in those formative years in Malta. Apart from a natural athletic flair, nothing seemed to interest him. After scoring 365 not out in a house match, his name was noted by the county and he played three games for them as an amateur. Cricket seemed a pleasant enough diversion as a career (he lacked the early commitment of Hobbs, Grace or Bradman) and he was preparing himself for his first year as a professional when the rulebook thwarted him. Lord Harris, that influential martinet at Lord's, was piqued that a boy born in Dover had slipped through the net of his beloved Kent and he insisted that Hammond serve a two-year residential period in Gloucestershire before being allowed to play county cricket. Although irked, Hammond had little else on the horizon apart from resisting the blandishments of professional soccer (he felt the money was not sufficient), so he settled down to serve his penance. He became assistant coach at Clifton College, under the dictatorial guidance of John Tunnicliffe, 'Long John' of 'caught Tunnicliffe bowled Rhodes' fame. They did not see eye to eye on attitudes to batting, but there is no doubt that Tunnicliffe's advice and example helped Hammond become one of the greatest slip fielders of all time.

After three years, Hammond had played just sixteen first-class innings for Gloucestershire and when he finally entered county cricket in 1923, his rashness revealed how the delay had frustrated him. For the next three seasons, his average hovered around the thirty mark and although his class was obvious, influential judges agreed with Tunnicliffe that the boy was too headstrong, he had too many shots to offer. They agreed his off-driving was superb, but criticised the way he hooked in the air. He had never been coached until he joined the Gloucestershire staff and, even then, the only man who occasionally offered some advice was George Dennett, the eminent slow left-arm bowler. It looked as if Tunnicliffe, the sage of Pudsey, might have judged his man astutely; perhaps he would always be just an 'iffish' county batsman.

One innings altered the balance. On 19 August, 1925, Hammond scored 250 not out at Old Trafford against the best fast bowler in the world (MacDonald), the outstanding off-spinner (Parkin) and an England leg-spinner of the future (Dick Tyldesley). Gloucestershire were 20 for 2 when Hammond strode to the wicket and he stayed another five-and-a-half hours. No longer could there be any doubt over his quality. The England selectors prepared to see him bat at number four in the following summer against the Australians. He looked the ideal man to help wrest back the Ashes.

Alas for fond hopes. Hammond was bitten by a mosquito on a tour of the West Indies during the winter of 1925–6 and he contracted a desperate illness that was beyond the medical skills in the Caribbean. He was shipped back to Bristol, entered hospital and spent the bulk of the 1926 season on his back. Sir Pelham Warner, that thoughtful encourager of the young and talented, visited Hammond and assured him he would one day play for England. For a time in that season, it was enough to hope he would live.

He returned to English cricket a great batsman. Something had happened during his convalescence that fused his talents into a whole; no longer did he charge recklessly after the bowling, now he would trust to his delicious footwork, his sportsman's eye and a straight bat. He scored a thousand runs in May, the third batsmen to do so. Throughout that 1927 season, he made bowlers pay for that malevolent mosquito, for the pettiness of Lord Harris, for the arid years of his youth. One innings that season encapsulated his grandeur – and again it was at Old Trafford. One Friday morning in May, the Lancashire team had their eyes on an early finish and a trip to the races. No one could quibble at their optimism: Gloucestershire, with two wickets down, were just 44 ahead and only this young dasher Hammond barring the way. In the first over of the morning – bowled by the great MacDonald – Hammond drove five fours in succession. He then hooked MacDonald with the arrogance that stems from complete mastery. In three hours, Hammond made 187 devastating runs and saved the game.

Eighteen months later and he was ready to conquer a bigger stage. Percy Chapman's 1928–9 side to Australia contained a marvellous array of talent, but Hammond, with 905 runs in the series, dwarfed everyone. Bradman's capacity for gargantuan scores had not yet reached a worldwide audience and so Hammond was the wonder of the age. His methods were simple: he realised the wickets were good enough to accelerate retirements among the bowling fraternity, so he decided to eliminate risk, occupy the crease for as long as possible, playing 'through the V', that arc between extra cover and midwicket. The hook was dropped from the plentiful repertoire, and so was the glance. He only used the cut in the last Test, after some of the Australian players had ribbed him over dinner that he could not play the shot. Hammond, so determined to prove himself a great batsman, vowed to show the cocky Australians; he was out for 38 and 16 in the last Test, on each occasion caught in the gully off square cuts. Henceforth, Hammond would never take any notice of Australian whimsy.

By 1929, Hammond was the greatest batsman in the world, even if he judged the hook shot too risky and the pull a lottery on wickets favouring seam and swing bowlers. He compensated in many other areas, and his disciplined technique allowed him to make stately progress through the pages of cricket history. Yet his superiority lasted just one year: at the end of the 1930 season, Don Bradman had surpassed him in quantity and he looked even more infallible. Bradman's dominance throught the 1930s gnawed away at Hammond; it seemed that whenever he made a hundred, Bradman would reply with a double hundred. When England amassed 903 for 7 declared at the Oval in 1938, Hammond would not declare until he had received medical assurances that Bradman's injured ankle would prevent him from batting. Again in 1938 Denis Compton threw his wicket away after making a joyous hundred in his first Test against Australia only to be told by his captain: 'Don't ever do that to me again. Never give the Australians your wicket.' John Tunnicliffe would have approved of such ruthlessness.

Bradman seemed to rattle Hammond even when he did not wear pads. In the third Test at Adelaide in 1933 Hammond was established in his cool mastery as the end of play neared. Bradman was brought on to bowl on a captain's whim and Hammond walked down the wicket to his partner, Les Ames, and warned him not to take risks against such innocuous bowling. Hammond was bowled with a high full toss and stalked away in fury. Recalls Ames, 'I have never seen him so angry. He was outraged at showing weakness against Bradman.'

In the 1934 series, Hammond had a miserable time and did not score one fifty; Bradman won the rubber with a double and a triple century. At Sydney in 1936, Hammond's double hundred set up a two-nil lead in the series, but Bradman turned the series with scores of 270, 212 and 169 and Australia won three-two. An incident in the fourth Test at Adelaide illustrated the difference between the two great batsmen of the age – England started the final day on 148 for 3, needing another 244 to win. Hammond was not out and clearly the man Bradman had to dismiss early. He was bowled third ball of the morning by Fleetwood-Smith and he strode off with that air of unconcern that was so maddening in failure, so coldly impassive on his days of plenty. George Duckworth, who was sitting with the shattered England side, voiced the thoughts of many: 'We wouldn't have got Don out first thing in the morning with the Ashes at stake.' Australia won that Test and the final one.

Hammond knew all about the unflattering comparisons and they only served to drive him deeper into his shell of introspection. Bradman and Hammond were the rival captains in 1938, and their relationship was cool and wary. After an incident on the first morning of the opening Test in the 1946-7 series, they only spoke to each other when the coin was being tossed. Hammond thought Bradman had been caught by Ikin at slip and felt he should have 'walked'; Bradman went on to score a rehabilitatory 187 and Hammond resigned himself to being bested by the malign finger of fate that had brought two such masters together in opposition at the same time. Why, even on their first appearance on the same field Bradman gained the upper hand: he ran Hammond out with a brilliant pick-up from cover and answered Hammond's double hundred with 87 and 182 not out. From that moment at Sydney in November, 1928, Bradman had Hammond in his sights.

If the little Australian had the edge over him throughout the 1930s, no one else did. He could be comparatively passive against Bill O'Reilly's accurate leg-stump attack, but apart from the inexplicable lapses in the 1934 series, O'Reilly did not enjoy much success against him. O'Reilly would have none of the talk about his superiority over Hammond: to this day he speaks of him in the most glowing terms. Hammond went through periods of famine, but he felt that was due to lack of challenge, rather than any deterioration. When he was needed, he showed his mettle, especially on bad wickets. Doug Wright still talks about the game at Bristol in 1939 when Hammond scored 153 not out in a total of 284 all out. The wicket was so bad that no Kent player got more than forty and, with Tom Goddard taking seventeen wickets in the match, Gloucestershire won by an innings and forty runs. Wright took 9 for 47, including the hat-trick, yet, as he told me, 'I just couldn't bowl at Wally. It was the most fantastic performance I've ever seen, the work of a genius.'

At Melbourne in 1936, he played an innings of 32 that, on a rain-affected pitched threatening throat and temple, was remarkable. Ten years later, Alec Bedser witnessed another miraculous effort at Brisbane; two inches of rain had fallen in the night and the wicket was spiteful. The ball took divots out of the pitch every time it landed. Keith Miller, that chivalrous cricketer, kept the ball well up to the batsman, yet one of his half volleys at medium pace spat off the pitch and knocked Cyril Washbrook's cap off as he played forward. Only Hammond looked comfortable, as Bedser recalls: 'When it was short, he stood aside and let it go. If pitched up, he let fly, playing straight past the bowler to eliminate risk. He hit cleanly and sensibly and in the circumstances, it was the best bad-wicket innings I've seen.' He made 32 in two hours and was not hit once; at the other end, Bill Edrich was battered black and blue while making 16.

Adversity saw him at his best. At Lord's in 1938, the fast bowling of Ernie McCormick swept away Hutton, Barnett and Edrich for just 31 runs. Hammond made 240 of the most perfect runs imaginable, crashing the fast bowlers away off front and back foot like a mixture of Dexter and Cowdrey at their best. It was utterly safe, dignified and breath-taking. 'A throne-room innings,' Cardus called it. Even then, Bradman's shadow stalked Hammond – on a damp pitch, the Australian captain saved the match with a brilliant, quick-footed 103 not out.

Hammond was an unemotional cricketer, yet he liked to demonstrate his astonishing virtuosity when the mood was on him. One day at Cheltenham Tom Goddard was quaffing a lunchtime pint after bowling out Leicestershire on a typical Cheltenham turner. Goddard was no blushing violet and Hammond became restless at his confident assertions. He told Goddard that he was not really much of a bowler and sat back for the expected reaction. When Goddard finished his expostulations, he was invited to go out onto the pitch where he had sent the opposition packing an hour earlier. The other Gloucestershire players followed, and took up their fielding positions as Goddard bowled an over at Hammond. 'I'll play you with the edge of my bat, Tom' he said, and proceeded to play six sharply-turning deliveries with an area of willow no more than an inch and a half wide. He blocked all six deliveries, walked away and en route to the dressing room, called out, 'I told you that you couldn't bowl, Tom.' My source for this story is Reg Sinsfield, one of the fielders that day.

Hammond once indulged himself in similar fashion in the nets at Bristol. He had just returned from an Australian tour and did not know that the club had prepared a practice wicket for the spinners. The idea was to familiarise Goddard, Sinfield and Parker with a turning wicket early in the season so that they could judge their line and length and avoid turning the ball too much. None of the first-team batsmen could last more than four overs on the pitch until Hammond had a knock. Not one ball passed him until he felt sorry for the bowlers, dropped his bat and took up a baseball bat that he had brought back from his tour. He played the three spinners easily enough with that until Charlie Parker, frustrated and humiliated, threw a ball at him. He caught the ball and sent it soaring out of the net with his baseball bat. He laughed, walked off and when out of earshot, Parker announced, 'You have just seen the greatest exhibition of batting you will ever witness – but don't tell him I said so!'

He was not popular with his team-mates at Bristol. They felt he should have bowled more often – Reg Sinfield thought they would have won two championships if he had done so. He sometimes seemed in a world of his own, occasionally saying nothing to anybody for two days, yet carrying on with the game. When he batted in the nets he would ask the fast bowlers to use a new ball and then he would take a fiendish delight in smashing it straight back at them. When he was captain, he had his own way of dealing with young players, as George Emmett discovered. Emmett, a strokemaker of great ability and charm, was left out for several games and went to see his captain for advice. He received one sentence – 'Well, Emmett, you're not a very good player, are you?'

Like most great batsmen, Hammond wanted the strike when the pickings were easy and would be happy to get away from it at certain strategic times. When he batted with Reg Sinfield, he would say, 'Reg, you take it for the first few overs, you're more used to it than I am' – and after that, Sinfield would be just a runner for him. Joe Hardstaff remembers having a furious row with him in 1937 during that ill-fated Adelaide Test; Hardstaff was nearing his fifty towards the end of play and he wanted to reach it before the close. 'I played O'Reilly off my legs for a comfortable single, possibly even two. Wally stayed rooted at his end and wouldn't come. I was amazed and two balls later, with my concentration upset, he bowled me with a beauty. I was so annoyed at Wally – he wanted to keep clear of O'Reilly.'

Hammond was respected by some team-mates and opponents, but he lacked the intimate touch that makes friends. He knew the loneliness of greatness just as he knew the isolation of youth. He was made captain of his county and country because he was the best cricketer in the land, not through any skills at the job. F.R.Brown reckoned he was the worst captain he had ever played under – 'he did everything by the clock, rotating his bowlers at set stages.' On the 1946–7 tour, he was apart from his side except during matches; while the team travelled on sweaty, interminable train journeys, Hammond journeyed by expensive car. He could never understand that experienced players held him in awe, that they looked to him for guidance. Hammond felt he should captain by inspiration and when his flow of runs dried up through fibrositis and the weight of personal problems, the tour was doomed. He even criticised his players for fraternising with the opposition over a few post-match drinks.

With his batting crippled by fibrositis, his personal life was also in a mess on that tour. News of his impending divorce broke as the team landed in Australia, and Hammond could not see why his personal affairs should be a matter of public interest. He had fallen in love with a South African beauty queen and, worried about the reaction from the Establishment, had installed her with his mother in a house in Gloucestershire. Throughout that Australian tour, Hammond was taking telephone calls from either woman, each giving their side of their continuing quarrels. It only served to darken a nature that was gloomy enough.

He remarried, left abruptly for South Africa and settled in Durban. After Australia, he was lost to first-class cricket, apart from a couple more matches when he turned out to boost Gloucestershire's coffers. His final appearance was in the 1951 Whit Bank Holiday game at Bristol against Somerset; public interest was huge and the ovation accorded Hammond would have melted many men. If his waistline was thicker, his chest rather stouter, he still moved with that old liquid grace on his way out to bat. There the good news ends: he scratched around for half an hour to score seven singles before Horace Hazell bowled him and put him out of his misery. Arthur Milton partnered him and recalls, 'It was terribly sad to see him struggle. I had been brought up on his exploits and longed to see him do well. Yet there he was, cursing quietly as he mistimed balls he once hammered.' He strained a muscle while batting, did not re-appear for a second knock and fielded immobile at slip. That was the last time Bristol saw him in the uniform that always seemed to fit him better than any mortal man – cricket whites.

Bad luck dogged him in South Africa. He took a partnership in the motor trade and his partner ran off with all the money. He suffered a fractured skull in a frightening car crash in 1959, when his legs were trapped under the dashboard and he could not escape as a train bore down on him at a level crossing. The doctors said only a man with a marvellous constitution could have survived. He was glad enough to take a job as a coach/groundsman at Natal University and happy to fly over to Bristol in 1962, to try to boost Gloucestershire's membership drive. Visits by members of successive England touring sides found him cheerful enough, but reluctant to discuss his great days and uninterested in modern cricket. He never really recovered from that horrific car smash, and died in 1965, at the age of sixty-two. An appeal was launched in Bristol for his widow and dependants and his redoubtable mother attended a memorial service. A decade later, a poignant reminder of Hammond turned up in a Gloucester antique shop – the silver cigarette case given to him by his team-mates when he remarried.

Nothing in life came easy to him, apart from his glittering athletic prowess, small comfort to him when misery cast its hand on his psyche. Little things used to upset him; he could not see why Hobbs and Sutcliffe were each given £100 by a newspaper after their wonderful bad-wicket performance at Melbourne in 1929, when Hammond received nothing for his double hundred earlier in the match. Slights and insults would arouse him, as J.W.H.T.Douglas discovered once at Chelmsford. Hammond was caught at cover, but he stood his ground, convinced it was a 'bump' ball. At the interval, Douglas called him a cheat, Hammond kept his own counsel and scored 244. The following day, as Gloucestershire walked out to field, Hammond announced quietly to his captain, Harry Rowlands, that he would like to bowl. He proceeded to bowl frighteningly fast, knocking the bat out of Douglas's hands.

Les Ames and G.O.Allen think him the best offside player they ever saw and both make the point that he was pulverisingly effective off both back and front foot. R.E.S.Wyatt believes him to be the hardest hitter of all the great batsman he has seen. Bill Bowes recalls being told by Hammond that every ball should be hit hard enough for two; he felt his back foot excellence gave him a crucial yard extra to see the ball.

The general view among his contemporaries is that he would have to adapt more to the modern game than the other great players. G.O.Allen points out that Hammond set himself to play on the offside, his body was locked into a certain position; by getting inside the ball, he was slightly off balance for legside shots. Les Ames thinks that short-pitched bowling would unnerve him and the alteration of the bowler's line to middle and leg would restrict him. Norman Yardley says he loved batting against spinners and that his majestic drives off the back foot would be difficult against fast bowling aimed at the heart.

Joe Hardstaff confirmed that Larwood always like to bowl at Hammond, he felt he was apprehensive. Certainly Learie Constantine rattled him at Old Trafford in 1933; after being hit on the jaw, Hammond gave himself up in the leg-trap soon afterwards and entered the England dressing-room with the words: 'If that's what Test cricket has come to, I'm giving it up.' More than once he was troubled by Farnes and Nicholls when Essex played Gloucestershire.

If he battled today, perhaps he would simply ride the fast bowlers, duck out of the way of the short-pitched deliveries. Perhaps, protected by a helmet, he would hand out the kind of medicine suffered by MacDonald in 1927. It may be that he would learn how to play the hook, the cut and the glance. A man who can humiliate Parker and Goddard on turning wickets cannot be without resource. The spinners and the fast-medium bowlers would be no problem; he always played spin off the pitch, rather than from the hand and his back-foot driving would relish medium pace. During the England tour to South Africa in 1956–7, he confessed that he would not be able to score quickly against the nagging bowling of Trevor Goddard, left-arm medium pace over the wicket to a legside field. That is hard to believe – he would surely adapt while using the patience that drove the 1929 Australians to distraction.

Whatever his alleged shortcomings, Hammond was a genius of his time, worshipped by crowds and revered by his colleagues. When Gloucestershire won the toss and batted at Bristol, Tom Goddard would say to the bowlers: 'Right, lads, we can go off to the beach at Weston-Super-Mare now, Wally will see us all right.' Among all the tributes to a great batsman, one sticks in my mind and it comes from Sam Cook, the Gloucestershire slow bowler and now a first-class umpire. In his first season, Sam needed a blazer for the team photograph and Hammond gave him one of his. Now Sam lacked the awesome physique of his captain, yet if he noticed that the shoulders came halfway down his arms, he did not care. He posed proudly for the photo, took the blazer home to Tetbury on the bus, and it has stayed in his home ever since. He sometimes wears it when pottering in his garden, but usually it hangs in his wardrobe, a cherished family heirloom. When Sam shows you that blazer and tells you who first wore it, he rolls his Cotswold burr round the two words – 'W.R.' The pride in his voice tells you everything about the greatness of Walter Reginald Hammond.

10

Andrew Sandham

'With Andy, it was simply a case of bowl and wish'
(Jack Mercer)

The picture in the Oval pavilion just about says it all concerning the career of Andrew Sandham. It is dated 1925 and the adoring crowds are welcoming back Jack Hobbs in his first game at the Oval since breaking W.G.Grace's record of centuries. The Master is walking out to bat, shyly acknowledging the acclaim with that endearingly modest way of his. His partner, Andrew Sandham, can be spotted behind a knot of spectators who have dared to get that little bit nearer to Hobbs. Sandham is quietly fastening on his batting gloves, getting ready for the business of the day once all the fuss has died down. He was always one step behind Jack Hobbs.

A batsman who scored 107 centuries, more runs than Compton and Hutton and who once held the record for the highest score in Test cricket would, by all the canons of fairness, be expected to enjoy a few slaps on the back from his home crowd. It never happened to Sandham; he even contrived to score his hundredth century at Basingstoke, away from the Oval ground he adorned for so long. He was overshadowed too long by Hobbs to be called a great batsman, but he never allowed the fact to obscure his wry, balanced view of life. At the Oval in 1931, Hobbs had the rare experience of a first ball dismissal against Leicestershire. Stan Squires went to the next ball – Surrey 0 for 2. Sandham batted five hours for a skilful, composed century and as he walked out of the Oval that evening, reasonably content with his labours, he noticed the newspaper placard: 'Hobbs 0 at the Oval'. Sandham grinned and said: 'Well I suppose you've got to be a pretty good player to get a placard like that when you get a duck.'

If he ever felt irritation at being pigeonholed as Hobbs' partner, he did not show it. He once said: 'He was a great man, Jack. It used to annoy my wife, who didn't know anything about cricket at all. She'd say

93

there were ten other people playing besides Jack Hobbs.' There was never any rivalry between the two men, just a bond of mutual respect and affection. Sandham knew the needs of the side and he was content to run the singles that Hobbs wanted and to take the bowling when necessary. They ran beautifully between the wickets; Sandham was always ready to run for the last ball of the over and no calling was needed. He could see the humour in the situation, particularly the time when he faced one ball in a quarter of an hour and was criticised in the press box for being slow. They had 63 partnerships of a hundred to their credit – six behind Holmes and Sutcliffe – and during their fifteen-year association, they ran each other out just once. Reg Sinfield has painful memories of the speed between the wickets of Hobbs and Sandham; Gloucestershire came to the Oval and fielded first on a typical featherbed. Sinfield fielded at short leg in those days and opened the bowling. His first over at short leg did not equip him for a long stint with the new ball: 'Jack pushed the first one past me and I had to chase after it because we had a few slips and other fielders behind the wicket. On that vast Oval outfield, they ran five. I came puffing back for the second ball, and Andy pushed it past me – they ran another five! Ten runs in two balls, all run, and they were both no youngsters. My word, they could run!'

It was always Hobbs and Sandham, never the other way round; it could not be otherwise, for Hobbs was the greatest player of his generation. Sandham, however, was a beautiful batsman – the word 'dapper' might have been coined with him in mind. He was small, wiry and beautifully balanced, a player with an on-drive as good as that of the Master and a darting late cut that was not in his partner's wondrous repertoire. Sandham was a touch player – a deflector of fast, rising deliveries, a glider of the break-backs. Like W.G.Grace, he cocked his left foot in the air as the bowler braced himself for the delivery. He executed exquisite wristy shots, played the hook with disarming ease and at all times looked poised, unyielding and efficient. R.C.Robertson-Glasgow described him as 'a first fiddle who, for most of his time, played second fiddle in the orchestra.' Sandham would be the last man to suggest a roll of drums on his behalf.

R.E.S.Wyatt, who toured the West Indies and India with Sandham, told me how much he had learned from him by batting at the other end. 'He never moved too soon, his head was always so still. He was a most beautiful player who would walk into the England side today. His cutting and hooking would plunder all this short-pitched stuff.' Even when he retired at the age of forty-seven, Sandham was still playing immaculately straight, the result of learning his trade on good, hard wickets. One day at the Oval, Hobbs and Sandham were moving elegantly towards yet another big stand against Sussex. Hobbs was content to coast along for a time, while Sandham saw an unusual proportion of the strike. It all became too much for Maurice Tate, who spluttered: 'For heaven's sake, let me have a go at Jack! At least he gives you half a chance!' Jack Mercer, a great friend of both openers, agreed: 'I'd always prefer to bowl at Jack, because he had so many shots that he might just play one too many. With Andy, it was simply a case of bowl and wish!' Barring accidents, Hobbs was usually the first to go – normally as soon as he had reached his hundred and picked out an old friend to be the lucky bowler – but Sandham would invariably be still there after tea, inscrutably clocking up the runs at forty an hour. He knew how to rattle a fast bowler; within earshot, he would say, 'he's lost a yard of pace since last season, hasn't he?' and then wait for the inevitable bouncers on which to feed his peerless hook shot. He really loved batting against fast bowling, relishing the demands placed on his superb footwork, his orderly technique; Harold Larwood maintained that no one played him better than Sandham.

He was, of course, lucky to assess the methods of Hobbs at the other end and adapt them accordingly. He also admitted his indebtedness to Tom Hayward before the Great War. When still at school, Sandham – who lived just a few miles away from the Oval – idolised Hayward. After he joined the staff, he would spend every available moment watching him and analysing his technique, especially against fast bowling. After Sandham established himself in the Surrey side, he displayed much of Hayward's soundness, and none of his fielding defects. He became one of the finest outfields in the world, with blistering speed and a marvellous pick-up and throw.

His apprenticeship was a long one. He first played for Surrey in 1911 at the age of twenty and although *Wisden* said kind things about him, he had to be content with five games in two years. In 1913, he scored his first century and a good one it was – 196 against Sussex after his side had slumped to 64 for 4. But it was not enough to keep him in the first team. Donald Knight, the captain of Malvern College, was available during the school holidays and in those days the amateurs were chosen ahead of promising young professionals. Sandham managed just nine matches that season and five in 1914.

During the War, he was invalided home from the front line after being badly injured. When cricket resumed in 1919, he was still kept out by Knight once he had finished his term at Oxford. Despite one innings of 175 not out against Middlesex, Sandham was still on trial at the age of twenty-nine. The following season, he gained a regular place and when Jack Hobbs missed most of the 1921 season through illness and injury, Sandham made over 2,000 runs and looked a high-class player. The England selectors agreed, although they hedged their bets. He was picked just for the final Test at the Oval and made a modest enough 21 before Ted MacDonald bowled him. His chief merit was to keep Phil Mead loyal company while he soldiered on to his 182 not out. Sandham had to play second fiddle for more than just Surrey.

He played in just one more Test at home, against South Africa in 1924 and had to tour to pick up twelve other caps. He played twice against Australia on Arthur Gilligan's tour, but, for some reason, batted number six in the first innings and seven in the second. As he watched Herbert Sutcliffe consolidate a partnership with Hobbs that became a byword for reliability and temperament, Sandham knew he would never be centre stage for England. He never opened for England with Hobbs, whereas Sutcliffe and his splendid partner, Holmes, did manage it against India in 1932. Technically, Sandham was a better player than Sutcliffe, but the Yorkshireman was so positive, such a competitor, that there was only one man who could open with Hobbs against the best in the world. A total of 49 runs in five innings against Australia did not recommend Sandham for the task.

Sandham knew he would never need a special cabinet to hold all his England caps but his last game for England amused him greatly. He remains the only man to score a triple hundred in his last Test. His 325 at Kingston in 1930 took him ten hours; he used his captain's long-handled bat (he had sold or broken all his own) and batted in Patsy Hendren's shoes, which occasionally slipped off as he scampered a single. He started off with sore feet and shins, a legacy of the hard grounds, and as the day wore on, he was near to exhaustion. The bat did not suit him, it was too hot and, at the end of a hard tour, he wanted to put his feet up. Sandham swore till his dying day that he only stayed out at the crease to keep Joe Hardstaff Snr happy; Hardstaff, who was on the county umpires' list, had been brought over to show the West Indians the rudiments of umpiring. When Sandham reached his century, he told Hardstaff he was going to get out. 'Don't do that, Andy' the umpire replied, 'I don't know anybody out here and I'll feel lonely. Stay a little longer, try for two hundred!' Throughout the day, Hardstaff prevailed on Sandham – 'hang on till tea now', 'go for your three hundred, you've never scored one, you know', and he lasted till the close, unbeaten on three hundred. He faced two additional hazards – Patsy Hendren and Les Ames. Both men came out to bat, breathing aggression and demanding quick singles. On each occasion, Sandham had to call a halt to the frenzy. Les Ames remembers Sandham's words of wisdom: 'He said to me, "Young man, do you see that scoreboard up there? It says I've got 220, and it feels like it. I'm not having any youngster coming in and running me off my feet. Run when you're told to!" He said it all with a poker face and I did what I was told.'

Sandham was bowled the next day for 325 and yet he still had not finished with batting in that Test. He came in at number seven in the second innings, cursing his stiffness and wincing during the singles. He made fifty and his total of runs in one Test remained a record until beaten by Greg Chappell in 1974. Sandham's 325 did not last quite so long as the record for an innings – six months later, Don Bradman made 334 at Leeds. Somehow it seemed typical of Sandham's self-effacing batting that his record would not stand for any length of time; he was the second fiddler, not the cymbals crasher.

In the last few years of the Hobbs-Sandham partnership, the older man was carefully nursed through some sticky moments by his devoted junior partner. Sandham would notice when fatigue had gripped Hobbs and, calmly and quietly, he would take the bowling for a while. Hobbs always lauded the unselfishness of his friend and often pointed to Taunton in 1925 as a great example. In the first innings, Hobbs had gratified the tastes of the mass media and his own fretting supporters by scoring the century needed to equal the record of W.G.Grace. The posse of cameramen, news reporters and sensation-seekers had moved on by the time Surrey's second innings had started. Hobbs batted without care for an hour until Sandham confidently hazarded that another hundred was there for the taking. Surrey needed 183 to win and Sandham ensured that his own score would not threaten the pursuit of Hobbs's century. It was reached within nine runs of victory, Grace had been caught and passed within three days and although the laurels were placed on the head of a superb batsman, much of the credit goes to the unselfish Sandham.

He was to have his own day of glory, and it came on 26 June 1935 when he scored 103 against Hampshire at Basingstoke – his hundredth hundred. He was a worthy successor to his partner, Hobbs, and the idol of his youth, Hayward. Nearly fifty years later, Sandham could remember the stroke that brought him the hundred – a push off his legs for a couple of runs. Typically deft, typically safe. That night, over a celebratory drink, he allowed himself the rare luxury of basking in his glory and quipped: 'I ran a lot for old Jack as well, you know!'

Sandham did not outlast his usefulness on the field of play. He retired in 1937 while still a good player, proving that with a hundred in his last championship match. He finished his career on exactly a thousand innings – a neat, well-rounded end, in keeping with the methodical precision of his batting.

His association with Surrey cricket was to last till 1970, a round total of sixty years. He ran a cricket school with Alf Gover at Wandsworth – he never strayed far from South London – then returned to the Oval as coach. The Surrey captain, Stuart Surridge, called him 'Mr Producer' as he turned out class substitutes for the household names who were called away on England duty. He did much for Ken Barrington and John Edrich in their formative years at the Oval, instilling in them the virtues of playing straight and building an innings. He was proud and delighted when they became England regulars and Barrington and Edrich always called him 'Mr Sandham', with a touching blend of respect and warmth. He was a whimsical man with the same sort of dry humour associated with Jack Hobbs. Once Stuart Surridge returned to the dressing-room after picking up several respectable wickets and he was looking for some praise from his coach. In front of the rest of the side, Surridge said: 'Well, coach, what do you think of that?' Sandham sipped his tea, winked to the other players and said 'You bowled two very good balls – and they hit 'em both for four!' He did not lose his timing when he put his bat in mothballs.

Alec Bedser recalls his kindness as a coach: 'He was so pleasant, yet authoritative. He spoke rich common sense about the game; I can hear him now saying, "make your elbow hit the sky when you play back" to the young professionals. A great man for the basic principles of cricket.' He had no time for the biff-bang style of batting, he liked to see class in the nets. He would say: 'Now come on, my son, let's have a bit of ease and grace.' Alf Gover remembers Sandham's frustration at one cricketer who visited the indoor school at Wandsworth. 'Andy used to say to me "this bloke can't bat, why does he keep coming here?" Andy would try his darndest to get him to play properly, but he just wanted to whack it all the time. Finally, Andy got fed up of the ball whizzing back at him, he threw down his box of balls and walked out of that net for good. His version of the art of batting was being insulted in his eyes.'

He loved Surrey cricket with a touching devotion. After retiring as coach, he became the first team scorer, a well-loved, kindly figure always delighted to talk about the old times and forever speaking up for the latest addition to the Surrey first team. The tea room at the Oval was redesigned and named 'The Sandham Tea Room,': Hobbs had his gates at the Oval, Sandham the tea room. He left the scorebox in 1970, but he was not finished with Surrey; he would often be found watching the Club and Ground side, hoping to be able to put a word in for some promising youngster.

He lost part of his sight in his last years but bore his affliction with stoicism and dignity. He enjoyed the Centenary Test in 1980, meeting up with so many old friends and modestly fending off media questions such as:.'Mr Sandham, why didn't you play more times for England?' Les Ames saw him for the last time in December, 1981, when the Master's Club convened to pay its annual homage to Jack Hobbs. He seemed cheerful enough, although frail, and his last words to Ames were poignant: 'Les, don't ever live till ninety.'

He died in April 1982 at the age of ninety-one. Generations of cricketers mourned him and his former captain, Percy Fender, told me: 'He was a very great batsman and an even greater gentleman.' Few cricketers can have been so popular or given such distinction to the game for such a long period of time.

11

Sir Donald Bradman

'My feet feel tired when I think of him'
(Joe Hardstaff)

When considering the batting record of Sir Donald George Bradman, it is almost impossible to still a sense of wonder. His figures are quite staggering, but so is his impact on modern batsmanship. He was the third link in the chain that began with W.G.Grace – the Doctor evolved the basics of back and forward play against new styles of bowling, then Jack Hobbs developed those principles and adapted them to the demands of new bowling methods. After Hobbs, top-class batsmen aimed for quantity on predominately good pitches. But then came Bradman. He was a batsman who could score more runs than anyone else – but also at a faster pace. His genius lay in the art of doing things simply, clinically and with phenomenal success; his detractors thought he was unorthodox in technique, but it was his attitude that was unorthodox.

Don Bradman was just too good. He destroyed the contest between bat and ball that had always been one of the chief attractions of cricket. From 1930 – his first tour of England – till his retirement in 1949, Bradman was in the driving seat, and the rest nowhere. By his deeds, he changed the emphasis of Test cricket. In 1930, the attitude was still fairly Corinthian; England, under the uncomplicated, optimistic captaincy of Percy Chapman, tried to bowl Bradman out, even when he was scoring at forty runs an hour. When Maurice Tate was asked why he had failed to curb Bradman's scoring rate, he replied with engaging ingenuousness: 'Pin him down? of course not! I bowled every ball to get the little devil out!' On the first day of the Leeds Test, Bradman scored 309 not out; no less than 46 overs were bowled before lunch and the hourly average for the day was 22. Chapman's field placing during the series was, in retrospect, foolhardy; he should not have attacked such a devastating batsman. It was the last time a Test series was conducted in the spirit of the pre-1914 code; Chapman lost the captaincy for the final Test and the pragmatic R.E.S.Wyatt ushered in a new era of sensible, ultra-professional captaincy. Never again would a series in England see so much leg-spin bowling from so many: 300 overs from Peebles, Robins and Tyldesley for England and nearly 350 from Grimmett. Douglas Jardine and Wyatt realised they could not curb Bradman with leg-spin, so 'Bodyline' was born for the 1932-3 series. It was specifically designed to bring down Bradman to the status of ordinary mortals and it remains the greatest compliment ever paid to one player. At no other stage in cricket history has a tactical innovation been aimed at a single cricketer.

The scope of Bradman's achievements is so wide that a sense of perspective is needed: the eyes easily dull when confronted with page after page of statistics. I have always felt that the statistical evaluation of his career has unfairly overshadowed his genius, his certainty of strokeplay, speed of scoring and impact on generations of cricket-lovers. A few comments from those who played with and against Bradman may redress the balance somewhat:

> G.O.Allen: 'He had two shots for every ball when he was going well.'
> Alec Bedser: 'The more I bowled at him, the more I learned about bowling!'
> Jim Laker: 'The only batsman who ever gave me an inferiority complex.'
> Alf Gover: 'He would get runs off your best deliveries and murder your bad ones.'
> Jack Fingleton: 'Music to him was the crash of the ball against the fence. His bat was an axe dripping with the bowler's blood and agony. He knew no pity.'
> Joe Hardstaff: 'My feet feel tired when I think of him.'
> Les Ames: 'If he came back today, he'd be streets ahead of anyone else.'

I can hear the modern first-class cricketers scoffing at that remark by Les Ames, a man who has been intimately involved in first-class cricket since 1926. Of course, the fielding is better (although catchers like Hammond, Woolley and Duleepsinjhi, and outfielders such as Bradman and Sandham would have glittered in any age), of course today's wickets are inferior, and indeed, the turgid over-rates would clip Bradman's scoring rate. Yet I cannot believe that a man whose footwork was so dazzling, a man whose powers of concentration were legendary, a batsman who co-ordinated mind, feet and bat to an astonishing degree, would not still dominate today. His mastery of length meant that he was stumped just 22 times in a twenty-year career, even though against slow bowlers, the crease to him was just a place to take guard. Today's cricketers rightly set great score on speed between the wickets, running two to third man if necessary, and putting pressure on the deep fielders. Bradman was run out four times in first-class cricket, and three of those came before he was 22. Bill Bowes has told me how masterful Bradman was at placing the ball from where a fielder had just been moved – 'he just toyed with the field.'

No batsman has been more likely to despatch a bad ball to the boundary, or with such certainty. Bradman did not believe in lofting the ball: on his triumphant 1930 tour to England, he scored 2,960 runs, yet hit only two sixes, one off a no-ball. He expected to score off every ball; at Southend in 1948 he scored 187 in just over two hours against Essex and the last over before lunch was classic Bradman. Frank Vigar bowled it (leg-breaks) and Bradman hit five of the six deliveries to the boundary. The odd one out was hammered straight to mid-off and Bradman punched the palm of his hand with irritation. The old hunger was still there, at the age of nearly forty.

His attention to detail would surprise the modern sceptics who feel this 'action replay' age is the zenith of thinking, 'scientific' cricket. In 1930, Bradman began his first tour of England's unfamiliar, slow wickets with 236 at Worcester. Fred Root, one of the Worcestershire bowlers who toiled in vain, congratulated Bradman after his innings and was astounded to be asked: 'Does George Geary turn the ball much on English wickets?' He was due to face Geary and Leicestershire in the next match. He made 185 not out.

Those bowlers of the 1930s were not unsophisticated; Bill Bowes called for some scoring charts of Bradman's innings before the 'Bodyline' tour, hoping that he and his fellow-sufferers might glean some comfort. His strokes on the chart looked like the spokes of a bicycle wheel. Bradman always scored all round the wicket. Wilfred Rhodes, a great slow bowler, canny Yorkshireman and hard taskmaster, played twice against Bradman in 1930, his last season in a wonderful career that began in 1898. The man who had been captained by Grace in his first Test, who had enjoyed many thrilling duels with Victor Trumper and admired the beautiful craftsmanship of his opening partner, Jack Hobbs – he had no doubt that Bradman was the greatest batsman he had seen. 'I once saw him come in and put his first ball straight back past the bowler for four. And the second. And the third. Just like that. Without getting his eye in or anything. Every one an offensive stroke off a good ball.'

Sir Pelham Warner captained England and enjoyed an association with first-class cricket that lasted seventy years, from Grace to Dexter. He likened bowling at Bradman to 'casting pebbles at the Rock of Gibraltar.' Victor Richardson, splendid Australian batsman of Bradman's era, thought that captains should offer Bradman a century before he batted, provided he was out as soon as he reached that target.

If Richardson's whimsical notion had been adopted, the results would have been instructive – after all, Bradman's average century was 174. If you took away his tally of 43 not-out innings, his career average would still be 83.13, the best by any accredited batsman in the history of the game. If he were to be robbed of his centuries, he would still average 58.20 in his other innings – eight points more than Hobbs, seven more than Sutcliffe and two more than Hammond, with all their centuries included. Bradman made nought in just sixteen of his 338 innings, and not one in a period of seventy innings between December 1936 and January 1940. On 27 occasions, he scored 200 or more in a·day, and he batted for more than six hours on just twelve occasions. The slowest hundred of his career took 253 minutes – a perfectly respectable time for modern cricket. His runs were scored at a devastating rate, yet – according to one of his biographers, B.J.Wakeley – he gave just 93 chances that were not accepted throughout his career. Just one more statistic – of his 117 centuries, only eight were for a losing side. Bradman influenced the result of a cricket match more than any other player.

His temperament was as impressive as his statistical prowess. At Melbourne in 1933, Bradman walked out to bat in the second innings of the second Test with immense pressures on him. He had missed the first Test through illness, yet he was already well aware that Larwood and Voce were aiming to intimidate him by fast, short-pitched bowling to a legside field. He was embroiled in a dispute with the Australian Board of Control over his right to play for Australia and also comment on the game in a daily newspaper; the board had already fined him £50 for alleged breach of contract following the publication of a book under his own name after the 1930 tour to England. Bradman had hinted that unless the imbroglio was happily resolved, he might have to give up cricket to earn a living. On the first day, he had issued a statement to the effect that his newspaper had released him from his contract so that he could play in the series, but the atmosphere between Bradman and the Board was a little strained. The public interest in his comeback Test was frightening; during his illness, bulletins on his condition had been posted up in shop windows. The Australian public was willing him to be the man to combat this terrifying 'Bodyline' attack and Bradman was trying to come to terms with living a normal life amid the hysteria. On top of all that, he was on a 'king pair', having been bowled first ball by Bowes in the first innings. A new world record crowd of 68,188 watched Bradman take guard, with humiliation a distinct prospect. His first ball from Larwood was a bouncer, a supreme test of nerve and reactions on those fast, unreliable wickets of that season: Bradman hooked him to the boundary with a crack like a rifle shot. He made 103 not out in a second innings total of 191 and Australia won by 111 runs. For the moment, the public's craving for revenge had been assuaged. In the circumstances, it was one of the greatest innings of his career.

At Leeds in 1934, he had to dig deep into his reserves of stamina and iron will to salvage his reputation. He had batted frenetically so far in the series – scores of 29, 25, 36, 13 and 30 were most unlike him. He had been troubled by ill-health and the cynics were having a lovely time. In the fourth Test, Bradman went in with the score 39 for 3, all the wickets having fallen to Bowes. Bradman drove the first two balls past the bowler to the boundary and the next wicket fell at 427. Bradman made 304 – at 42 an hour – and in the final Test, 244 and 77. He not only had to contend with indifferent form: his health had been poor for some weeks. Finally it broke in September and he underwent an emergency operation. His appendix was almost gangrenous, he lost a lot of blood and, at the height of his crisis, five bulletins a day were issued. He almost died. Skilful surgery, the presence of his wife at his bedside and his own blend of stamina and mental fitness pulled him through, but it placed his achievements on the cricket pitch into a new perspective. He had played for two months when he should have been in bed, but he carried on through sheer willpower to average 94.75 in the series.

In the following series against England, Bradman again had to prove himself. It was his first series as captain, and he lost the first two Tests. He made two successive noughts and left the Brisbane ground in dark glasses to avoid public scrutiny. He had suffered a personal tragedy just before the series started – the loss of his new-born son. In the third Test at Melbourne, Bradman dropped himself down the order while the effects of a thunderstorm turned batting into a lottery, but when he came out – at 97 for 5 – the match was delicately poised. He made 270, followed that up with 212 and 169 and Australia became the first side to win a series three-two after being two down. Once again, Bradman's personal example had been crucial.

The pressures on him were immense when he tried to resume his Test career after the Second World War. He had been discharged from the Army because of fibrositis; at one stage, he could not lift his right arm to comb his hair and his wife had to shave him. When Hammond's England team arrived in Australia in October 1946, they were shocked to see the change in Bradman: he was frail and far from fit. At thirty-eight, dogged by gastric troubles and slowly recovering from five years of fibrositis, he was far from the concept of the strong Australian sporting hero. The general consensus was that if Bradman failed in the early games of the forthcoming series, he would stand down and announce his retirement. One incident on the first morning of that opening Test altered the course of the series. When he had scratched together an unimpressive 28, Bradman played a ball from Voce hard to Jack Ikin at slip; while the England players appealed for the catch, Bradman stood his ground and waited the umpire to rule in his favour. At the end of the over Hammond growled to Bradman, 'That's a fine bloody way to start the series!' and certainly the majority opinion of the England players was that it was a clean catch, not a bump ball. Doug Wright, Alec Bedser and Norman Yardley have all confirmed their certainties to me. Afterwards, Bradman told the press he would have walked if he had thought it a clean catch. Whatever the opinions, Bradman battled through his bad form and made 187. In the next Test, he scored 234; another personal crisis had been weathered and his triumphant final tour of England was set up.

There is no doubt he was not the same player as pre-War, yet his performances were still massively certain after that Brisbane Test. He played straighter than ever before, eliminating all risks, yet still scoring very quickly. He played closer to the ball, still using his feet to the spinners, but playing his shots when the ball was between his legs to ensure perfect balance. When Alec Bedser rattled him temporarily with the 'caught Hutton bowled Bedser' ploy (caught at backward short leg off deliveries of a full length that moved in to him late) his reaction was typically thorough: he went into the nets and ordered his bowlers to bowl that type of delivery until he had mastered it. Bedser never got him out again that way.

When Alec Bedser and Jim Laker are told that the pre-War Bradman was an even more frightening proposition, they count their blessings.

Both great bowlers affirmed he was the best batsman they bowled at. Bedser: 'No matter the setting of the field, he couldn't be tied down. At such an age, his speed between the wickets was amazing. He could alter the angle from which the ball left the bat with a slight change of grip and he left the bowlers with no margin of error.' Jim Laker conceded nearly a thousand runs against the Australians in 1948 without ever getting Bradman's wicket and he said: 'I can never remember Bradman letting a ball go by without playing a shot. He was streets ahead of anyone else and just couldn't be rattled. In the Lord's Test, I beat him with almost every ball of one over; he looked up at me and said: "Well bowled Jim – now you've got that out of your system we can get on with the game." He went on to score 89.' Laker remembered a shot Bradman played in the match against Surrey: 'Jack Parker was bowling medium pace and he sent down one that was a little short. Bradman hit it so hard off the back foot through the bowler and mid-on that the ball had bounced back off the pavilion rails as Jack was finishing his run-up.'

Bradman brought to his batting a strength of mind and purpose that was rock-solid and pitiless. He did not espouse stylish play for the sake of it, he was interested in results. He knew that bowlers hate to see the full face of the bat and good-length deliveries turned into half volleys and long hops by use of twinkling footwork. When he came into first-class cricket at the age of nineteen, he seemed astonishingly mature as a batsman. He had worked out the mechanics of batting for himself and was largely self-taught. The remarkable footwork and reflexes had been honed by practising a little game he devised as a boy: he would throw a golf ball at the brick base of an old water tank and then try to hit the rebound with the stump of a gum tree. The ball would come back at different angles and speeds, which of course developed his footwork. Unless he achieved 75 per cent success, he would keep plugging away.

At the age of twelve, he was taken to the Sydney Cricket Ground to see the visiting England team in the fifth Test. He watched the dazzling Charles Macartney score 170 for Australia and calmly informed his father: 'I shall never be satisfied until I play on this ground.' A lonely childhood, albeit within a loving family, had equipped him with that practical, calculating streak he later showed in all facets of life and when he made his debut for New South Wales in first-class cricket the resultant hundred seems, in retrospect, a formality. His opening boundary and the one that brought up his hundred were both pull shots – the stroke that became his trademark. He had worked out the grip that suited his fondness for the pull; both hands were turned over the handle, which rested against the ball of the right thumb. That enabled him to close the face of the bat over the ball, enabling him to hook, pull and cut down rather than uppishly. The right hand emphasis meant his onside play was stronger than on the offside, but he compensated with venomous straight driving. Everything else was textbook and remained so for the next twenty years.

His orderly mind played a vital role in his batting. He treated it like a business, something to be approached with dedication and professionalism. Jack Fingleton, a colleague many times in the Australian side, gave a fascinating insight into the personal habits of Bradman during a lunch interval when he was not out. Fingleton wrote that he would place his pads, gloves and bat on the table, have a wash, then take off his trousers, put a towel round his waist and sit down to a light lunch of rice custard, stewed fruit and milk. 'Each slow mouthful was an essay in method, in digestion, in relaxation, in cold planning and contemplation of the real feast soon to follow in the middle.'

One can only guess if Bradman would have been so ruthless if he had started his first-class career in a more encouraging, tolerant environment. The hard-nosed leg-pullers of the New South Wales team soon found Bradman a fertile source of amusement: the farmer's son from the outback was nineteen before he ventured outside the state of New South Wales and his gaucheness and naivety stood out. On his first trip to Adelaide, one of the players sent him on a fruitless errand to a suburb eight miles from his hotel; when the team discovered he had musical talent, he was made to play the piano with his shirt off, so they could examine his back muscles as he tinkled the keyboard. Bradman swallowed the 'country boy' jibes and vowed to answer back in the most satisfying way: on the cricket field. After his debut century, he was never again a laughing-stock.

Then he had to convince the Test selectors that he was the genuine article. From this distance it seems one of the great misjudgements of all time to drop Don Bradman after just one Test against England in 1928 – yet he only made 18 and one, and did not look at all comfortable on a rain-affected wicket in the second innings. He was back for the Third Test, scoring a hundred, but there were still doubts about his technique. Maurice Tate called him his 'rabbit', Warwick Armstrong thought he was not, at present, Test class and Charles Kelleway, a team-mate in that series, said he would be found out in England, because he used a cross-bat. All this steeled Bradman even more to greater deeds and his subsequent career is a triumph of willpower as much as natural ability.

The envy and pettiness of others inevitably kept pace with Bradman's burgeoning prestige. On his ascent to cricketing greatness, he seemed to attract a motley assortment of denigrators, eager to misjudge an imagined slight, exacerbate differences of opinion and accept damaing rumours. The press did not always acquit itself nobly and the strain on Bradman's private life must have been unimaginable. Much was made of the night at Leeds, in 1930, when Bradman retired to his hotel room to play classical music after he had scored his marvellous unbeaten triple hundred. Some of his team-mates felt he should have bought them a drink and joined in an orgy of back-slapping. Bradman's retort: 'What did they expect me to do? Parade around Leeds?' may have seemed tactless, but there is no playing regulation that ensures that a star batsman should spend his social hours in a way foreign to his nature. His successful business ventures while still a player also attracted disparaging remarks from some with inferior financial acumen and playing ability. Certainly he seems to have been a tough negotiator with those desirous of his services and name, but there were never any criticisms of his integrity. His relationship with the Australian Board was a fluctuating one, but he never dissembled and would stick out on a principle that was important to him – like the row over Bradman's book on the 1930 tour and the fact that he was barred from making newspaper pronouncements on the 1932–3 series, while some of his team-mates were allowed to broadcast their views every night on radio. To Bradman's logical and clear mind, that was nonsense and it is difficult to disagree with him.

His greatness as a public performer inevitably meant that his shy, reserved persona would occasionally be stripped bare of defence against the demands of a mass media age. Jack Fingleton, no lover of Bradman, has paid tribute to his remarkable tolerance with the hordes of autograph-hunters who besieged him for two decades. On one England tour, a former Test captain who had drunk rather too much was refused entry to see Bradman at Lord's because of his condition; he took his feelings of outrage to Fleet Street, who gleefully printed the story without seeking the view of Bradman. In the first year of Bradman's touchingly happy marriage, his wife overheard a conversation about their alleged pending divorce.

The flame of publicity also burned his son, John. In 1964, John booked into a guest house in South Wales; when he signed his name in the residents' book, he immediately attracted interest. The guests never left him alone that night, quizzing him about his father. Finally, in 1972, John could stand it no longer, changing his surname by deed poll to Bradsen. As late as 1980, Bradman attracted ill-informed publicity over his decision not to attend the Centenary Test celebrations in London. The Fleet Street whisper was that he did not wish to share the limelight with the other eminent cricketers of yesteryear. A couple of phone calls to sources close to Bradman would have yielded the truth – he was worried about the health of his wife, who had undergone open-heart surgery in recent years, his daughter Shirley (a sufferer from cerebral palsy since early childhood) and his son, John (who had contracted polio at the age of thirteen). All that was enough to tax the morale of even Bradman.

I am happy to acknowledge innumerable acts of kindness by Bradman to the famous and the insignificant. G.O.Allen told me Bradman was the most sporting captain and gracious loser he had played against – despite his toughness on the field. Bill Edrich became the last Englishman to reach a thousand runs in May due to Bradman's willingness to share the spotlight of glory. It was in 1938 and on the last day of May, the Australians were playing Middlesex. Bradman reached his thousand runs in May and then declared twenty minutes from the close to give Edrich the chance to follow suit. He needed ten runs, opened the innings and Bradman was the first man to congratulate him. Edrich's great partner, Denis Compton, also has a fond memory of Bradman from that 1938 season; it came during the Lord's Test, when the twenty-year-old Compton played an innings of genius on a damp pitch. As Compton walked off the field – unbeaten on 76 – Bradman walked over to him, shook his hand and said: 'Denis, that was one of the finest innings I've seen.' Alec Bedser remembers two warm gestures – producing a sack of chilled beer for the England party as they prepared for yet another hot, sticky train journey in Australia, and bundling Bedser off to bed in his Adelaide home when he arrived in the city with 'flu and his hotel room not yet ready. Bill Bowes treasures the moment when, after beating Bradman all ends up, he was told: 'Well bowled Bill – that's one up to you.' Reg Sinfield's first wicket in Test cricket was that of Bradman, caught behind by Les Ames at Nottingham in 1938; as he walked away, he said to Sinfield: 'Well done, Reg – I give you best.' Nor did he hog the limelight when Australia batted. His exhortation to the rest of his side ('come and watch this, you'll never see the like again') during Stan McCabe's priceless 232 at Trent Bridge in

1938 reflects great credit on both captain and batsman. Neil Harvey will not readily forget the way Bradman blocked an over from Dick Pollard, so that young Harvey could hit the winning run in his first Test, at Leeds in 1948, nor the way his captain ran to him with congratulations, oblivious of his own 173 not out that set up that victory.

He did not confine spontaneous acts of human decency to the great and the good. At Trent Bridge in 1934, Bradman was on his way into the ground when he noticed a man standing outside the gates, looking wistful. Bradman stopped for a word, discovered he was an unemployed miner and invited him into the ground, paying his admission, finding a good seat and handing over some spending money. When he discovered he had a wife and eight children to feed, Bradman organised a collection for him in the Australian dressing-room and topped the list with his own contribution. On that same tour, he was walking along the Embankment in London, reasonably pleased with life; he had scored 244 that day in the Oval Test and then enjoyed a pleasant evening at the theatre. He spotted some tramps and was visibly moved at their condition; he took them to a coffee stall, forced food and drink on them and when one hungry tramp said suspiciously, 'who are yer?', Bradman wordlessly put a half crown in his hand.

All these were hardly the actions of a ruthless automaton, a man who carried the same merciless principles of his batting into his private life. He simply seems a person who knew his own mind, whom to trust and whom to avoid. Like any other member of the human race, his adult life was shaped by the circumstances of youth; because he had to play a lot on his own, he developed into a self-sufficient, wary individual. Yet he never forgot his family, writing every week to his mother from England in 1930, and making characteristically thorough financial provision for her future as his own prospects improved out of all recognition.

So much for Bradman the man. The batsman has only one worthwhile charge to answer when his claims to pre-eminence are considered: his performances on bad wickets. It is generally held that Bradman did not see why he should be expected to bat on surfaces that made the game a lottery and that is why Jack Hobbs remains the *nonpareil* in the eyes of many good judges. It is true that Bradman looked very unimpressive in 'Verity's Match' in 1934, when he slogged the spinner up in the air soon after he came in on a turning wicket. Woodfull, his captain, gave him a schoolmasterly stare as he walked from the wicket and the legend of Bradman and damaged wickets was born on that day. Closer scrutiny of his record in England does not substantiate the allegation; he came on four tours to England, totalled 120 innings and scored more than 2,000 runs each time. One-third of his total career innings was therefore played in England. Surely in such a climate, with the wickets uncovered, surely he faced wickets that were occasionally as tricky as Lord's in 1934? He did, and acquitted himself well. Norman Yardley remembers his superb hundred on a turner that won the Leeds Test of 1938: 'No one could have played better – wonderful footwork, immaculate defence and impecable stroke selection.' Hedley Verity, the unwilling agent of the slurs on Bradman, would not agree that he was susceptible on unreliable wickets and he would cite Bramall Lane, 1938, as an example. On an authentic 'sticky' wicket, Bradman batted for nearly four hours to total 59 and 42, playing most deliveries in the middle of the bat and living off his considerable wits. Again, in that season, his performance on a dry, dusty wicket in the Trent Bridge Test won high praise; on the last day, Verity and Wright spun the ball sharply, yet Bradman scored 144 not out in an innings of judicious defence and clean striking of the bad ball.

Bradman played most of his Sheffield Shield career on covered wickets and on the rare occasions when he came up against a 'sticky' wicket during Tests in Australia, he did not fare well. It seems he had cashed in his psychological chips by the time he came out to bat on these uncertain, physically dangerous surfaces, but I believe he would have adapted if necessary. The man who improvised against the terrifying 'Bodyline' onslaught to average 56.57 (better than Sutcliffe or Hammond) in that series need have no qualms about any other type of bowling or cricketing surface. Jack Hobbs thought he would have been the best in the world if given the opportunity to play regularly on rain-affected wickets and with his gifts of timing, concentration and footwork it is hard to disagree.

The man was a marvel. Other batsmen of his age would make more charming hundreds (McCabe, Woolley), others were more thrilling (Hammond, Compton), more resolute in unfavourable conditions (Sutcliffe, Hutton) but Bradman's was always the wicket to prize. Ask Reg Sinfield – he still talks about the day Les Ames caught a legside tickle in 1938. Alec Bedser, bluff, unsentimental veteran of countless Tests as player and selector, still treasures the ball that bowled Bradman for nought at Adelaide in 1947. Ian Peebles used to recount the newspaper placard that greeted him after he dismissed Bradman for 14 in the 1930 Old Trafford Test – PEEBLES DOES IT. It was left to a hale and hearty inswing bowler from Somerset to put Bradman's prestige in a nutshell. Bill Andrews is a splendid character with an engaging raconteur's wit, an enviable ability to remember the punchline and an endearing way of beginning a sentence with 'Did I ever tell you . . .' At Taunton in 1938 he sent down one delivery that has kept him in after-dinner stories for the next forty-five years: he clean bowled Don Bradman. He had made 202 at the time and had relaxed his customary vigilance at the end of the Test series, but no matter. In 1973, Bill Andrews's book of reminiscences was published, entitled *The Hand that Bowled Bradman*. All because of one carefree shot at a time when Neville Chamberlain still believed Herr Hitler was a man of honour. A Bradman dismissal really was that special.

12

Les Ames

'Taking on the bowlers was my idea of cricket,
not worrying about dropping a catch'

Of the twenty-one batsmen who have scored a hundred centuries, four can be classified as all-rounders. W.G.Grace, Frank Woolley and Walter Hammond were all match-winning bowlers at some stage in their career, but there is a strong case for nominating Les Ames as the best all-rounder in the pack. Ames has been the outstanding wicket-keeper/batsman of all time, and if I concentrate on his orthodox, attractive batting for the bulk of this chapter, his abilities on the other side of the stumps should never be forgotten.

He made 102 centuries, most of them in aggressive, hard-driving style. His temperament was excellent, as eight Test hundreds testify. A little matter of 37,248 runs (average 43.57), a hundred in each innings on three occasions and 3,000 runs in one season – all these qualify Ames for honourable mention in any assessment of the premier batsmen of his time. When his wicket-keeping is considered, one can only marvel at his consistency and fitness.

Three seasons in particular demonstrate the all-round talents of Ames. In 1928, he took 121 victims behind the stumps and supplemented that with 1,919 runs; the following year 127 and 1,795; in 1932, 100 victims and 2,482 runs. The 1928 and 1929 total of victims has never been beaten and only J.T.Murray has combined a hundred victims and a thousand runs in a season – and then just once. Ames did it three times.

The breakdown of Ames's victims graphically demonstrates the kind of cricket played by Kent in the 1920s and 1930s: challenging batting, geared to making enough runs to give 'Tich' Freeman sufficient time to bowl out the opposition twice with his leg-breaks. What fun it must have been to watch Kent in those days! Woolley, Chapman, Ashdown, Valentine and Ames would attack the bowling in their various styles and then Freeman, Marriott, Woolley and Hardinge would bowl assorted degrees of spin. Ames fitted to the manner born into this atmosphere; he needed no second bidding to play his shots and what could be more enjoyable for a wicket-keeper than to stand up at the stumps for ninety per cent of one's career, picking Freeman's googly and enjoying the abortive attempts of callow amateurs to discern which way the ball would break? Bob Taylor, Jack Richards and the rest today would give their leather inners to learn their wicket-keeping trade at such a time.

A casual leaf through *Wisden* gives a flavour of Kentish cricket during the Ames/Freeman partnership. 'Stumped Ames bowled Freeman' leaps out of the pages – four of them against Glamorgan in one innings (later, 130 runs from Ames), five against Northants (Ames 149), another four in one innings against Warwickshire and even four of the dour men of Lancashire perishing to the combination. In 1932, Ames stumped 64 of his 100 victims – a record that will only be threatened when wickets are better prepared, when spin bowlers are encouraged to bowl properly in long spells and batsmen go down the pitch to play them. In other words, never. Nor is Ames's career record of 418 stumpings likely to be surpassed, nor the 259 times that the Kent scorer wrote in his book: 'stumped Ames bowled Freeman'.

So much, for the time being, on Ames the wicket-keeper. Ames the batsman is worthwhile enough to examine. His method was disarmingly simple; he believed in hitting the ball, on the ground or in the air, as hard and as often as possible. With Ames in the side, a run chase was always on – twice he won the trophy for the fastest hundred of the season during the 1930s. Essentially, he played 'through the V', showing the full face of the bat to the bowler. He liked to settle in for the first half hour or so, then press on. Of all the batsmen who scored a hundred centuries, I would have thought that Ames played further down the wicket than anyone. Godfrey Evans, who kept wicket after the War with Ames in the side as a batsman, recalls: 'He used to go yards to get to the pitch of the ball. He'd love to play a low skimmer over cover point, like a three iron golf shot. I called him "twinkletoes" and I've never seen a major batsman play so far out of his crease.' Doug Wright, another team-mate, admired his footwork immensely: 'As a quickish leg-spinner, I never had many batsmen give me the charge, but I'm sure Les would have tried it if we hadn't been in the same side. He was fantastic on his feet and played the same way through his forties.' Norman Yardley, who toured South Africa with Ames in 1938–9, feels Ames has never been given his just deserts as a batsman: 'In his early England days, there was Sutcliffe, Hammond, Woolley and the rest, then later Compton, Hutton, Edrich and Leyland. Les was always a little overshadowed by them, yet his record was first-class. He was a beautiful striker of the ball.'

As one of just three batsmen to hit Larwood for six, Ames could fairly be said to be comfortable against pace – with characteristic candour, Ames tells me that he simply followed Larwood's delivery around on the legside, helped it on its way and the strong wind did the rest! His most glorious displays, however were against the slow bowlers; Reg Sinfield told men how much Ames enjoyed wading into himself, Goddard and Parker whenever Kent played Gloucestershire: 'I remember the time when Tom Goddard had him caught in the deep – Les walked past me and grinned: "Well, I'd rather be caught out there than at short leg." That's the way Les played his cricket.' It is generally acknowledged that Ames played Goddard better than anyone after the lbw law was revised in 1935; afterwards, Goddard reaped a harvest of wickets because the right-hander just had to play the ball coming in on him. Ames counteracted that by splendid footwork and the courage to attack Goddard. He told me: 'It was either me or Tom who would win. I reckoned that if I stayed in the crease he would dictate the length to me. Tom didn't like the long handle at the best of times and I loved to see his reaction if I got hold of him. Mind you, he made a fool out of me a few times!'

Both Jim Laker and Tom Graveney have assured me that the postwar Les Ames played essentially the same way as a decade earlier. Graveney recalls four hundreds in a row by Ames against Gloucestershire when Ames was well over forty, dogged by lumbago and putting on weight. 'I couldn't believe it when I first saw him,' says Graveney, 'He gave our spinners some terrible hammer. I envied his footwork and confidence.' Jim Laker's cricket education was occasionally rudely interrupted by violent assaults from Ames in county matches: 'I think perhaps he couldn't pick my flight, but it made no difference to the way he attacked me. He'd take a chance, get down the pitch and crack me all over the place. He told me that was the method he used against Tom Goddard, so it would do for all the other spinners.'

G.O.Allen recalls affectionately his partnership with Ames against the 1931 New Zealanders – not for the achievement of adding 246 for the eight wicket (a record for England against all countries), but for the attitude of Ames to a crisis. When Allen joined Ames, England were 190 for 7, still 34 behind. Ames discussed Bill Merritt with Allen and said of that very good leg-spinner: 'He doesn't like the tap, Gubby, let's get after him.' They added 246 in just under three hours and Allen recalls: 'That remark was typical of Les. He believed in getting at them.'

Even when becalmed, Ames could always pick up ones and twos by dint of his speed between the wickets. He was a wonderful judge of a run – Frank Woolley was happy to leave the calling to his junior partner – and he was one of the first batsmen to realise how to put pressure on a fielder. He would run the first one as quickly as possible, in the hope of getting another if the fielder fumbled the ball by taking his eye off it, or panicked. Both Godfrey Evans and Doug Wright thought Ames the best runner between the wickets of their time, and that quality must have been invaluable during the many thrilling run-chases he guided. Alf Gover tells an amusing story that sums up his own lack of fielding mobility and the effervescence of Ames. 'It was at Blackheath and I turned from mid-on to chase his shot. I though I'd kid him to try for the second run, so I trotted after the ball, ready to turn round, whip it in and get him stranded going for the second run. It all worked according to plan, except that when I turned round with the ball in my hand, Les had run three! He's laughed about that for years . . .'

Ames believes his ability as a soccer player was more central to his batting success than his wicket-keeping. He played on the wing for Second Division Clapton Orient, and shared with Denis Compton the fleet-footed skills of both the winger and the dashing batsman. He does not feel that standing up to the wicket for the bulk of an innings helped give him an insight into the pitch's condition when it was his turn to bat. 'I always separated the two in my mind. When I kept wicket, I concentrated on the batsmen and worked out what our bowlers were trying to achieve. I didn't have time to think about how I would play during our innings.' He does agree that his success behind the stumps gave him extra confidence: 'When you're double-barrelled, you can console yourself when you do badly early in the game. If I made nought with the bat, I'd think "Ah well, I've been picked as a keeper", and vice-versa.'

He became grateful for the advice given him by Gerry Weighall, the captain of the Kent Second Eleven when Ames joined the staff in 1926. Before then, he had kept wicket just twice at school and had no ambitions in that direction. In his first Club and Ground game, Ames was sent in to open the innings and did reasonably well. Weighall asked him if he could bowl and when Ames said no, he was told in no uncertain terms: 'When you take up this game, you must have two strings to your bow – you'll keep wicket.' To his great embarrassment, Ames was handed the regular wicket-keeper's gloves and told to get on with it. He had to keep on a turning wicket, with two slow left-handers in the side, but the Ames temperament showed its mettle for the first time – he took five victims.

He never thought of himself as a natural wicket-keeper and compares himself unfavourably with his brilliant successors in the Kent and England sides, Godfrey Evans and Alan Knott. At five feet nine inches, with a strong physique, Ames always looked a little out of place behind the stumps, yet he prospered by dint of an unfussy technique. W.H.V.('Hopper') Levett, who deputised on occasions for Ames in the Kent side, told me: 'He was quiet, unspectacular and extremely competent. "Tich" Freeman got him many victims, of course, but he also pulled off some brilliant stumpings.' Godfrey Evans makes the point that the style of wicket-keepers in those days suited Ames – 'They never believed in throwing themselves around as we did. If a throw was wide, they would leave it to the fielders to gather it. Les was one of the very best of those kind. He was no goalkeeper, but he missed very little.'

'Gubby' Allen says Ames did not really like keeping wicket: 'In his heart, he would love to have been a number four batsman, brilliant outfield and occasional leg-spinner. When we played together for England, it was clear that Les preferred batting – when we came off the field, Les would be out of his wicket-keeper's gear very swiftly, getting himself prepared to bat, even if he was low down in the order.' Ames agreed: 'I never thought of myself as a natural keeper but I loved to bat. Taking on the bowlers was my idea of cricket, not worrying about dropping a catch. You've no idea what it was like keeping to Bradman, all the time thinking, "Gosh, I can't afford to drop this fellow." It was much more fun when I let their 'keeper do the worrying.'

For all his modesty, Ames was first choice for England as wicket-keeper from 1931 to 1939 as well as an authentic batsman. His work behind the stumps on two Australian tours drew high praise and the team was fortunate to have such a splendid player going in at number seven. When necessary, he would play within himself for the side. At Lord's in 1938, Ames played second fiddle to Hammond as his captain compiled one of the greatest double hundreds of his career. When he joined Hammond, the England score was 271 for 5 – almost a crisis against an Australian side containing Bradman and McCabe. Ames settled in to play for the morrow, giving the strike to Hammond, taking his measure of the bowlers. The next day, he took his score to 83, the partnership added 186 and England thereafter could not be threatened by Bradman.

He was even more obdurate against the Australians at Lord's in 1934.

Posterity has accorded this Test as 'Verity's Match', but without the solidity of Leyland and Ames, England would not have won so resoundingly. They came together at 182 for 5, with O'Reilly and Grimmett smacking their lips. England, already one down in the series, needed a large total to thwart the run-making greed of Woodfull, Bradman and McCabe. Leyland and Ames both battled through for centuries, Ames then encouraging Geary to add 48 precious runs and putting on another fifty with Verity. Ames is honest enough to remind me that he was badly missed by Bertie Oldfield on 96, but that was his only mistake in an innings of 120 that took him nearly four-and-a-half hours, slow going for such a natural strokemaker, but, in the circumstances, an invaluable performance. When he caught Bradman off a skier in the second innings, Les Ames thought Christmas had come early.

Lord's 1934 remains his most memorable match, but there are many other moments to treasure. Another Test hundred that gave him particular pleasure came at Kingston in 1935; England lost the Test but without Ames, they would have been ignominiously brushed aside. Overnight, five men including Leyland and Hammond had gone and the captain, Wyatt, had a broken jaw, courtesy of a fast delivery from Martindale. Ames scored 126 of the bravest runs imaginable, against fearsome fast bowling from Constantine, Martindale and Hylton on a very quick wicket. He did not just hammer slow bowlers.

His all-round skills were devastatingly revealed at Brentwood in 1934. Kent slaughtered the Essex bowling for 803 for 4 declared – 632 runs coming on the first day – and Ames made 202 not out in two hours and fifty minutes. That would be enough in one match for a normal man, but as Essex succumbed twice to the spin of Wright and Freeman, Ames picked up seven victims – including four more stumpings off Freeman. When he won the trophy for the fastest hundred of the 1939 season, it was made in typical style, to win a county match. Surrey asked Kent to make 231 in 145 minutes and Ames – 136 not out – saw them home after reaching his hundred in 67 minutes. Other batsmen may have relaxed and played their shots in festival games at the season's end, light-hearted affairs when a bowler could always get the handful of wickets to reach his hundred for the season, or a batsman was able to get enough to reach a personal milestone – Les Ames played his shots right through the season, whatever the opposition and state of the wicket. He was a festival cricketer all year round.

The manner in which he achieved his century of centuries was quintessentially Ames. It came in Canterbury Week, 1950 – an appropriate venue for such a happy, colourful cricketer and achieved in the best possible manner. Middlesex asked Kent to score 237 at about eighty an hour and Ames went in with the score 0 for 1. He scored 131 in two hours, driving the spin of Jack Young and Jim Sims to all parts of the ground and handing out a thrashing to John Warr, who was deemed good enough to tour Australia with England that winter. He was dismissed in the most satisfactory way – caught in the deep, going for another big hit. Kent won a marvellous match by seven wickets. For good measure, Ames kept wicket in the second innings, while Evans rested an injured hand. He was in his forty-fifth year and surely good for a few more run-chases.

He never played a full game for Kent after that season. The dreaded lumbago struck with a vengeance when he returned from a tour to India and that was that. Typically, he can see the funny side to his retirement: 'If I hadn't got a move on at Canterbury that day against Middlesex, I might have died on 99 hundreds! The two centuries I got in India were later ranked as first-class, but I didn't know that at the time, so when I retired I thought I was on exactly a hundred. I shall always be grateful Jack Young for slipping me one down the legside for a free hit.'

Cricket never stopped being fun for Les Ames. If you talk cricket with him for any length of time, he will tell you how lucky he was to play for Kent: 'All our captains had the right idea – get the runs quickly and attractively. We were never given a rollicking if we got out playing shots and no one dared play for his average.' His top score of 295 is proof of that – 'It was against Gloucestershire and when Bryan Valentine came in, I was told to get a move on, because the skipper wanted to declare as soon as I got my three hundred. I only needed five more, so I tried to get down the other end with a quick single. I went to turn Charlie Parker to leg, it spun a little and I was dismissed by the old firm – caught Hammond bowled Parker. No regrets, though. When you saw Frank Woolley carry on playing his shots when he reached the nineties, you followed suit.'

Of the old players, Les Ames remains one of the most balanced and thoughtful of judges and a highly-respected bridge between generations. He has kept in touch with modern trends, as England selector and manager of MCC teams abroad, and secretary-manager of Kent until 1974. He gave invaluable assistance in coaching at Canterbury after his retirement and then became the first former professional to be president of the county. Today he can still be found at the ground every day during the Canterbury Festival, those twinkling feet carrying him from one group of friends to another, a perennial smile on that cheerful, freckled, face. When pressed, he will pay due homage to the players of his day, but he is no *laudator temporis acti*; he marvels at the fitness and consistency of Alan Knott and no one is keener to see Kent prosper. His view of cricket over an active participation of nearly sixty years is unprejudiced, sensible and charitable. He concedes that the paucity of slow bowling would perturb him if he had to bat today, but concludes that he would probably get by reasonably enough. Les Ames, the Mr Micawber of cricket, invariably ensured something would turn up.

13

Sir Leonard Hutton

'You've got to think it through, you know'

They did not waste words in the Yorkshire cricket hierarchy of the 1930s: no need, they had the best side in the land. When George Hirst, the county's great coach saw a slender sixteen-year-old play in the nets for the first time, he contented himself with four words: 'Keep on wi' that.' A few weeks later, he doubled his output to the lad: 'Booger off, there's nowt we can teach thee.' George Hirst knew a great player when he walked into his nets – and Leonard Hutton did not let him down. Bill Bowes, fresh from bowling Bradman first ball, was asked by Hirst to assess the boy; apart from a slight technical defect on the leg stump that was soon rectified, Bowes pronounced him perfect. Herbert Sutcliffe, legendary opening batsman and a meagre singer of praises of other batsmen, could not contain himself. He wrote; 'He is a marvel – the discovery of a generation. At the age of 14 he was good enough to play for most county sides.'

If Hutton was disturbed by such uncharacteristic eulogy, he did not show it. He became one of the greatest opening batsmen in history, a man who carried innumerable weak England batting sides after the War. Few batsmen have been more technically perfect, more interesting to watch even when scoring slowly. He had as many shots as Hammond and Bradman, and if he kept them on a tighter reign, the occasions when he unfurled his flag of batsmanship have never been forgotten by those who witnessed them. He was a natural and worthy successor to the honourable line of famous batsmen who have gone in first for England – Shrewsbury, Hayward, Hobbs and Sutcliffe. There was a professional certainty about his batting, an elegance that beguiled and a quiet determination that compelled admiration. Colin Cowdrey says he was the most complete batsman he has seen, Brian Close, Ray Illingworth and Johnny Wardle will not be shaken from the same opinion and Fred Trueman calls him 'a batsman whose bat had no edges'. When Hutton was dismissed, it came as a jolt to the system, an affront to the well-ordered nature of things. On the opening morning of the Leeds Test of 1953, Ray Lindwall bowled him second ball with a classic yorker; the crowd and the England batting seemed to go into mourning. England laboured to 142 for 7 on the first day and the shadow of one delivery hung over the day's proceedings. No one seemed to give Lindwall credit for such a magnificent delivery. Hutton's dismissal in the first over was the big story.

He did not often fail the public that expected far too much of him. Just three batsmen have scored more runs for England, while seven have surpassed his 129 centuries. Hammond and Boycott are the only English batsmen to surpass his career average of 55.51. All this despite the loss of six years through war, an injury to his left arm that hampered his postwar batting and an early retirement at 39.

If batting mastery in the nets came easily to young Hutton, little else did. He was overawed by the great men in the Yorkshire side of the 1930s, by the achievements of players who came from his home town of Pudsey – men like John Tunnicliffe, Major Booth and Herbert Sutcliffe. At the age of ten, he was reading M.A.Noble's book on captaincy and before he had needed to shave he was opening the batting for Pudsey St Lawrence with Edgar Oldroyd, a fine, bad-wicket player who had scored 37 hundreds for Yorkshire. As a wide-eyed teenager, Hutton would give anything just to carry out the drinks for Yorkshire and Bill Bowes remembers the youngster with great affection: 'He was a slow-speaking, naive lad who found it hard to believe what he was watching. He would say something like "Eeh Bill, doesn't Hammond hit 'em a mile off his back foot?" The next time he batted, he tried the same shot and trod on his wicket. It didn't matter – he wanted to learn.' Others in the Yorkshire side were less approachable than Bowes; in one of his early games for the first team, Hutton was sent to field alongside Arthur Mitchell in the slips. Mitchell, a man who played the role of the stage Yorkshireman to perfection, growled: 'What's tha' doin' here?' Nor did he mellow on the occasions when he partnered Hutton. Once the youngster essayed a rather ambitious cut that missed the ball by several inches; from down the wicket came the familiar Mitchell grunt: 'Nay, nay, nay – you're not playin' for Pudsey Prims now. You'd 'a wanted a clothes peg to reach yon.'

Fortunately better batsmen than Mitchell knew how to encourage the shy Hutton. When he followed his debut duck for the second eleven with another on his debut for the first team, Maurice Leyland consoled him with: 'Never mind, lad, tha's started at the bottom.' Herbert Sutcliffe billed and cooed about his protégé out of Hutton's earshot and when they batted together, the great man did everything possible to help – taking the difficult bowlers at strategic times, advising him what shots to play, praising his defensive technique. Hutton was always grateful that he was not expected to crash the ball all over the field in his early days in first-class cricket. Sutcliffe encouraged him to take his time and learn how to build an innings: he never forgot the formative years of his cricket education. Just after his first Test in 1937, Hutton was ushered into the presence of Bobby Peel, the slow left-arm bowler whose drunken exit from first-class cricket at the behest of Lord Hawke never obscured the memory of his classical bowling. Peel – then aged eighty-one – told Hutton: 'Once you start thinking about getting quick runs you're finished. We don't expect fireworks from an opening batsman.' Hutton, conscious of the cricket heritage of Yorkshire, drank in such advice avidly.

When he started his England career with 0 and 1, it was simply one of those aberrations that seemed to dog Hutton on every debut; by the end of that New Zealand series of 1937, he had scored his first Test hundred and Sutcliffe's successor for both Yorkshire and England was triumphantly confirmed. The Australian team of 1938 felt the brunt of a technique now classically moulded, and a temperament secure and rocklike. A century in the First Test was followed by an innings at the Oval that has dogged him for the rest of his life – 364, a new record for Test cricket. It took him 13 hours 20 minutes during eight sessions of play and the first Australian to congratulate Hutton was the man he watched make no less than 334 in 1930 – Don Bradman. As he observed Bradman from the stands at Leeds, Hutton did not cherish any particular ambition to topple that score – fourteen-year-olds from Yorkshire tend to aim for respectability before they climb the slopes of Olympia. Hutton's main memory of that Oval marathon is one of tiredness and nightmares about Bill O'Reilly on the night before he walked out to bat against him, needing just 35 to beat Bradman's record. His Yorkshire team-mates, Bill Bowes, Hedley Verity, Maurice Leyland and Arthur Wood kept him going while his captain, Walter Hammond, forbade him to play loosely. 'I remember I had got to about 130 when I started to play freely, to hit Bill O'Reilly over the top. Hammond came on to the balcony and gestured to me to quieten down. He wanted to grind them into the dust.'

Joe Hardstaff was at the other end when Hutton chopped Fleetwood-Smith through the slips to establish the record. He recalls a conversation with Hutton just before – 'Len said to me "will you take O'Reilly for me? I don't fancy him." Well I looked up at the scoreboard, saw about 340 against his name and said, "You've taken a long time to discover that, Len." But I did as he asked because he looked all in by then.' Bill O'Reilly remembers that Hutton was so grooved in his concentration that he did not take advantage of a no-ball from him when his score was 333. Denis Compton – who made only one after sitting with his pads on for over a day – recalls how calm Hutton seemed at the end of it all. 'As the champagne was flowing, Len just stood there, saying "Thank you very much" to all the well-wishers.' He had an old head on his shoulders even at 22.'

Compton told me that he had never seen anyone less likely to get out in that Oval innings yet Hutton does not dwell very long on it. He says that the wicket was far too good, that the Australian attack was unbalanced – just three regular bowlers – and that he would have preferred to play his shots. It all seemed an ordeal to him and the relentless demands of the media after that innings unnerved a young man who was trying to broaden his social as well as his cricket education. Hutton points out that he played a lot of shots in the last couple of years before the War and that the Oval marathon has overshadowed them. Compton agrees – he vividly remembers Hutton's glorious strokeplay at Lord's in 1939 against the West Indies. He and Hutton added 248 in 140 minutes and Hutton actually outscored the young genius during his 196. Norman Yardley, who toured with Hutton on the England trip to South Africa in 1938–9 remembers his commanding batting on those beautiful wickets. By 1939, Hutton was the best batsman in the world after Bradman. He was just twenty-three. War came at a cruel time.

Hutton believes he was never quite the same batsman after the War. The responsibility of opening for England became far greater because, apart from Compton, and the rugged professionalism of Edrich and Washbrook, there was little in the batting larder until May and Cowdrey came along nearly a decade after the resumption of Test cricket. Hutton knew that if he was dismissed early, the batting was vulnerable; a conscientious man to a fault, he was always imbued with the necessary team spirit. He was also hampered by a wartime injury that meant his left arm was an inch shorter than the other. At one stage there were grave doubts whether he would play again; twelve plaster casts were needed. He mastered the disability with characteristic determination, but a right-hand batsman with a left arm that does not function satisfactorily is at a disadvantage. That was not lost on Lindwall and Miller when they bowled intimidatingly at him in Australia in 1946–7; they knew he was struggling to come to terms with the lifting ball. The Australian wickets were hard and lively and Hutton – the best batsman in the side – was the main target. The barrage continued in 1948 and it is a measure of Hutton's greatness that his reputation survived intact, apart from the occasion when the England selectors, in their infinite wisdom, dropped him for one Test in 1948 because they felt he had not acquitted himself well enough against the bouncing ball at Lord's. They presumably took little account of the fact that Hutton had to use the lightest possible bat to counteract his disabled arm, that the regulations allowed one new ball every 55 overs in 1948, so that Lindwall and Miller never lacked incentive. Any England batsman who scored fifty against Bradman's side that series had acquitted himself nobly. Hutton managed it four times, plus an heroic thirty in England's all-out total of 52 at the Oval.

On occasions, he would slip the leash and take apart a high-class attack with a breathtaking range of shots. It happened in the Sydney Test of 1946, when he scored 37 out of 49 in the first twenty minutes. Veterans on the ground babbled about Victor Trumper as Hutton put together a cameo innings that was ended cruelly when he lost control of the bat – that arm again! – and it fell on his stumps. Today Hutton will concede, with his familiar caution: 'Yes, I played well that day. I decided to go at them and I played a series of judicious shots.' In the same series, he and Washbrook put on 87 in 57 minutes (Hutton 50) against another bumper barrage. In the opinion of Alec Bedser, Denis Compton and Bill Edrich – men who played during that fierce, intimidatory atmosphere – not enough credit has been laid at the door of Hutton for coming through the ordeal with such quiet tenacity. One bad match – at Lord's in 1948 – was enough to see him dropped. Norman Yardley, the England captain at the time, today concedes that it was, on reflection, a ridiculous decision but that must have been no consolation to Hutton after his buffetings. It only served to drive a reserved man further in on himself.

By 1950, Hutton had weathered the fast bowling barrage and re-established himself as the world's best player. He had come to terms with the ball that dipped late into him to trouble a technique getting used to a shortened left arm. He had made the necessary technical adjustments, and off-spinners and inswingers no longer perturbed him greatly. The rest of the technical equipment that had delighted Sutcliffe was still there, even if the left shoulder now pointed a little towards mid-on to thwart the ball that came into him. Everything was under control; the ball was played astonishingly late and his balance when playing the delivery was a model. To the fast bowlers he would play half-forward, with the weight easily balanced and they just could not get him out of position, turn him round with a seaming or swinging ball, and make him vulnerable to late movement. He allowed the ball to come to him and could delay the shot by opening the face of the bat and running it down into areas where there were no fielders. Johnny Wardle still talks about the match at Wellingborough, when the Northants captain, F.R.Brown, bowled seamers at Hutton – 'he had nine men on the offside, including two on the third-man boundary, yet he was still piercing the field. Freddie Brown got annoyed, bowled him a beamer, and Len just leaned back and cut it away close to the keeper to the boundary.' R.O('Roley') Jenkins was a brilliant cover point in his days with Worcestershire yet he could never outwit Hutton's mastery of placement. He told me: 'Once at Sheffield, I was busy watching Len's footwork from cover, trying to work out where he was going to play his off-drive. I managed to stop a magnificent drive on my right side but to the next half-volley, he played a little inside out and it screamed past my left hand. So I moved a shade towards my left and next time, it went whistling past my right hand. He just used his left arm to manipulate the ball away from me. A craftsman.'

Hutton was a master on bad wickets because of this ability to fashion runs, to manufacture them by deft manipulation of the bat face. If the bowler over-pitched, the most beautiful cover drive in the game would be brought into play, and in defence his masterly use of the dead bat would frustrate. Norman Yardley remembers his knack of playing the ball and deadening it at the same instant. He favoured playing with the bat rather than the pads, and from the crease rather than down the wicket – his rationale was that he was not a hitter of sixes and that he wanted to leave his stroke till the very last instant, so why go down the pitch? At all times, he was elegant and utterly composed, a master on surfaces that exposed the lesser players. His innings of 62 not out in a total of 122 on a foul Brisbane pitch was a classic which even pleased Hutton: 'I made them without an acknowledged batsman at the other end, as I went in at number six. Yes, that was a good knock.'

One innings at the Oval in the early 1950s made a deep impression on so many players that it is worth a closer analysis. Hutton made 79 out of

130 all out on a wicket made for the spinning talents of Jim Laker and Tony Lock. Ray Illingworth remembers he and the other batsmen playing and missing three times an over, while Hutton did so twice in his entire innings. Illingworth said: 'At the moment of contact with the ball, he was so relaxed. He picked the length of the ball up remarkably quickly. Without him we'd have been pushed to make thirty that day.' Johnny Wardle, no mean performer himself on turning wickets, was also in the Yorkshire side and he says: 'I defy anyone to have ever played better. He was playing Lock's quicker ones off his chest, yet somehow keeping it away from the leg-trap.' Jim Laker, one of the suffering bowlers, described it as one of the great bad-wicket innings he had seen. 'He just toyed with Tony Lock, hitting him that little bit squarer on the offside, just out of reach of the fielder. And he placed my off-breaks with uncanny precision.'

He had the capacity to surprise even his Yorkshire team-mates accustomed to his mastery. Just now and again he would play an innings of genius, when bowlers could not contain him. Ray Illingworth remembers a hundred in seventy minutes against Derbyshire's seam attack headed by Jackson and Morgan on a green wicket – it included a six over square cover off an astonished Jackson, one of the best postwar seam bowlers in English conditions. Johnny Wardle recalls the day when Hutton gritted his teeth and decided to play his shots. 'We were coming back from Northampton and we were due to play the South Africans at Sheffield. There had been some criticism about Len's batting against them in the Tests that year and it had clearly got on top of him. He told me in the car, "I just hope the sun shines tomorrow, because I'm going to show the boogers I can play." He was 93 not out at lunch the following day. He just toyed with them.'

By 1952, the England captaincy was available and Hutton was clearly the best-equipped for the job. He had stood in the slips alongside Freddie Brown during the 1950–1 Australian tour, and his captain had been vastly impressed by his tactical acumen. Some antedeluvian members of the Lord's hierarchy baulked at the idea of England having a professional as captain, preferring to quote Lord Hawke's famous dictum ('pray God no professional ever captains England!'), while ignoring the fact that the remark had been taken grossly out of context. Hutton made it clear – politely yet firmly – that he would not emulate Walter Hammond and turn amateur to secure his ambition. He was a proud professional and would stay that way. He won the day but, for the next three years, was acutely conscious that one or two sharpened knives had been placed on some tables in the district of Marylebone. This innate distrust of the Establishment, his own native caution and the quality of the players at his disposal inclined Hutton to a style of captaincy that was shrewd, realistic and unexciting. He unashamedly slowed down the over rate in Australia in 1954–5, and his success in that sphere has ruined many a day's cricket in later years as imitators perfected the ruses to avoid bowling too often. Apart from that, Hutton cannot be faulted, except for an emphasis on pace that stemmed from the days when he was battered by Lindwall and Miller: a keen desire to get one's own back is a human trait. Whatever the moralities, Hutton's means justified the end and he never lost a series. Nor – until that exhausting Australian tour – did his batting suffer the responsibilities of captaincy. The 1953–4 tour of the West Indies was a monumental strain, not just for cricketing reasons, yet amid all the political disturbances, riots at the grounds, ill-discipline of some England players and ludicrous umpiring decisions, Hutton stood firm. By his own example, he turned a two-nil deficit into parity by the end of the series. His 169 and 205 were innings of the highest class and character – as Tom Graveney shrewdly observed to me, 'Tests aren't usually won by batsmen on good wickets, but Len did it twice in one series.'

Even after such an inspiring performance, Hutton still was not sure of taking the side to Australia in the following winter. He had to endure the experience of seeing David Sheppard captain England twice against the Pakistanis in 1954 – Sheppard had graciously announced that he would delay his ordination if it meant captaining England in Australia. It seems an extraordinary sequence of events, and happily the attitude of the players influenced matters. Hutton led England in Australia, winning the series three-one. Victory was achieved at a cost. The tour finished Len Hutton as a cricketer. The strain was too much – he won the toss at Brisbane, put Australia in and somehow lost by an innings. He shepherded Tyson and Statham through the early part of the tour and they repaid his encouragement with a series of match-winning performances. Yet Hutton could not relax; he was still on guard against press criticism, ever conscious that he only had to slip slightly from his standards to lose both the captaincy and his place as batsman. He was so distracted that he forgot to take Alec Bedser to one side and explain why he had been dropped for the Second Test, harsh treatment to such a great, willing bowler. On the morning of the Melbourne Test, he refused to get out of bed; Godfrey Evans and Bill Edrich had to plead with him to come down to the ground. 'Don't feel

128

much like it,' he would only reply. Finally they cajoled him into playing. In the Fourth Test, he told Denis Compton, 'pad up, Denis, I don't feel much like going in again,' when England needed just 94 to retain the Ashes. Compton did as he was told and then noticed Hutton putting on his own pads. Compton asked if he had changed his mind and was told, 'Ah yes, I'll be going in first.'

By the end of the tour, Hutton was shattered. He was a sick man and the fibrositis that had plagued him for years was taking its toll. He was suffering from occasional black-outs; he revealed that during the Oval Test of 1953, he had suffered an attack of temporary blindness and literally could not see the ball after the bowler had brought over his arm. Hutton was ready to go; he had done more than enough and, with typical hard-headed clarity, he realised that there was now only one way his career could go – down. His retirement showed the natural timing that characterised his batting. His knighthood for services to cricket was fitting reward for a great cricketer, a highly successful captain, a model team man and a supreme professional. One can only wonder why he never gained the captaincy of Yorkshire, but perhaps it is best to leave that particular hot potato to cool.

His colleagues and friends have confirmed the enormity of the pressure he seemed to feel. At times, it was self-inflicted; Trevor Bailey says that Hutton genuinely believed that anything less than a century from him would bring press criticism raining down. Bill Bowes remembers being told by him: 'It gets increasingly difficult, this game. I have to get forty for the spectators because of my reputation, and only then can I think of playing properly.' Tom Graveney recalls; 'Len wasn't on this earth when he batted, he was in a trance. During an interval, he would sit down, drink his tea while someone unbuckled his pads and just look into space.' Norman Yardley remembers the day towards the end of his career when the strain was starting to show; he scored a hundred and when he came back to the dressing-room, he said: 'I never thought I'd see the day when I got tired of batting.' When Richie Benaud came into bat for Australia, Hutton would always greet him with a cheery quip of 'Here comes the festival cricketer,' a reference to Benaud's fondness for attacking batting. Benaud feels Hutton's remark was made wistfully, with a sense of envy. Certainly Hutton's attention to detail and scrupulous concentration would have satisfied even Geoffrey Boycott, as Trevor Bailey will confirm. One morning, Bailey came across Hutton in the nets trying to eradicate an imaginary fault in his cover-drive: this from a man who was unbeaten overnight on a century! His memory – like most Yorkshire and England cricketers – is faultless. When I asked him about the game when he scored his hundredth century, he gave me a potted summary instantly: 'Surrey v Yorkshire at the Oval in 1951. A cover drive for 4 off Owen Wait. He couldn't have bowled me a better one, you know. My favourite stroke. He was a Cambridge Blue, was Wait. Died young. Cancer, I believe.' He has slight regrets that he could not play his shots more often, but points out that he never had a sturdy physique, even before the War: 'I found it all very exhausting, you know. In a lot of cases, I've lost interest after I got to a hundred.' He gently demurs that he would not have fancied today's short-pitched bowling, pointing out that a lot of half-volleys go unpunished with the batsman in position instead for the short one. Godfrey Evans feels that Hutton would enjoy himself today: 'Don't forget that Lindwall and Miller were allowed to bowl plenty of bouncers. Len was used to the quicks, alright.' Johnny Wardle was adamant that Hutton would be a boon in limited-overs cricket, because of his ability to place the ball wide of fielders and his faultless judge of a run.

Hutton's former colleagues are immensely loyal to his good name, partly because of his classical batting gifts, but also because of the quiet, unfussy way he carried on batting under the most trying of circumstances. It seems that the fear of letting down the side, rather than himself, was never far from his mind. Hutton told me how much he admired Sutcliffe's conviction that luck was on his side and gives a game against Leicestershire in 1937 as an example. 'When we walked out to bat after tea-time, we had put on 315 and Herbert said, 'we only want 240 more, Leonard.' I didn't know what he was on about and he explained – the record of 555 that he and Percy Holmes had set up five years before. I couldn't get over his confidence and I was out within a couple of minutes. My concentration had been shattered by Herbert's conviction.'

If Hutton lacked the *sangfroid* of a Sutcliffe, he had a dry humour that his mentor lacked. Hutton could see the whimsical side of life, as Denis Compton recalls. 'It was during a particularly tense moment in the Lord's Test of 1953, when we were hanging on for dear life. Lindwall and Miller were giving us a terrible old time and, at the end of an over, Len motioned me towards him. I expected some sort of technical discussion with my captain, yet he said: "What are we doing here, Denis? We could have better jobs than this!" At that stage, I couldn't disagree.' Hutton had a droll way of dealing with fatuous questions from cricket journalists; once he was asked in a rather long-winded fashion why he had been dismissed by a particular delivery and his reply was succinct: 'I missed it.' At the Centenary Test celebrations in Melbourne in 1977, he whispered to Joe Hardstaff, his partner during a record stand in the 1938 Oval Test: 'Joe, I've caught O'Reilly's eye several times and I think he's ignoring me! What have I done to him?' When an earnest young cricket writer asked Hutton the best way to play fast bowling, he was told 'from the other end.' In 1957, Hutton, on one of his earliest excursions into the press box, was covering a match on the West Indies tour. Their two opening batsmen got into a fearful muddle, each was stranded and either could have been run out. Hutton, his sense of propriety outraged at the waste of a wicket, surveyed the West Indian recriminations with a mordant eye and said with resignation: 'Ay, and they want self-goovernment as well.' Once he was taken to task by Brian Sellers, his former captain, for not giving his young son, Richard, a very impressive bat with which to learn his trade. Hutton agreed it was not a very good bat, adding, 'But he's not a very good player is he, Brian?'

Well, Richard was good enough to play five times for England, watched by his father in the press box, but the stature of Hutton Senior was not threatened. Nothing could alter that. An instinctive, natural stylist who believed in stroking rather than hitting the ball, he was a batsman for the connoisseur. Resilient, undemonstrative and physically brave, he remains the hero of men like Ray Illingworth, who watched him as a boy, admired him as a playing colleague, and wishes fervently that another of his ilk would walk into Headingly from Pudsey with his Herbert Sutcliffe bat under his arm.

Hutton always seemed to know what to do with his feet and his bat. Once he walked out to open with a young partner, recognised as an attractive player, but a little slapdash in his approach. 'What are you thinking about?', Hutton asked him. 'Nothing' came the reply. Hutton persisted. 'Well, let me tell you what I'm thinking. I'm thinking about how the wicket's going to play, which bowler will have the breeze, what shots I should not try in the first hour, which fielders aren't too quick on their feet and I'm wondering about those sightscreens.' The learned discourse had lasted till the batsmen were almost at the wicket. As they parted to go to their respective positions, Hutton delivered the sting in the tail – 'You've got to think it through, you know.' No one thought it through better than Leonard Hutton.

14

Denis Compton

'He played cricket for fun and made it look fun'
(Godfrey Evans)

The very mention of Denis Compton's name is always good for a positive reaction from his contemporaries. They lean back, the features soften, the eyes mist over a shade, they smile and chuckle, 'Ah, Denis . . .' Two words that speak volumes. Denis Compton had that effect on everyone; he made you care for him. Anyone who ever watched him for an hour can remember at least one outrageous stroke, a moment of daring. When Denis Compton's genius was channelled in the right direction, no one went for an early tea or burrowed into the crossword. I am surprised that no Government of his day thought of slapping an Entertainment Tax on him; he would have cleared the National Debt in just one season.

It was always 'Denis', not 'Compton'. The great Leonard Hutton would sometimes be dubbed 'Len', even though his classic batting and demeanour marked him out as a 'Leonard'. Denis was always on first-name terms with the crowd, communicating his sense of enjoyment, gulling the spectators into believing it really was quite an easy game. Hutton, his only contemporary rival as a great batsman, would sometimes look careworn, racked by responsibility. Denis, on the other hand, brought cricket into the lives of many who had no knowledge of the game's technical niceties; he made it seem fun, an utterly natural way of passing the time. The shrill schoolboy cries of delight, the positive way their elders folded up their newspapers – that was the reaction Denis got when he walked out to bat. The crowd agonised if it was one of the days when his gifts had deserted him: they knew that the currency of genuis can sometimes be devalued, when mundane bowlers enjoy one satisfying day to warm their memories in retirement. When that happened, the account in the bank of goodwill marked 'Compton, D.C.S.' was stamped with the imprimatur of tolerance. He would make up for it.

He was the cheekiest of the great batsmen. His gifts of improvisation against slow bowlers are well-documented, but the way he tackled the fast bowlers was astonishing. He played Lindwall, Miller, Adcock, Heine and the rest from several yards down the wicket when the Muse of inspiration was with him. Tom Graveney, an England colleague and keen observer of today's styles of batting, told me: 'The players today just wouldn't believe you if you told them how Denis played the short-pitched stuff from down the track. He made everything look so easy.' Fred Titmus, who batted many times with Denis for Middlesex, says he was the only English genius he encountered in cricket – 'I'd be batting at the other end, watching him do things I could hardly believe. You'd think, 'No, he can't get away with that' and he usually did. I once saw him take Mel Ryan apart when we played Yorkshire. Mel took the new ball, and Denis hit the first two through the covers for four. The next ball was delivered in the same area and it went through mid-wicket. Mel said to me, "How the hell do you bowl at him?" and I confess I didn't know.

Denis was the scourge of slow bowlers. His reflexes and resourcefulness were so astonishing that he could not be contained when the fires of genius had been lit. His duels with Tom Goddard were vastly amusing to those who knew that bowling was no laughing matter to Goddard. At the Oval in 1947, Denis made 246 against the Rest of England, and during this innings he played a shot that has become legendary; he advanced towards Goddard, fell over and as his knee gave way, swept the ball to the square leg boundary. Goddard growled: 'One of these bloody days, Denis, there'll be no return ticket.' Goddard had his revenge, incidentally, in a subsequent season. Denis was left stranded, stumped by yards and Goddard pulled out a crumpled piece of paper and gave it to him. 'Off ye' go Denis,' he said, and as he walked back to the pavillion, he opened up the piece of paper. It was a bus ticket. Single fare.

Tom Goddard was not the only spinner to suffer from the Compton gift of improvisation. Doug Wright has told me he once cut him to the boundary after falling over and John Langridge remembers him doing exactly the same to his brother, James. He was irresistible on his good days; somehow he seemed to be making it up as he went along. No one could copy Denis's method – Jack Robertson was the coaching-manual batsman in his time at Lord's – but we could all identify with him. He was the eternal schoolboy, no matter what the hour glass indicated. Before the War he walked onto a cricket ground with a cheerful Cockney swagger, and batted like an errand boy who winked at the lady of the house while delivering the groceries. Denis was always worth a tip. He was twenty-eight when Test cricket resumed in 1946 and if the figure had thickened, he still played enchantingly for the next three seasons. A chronic knee injury restricted him thereafter but the way he adapted to his disability only accentuated his greatness. He managed to carry on until 1957 by guts and resilience, but also due to a technique that was fundamentally orthodox. Denis was lucky enough to learn how to bat on pre-War wickets at Lord's that were hard, fast and true; he developed a confidence from those good wickets that enabled him to play his shots later on. Much has been made of the 'Compton sweep', the stroke that will always be associated with him – but he only swept the deliveries that were on middle or leg stumps. The ones that pitched on the off-stump were driven peerlessly square through the covers with a beautifully delayed stroke. He had a high backlift, but he brought it down straight and played impeccably through the line of the ball. Like the great overseas batsmen who were brought up on good wickets, he was quickly into position even for a defensive shot. Back and across with the back leg covering the leg stump, he would always get behind the ball. When playing back defensively his deft footwork would take him almost back onto his stumps. Perhaps there was a little too much right hand in his cover driving, so that it would resemble a square slash, rather than a drive, but he could play the shot very late and guide it into the open spaces in the manner of Hutton. His strong right hand meant he could on-drive superbly and he was a magnificent puller and hooker, often delaying the hook until the ball was almost on his nose. He played the sweep shot perfectly – only when the delivery was just fuller than a good length – and he would always roll the bat over the top of the ball, making sure he kept it down. Denis told me that he discovered he could play the sweep when he was about fifteen; he practised hard at it and he believes it got him out just three times in his career. His mastery of the shot spawned a clutch of imitators in the 1950s and 1960s, but none could master it because they did not observe the basic principles. Denis Compton, despite the excesses of imagination and audacity, always had the basic principles in mind when he batted.

Those who warm to the entertainers of cricket must feel there really is a sense of destiny about Denis Compton. It was a delightful coincidence that saw him begin his career as Patsy Hendren was ending his in the Middlesex side. Patsy saw Denis as his logical successor as prolific batsman and darling of the crowd and he delighted in his success. He would guide him through technical teething problems – 'sit on the ball when you sweep', and 'never duck when hooking', he would tell him – and encouraged him to keep the crowd happy. When they batted together, Denis would watch how the old master would play 'Tich' Freeman or Tom Goddard and he soon realised with great pleasure that he was being encouraged to play his natural game. When we glory in the career of Denis Compton, we owe a genial glance in the direction of Patsy Hendren, Walter Robins and the other influential members of that attractive Middlesex side. Many other senior players would have tried to coach the genius out of him: one can only imagine what Arthur Mitchell would have thought of him.

In those uncomplicated pre-War days, the main problem for Denis seemed to be staying awake on the field when not batting. More than once, his captain, Walter Robins, had to bawl him out because he was not concentrating on the task. Alf Gover remembers Denis's first Test against New Zealand in 1937: 'Denis misfielded about four times and finally Robins roared: "Compton, I shall make it my business to make sure you never play for England again!" Typical Denis – he was always in the clouds, without a care in the world.'

He also batted in the same vein; before he was twenty-two, he had made Test hundreds against Australia and New Zealand. Life was good and easy to this natural athlete: his soccer skills were so impressive that he was allowed to miss the England tour to South Africa to play a winter's First Division football with Arsenal. Joe Hardstaff tells a story from the 1938 Australia series that epitomises the carefree Compton of that period – for that matter, the Compton of maturity and middle age as well. At Leeds, Hardstaff was due to bat at number five, with Compton at six. With two England wickets down, Hardstaff was on edge, expecting to have to go in at any moment. Batsmen of all standards know the feeling and, not surprisingly, Hardstaff suddenly felt the call of nature. As he walked towards the toilet, he saw Denis sitting reading the paper, fully clothed, without any cricket gear on. Hardstaff spluttered: 'Denis, you could be in any minute!' but Denis smiled and said: 'Don't worry, Joe, you'll be alright, I've got great faith in you.'

Those blissful days of 1938 seemed light years away when Denis and the other first-class cricketers tried to bring some enjoyment to a war-ravaged country in 1946. For the next few years, cricket enjoyed tremendous prosperity, and Denis Compton, of all players, must take credit for this. The summer of 1947 is burned deep into the memories of those cricket-lovers who lived through that season. With the brilliant support of Bill Edrich, Denis Compton made people realise what they had been missing for the last six years. Statistically no batsman has enjoyed a better season than Compton or Edrich in 1947, but the joy of their batting and the challenging cricket played by Middlesex are what people remember most. Day after day, the sun shone gloriously and Compton and Edrich hammered bowlers all over the country. They enjoyed six stands of over 200 and for good measure helped win Middlesex the championship by honouring Walter Robins's instructions that quick runs were essential. The crowds loved it. At one stage in that summer, the secretary of the MCC, Colonel R.S.Rait-Kerr, was summoned to Downing Street to answer allegations that cricket popularity was hampering industrial production. One can only assume that Prime Minister Attlee – himself a great cricket fan – realised what Compton and Edrich were doing for the morale of a nation starved of thrills and honest sporting combat, a country rationed of food, petrol and all the other things we now take for granted. There were no rations when Compton and Edrich batted in 1947, and if they had retired at the end of that season, they would never be forgotten by a generation for what they did. It did not matter that the bowlers were rather inferior, that the sun-burnt wickets were made for batting or that the field-placings were unimaginative and unsophisticated – Edrich and Compton reminded a nation of the contagious pleasure gained from watching fit, young men excelling at a sport and enjoying themselves in the process.

For good measure, Compton learned how to bowl left-arm 'chinamen' in that 1947 season. Jack Walsh, the splendid spinner with Leicestershire, took him out to the nets one morning and demonstrated the art. In just over half the season, Denis took 73 wickets with his new toy. Natural talent is not circumscribed by mundanities like apprenticeships.

Although Compton played like Victor Trumper, he had the backbone of Herbert Sutcliffe, even if he did not flaunt his competitive streak in the shameless manner of the modern, clench-fisted cricketer. He played two wonderful innings in a crisis against the 1948 Australians to demonstrate that a 'festival' batsman can also battle it out if he has the necessary temperament and bravery. At Trent Bridge, he made 184 in seven hours against a rampant Lindwall and Miller. He had to play himself in no less than nine times due to intermittent rain and appalling light; he was dismissed when he slipped on the wet grass, avoiding a Miller bouncer, and fell on his wicket. Not one spectator had been bored by an innings that, by his usual standard, had been positively ascetic. It was resourceful, at times punishing, always full of character and it proved that the Cavalier had steel beneath his finery. Two Tests later – at Manchester – he showed his class and temperament again. He scored 145 not out in five hours twenty minutes, after being knocked out of the fray by Lindwall when he top-edged a hook into his face. He retired to have some stiches inserted and returned with England 119 for 5; not once did he flinch, nor avoid playing the hook shot. It was a stern, unyielding effort, against the odds and in the face of deadly fast bowling.

By this time, Denis was getting used to battling against the odds: the knee that he first injured while bowling in 1947 was beginning to cause him pain. Three minor operations and one major one eventually robbed him of a kneecap and the remaining years were a story of grit, frustration and compromise with a body that had seemed certain to defy the march of time. He began to experience devastating periods of bad form – in the 1950–1 series in Australia, he scored 53 runs at an average of 7.57, choosing the most remarkable ways to be dismissed. Even the pragmatic Australians tried to give him one off the mark and Sir Donald Bradman took time out to give Denis some technical advice. It was a bad time for Denis; the news of his impending divorce was splashed all over the Australian newspapers and there were some snide remarks about his social life, remarks that were never forthcoming during his 'good old Denis' days of plenty. As vice-captain, he wanted desperately to succeed and he was acutely conscious that a consistent series from him would have altered the shape of that four-one defeat. Freddie Brown, the England captain on that tour, told me that such a low period in Denis's life did not affect his relationship with the rest of the side. 'He was the same lovable Denis, a little bit quieter on occasions, but never out to make excuses for himself or wrap himself up in his own misery.' I wonder how many other batsmen would react the same way?

Occasionally, he would roll back the years and the old Compton – the unfettered, natural Compton – would come storming through. There was the astonishing 62 in 40 minutes against Lock and Laker on a vicious Oval pitch; the 278 against Pakistan in 1954 when the bowlers just did not know where to propel the ball at him; a hundred at Lord's against Worcestershire when Reg Perks swung the ball prodigiously in the humid conditions and Denis attacked him from a long way down the pitch; the mellow 94 against Australia at the Oval in 1956, his first Test after having his kneecap removed. Yet the tour to South Africa in 1956–7 convinced Denis he had to retire: he could not get Trevor

Goddard's nagging medium pace away, while Tayfield's off-spin tied him down and the South Africans were pushed back in the field when he was on strike, because they knew he could not take quick singles. He knew that, in his palmy days, Goddard and Tayfield would have suffered the same fate as all the other bowlers; to his intense disappointment, he just could not do it anymore. He had been given everything by the gods in his youth, and now, at an age when Jack Hobbs was still to score 98 centuries, Denis was reduced to the ranks of the mortals. Typically, he ended his championship career with a century in his last match in 1957.

If only that knee had been whole; the surgeon said that it looked as if it had been gnawed by a rat when he opened it up. Johnny Wardle said he had never seen a sportsman's knee swell up so alarmingly when it gave Denis pain. Yet he never complained about his disability, never used it as an excuse for several worrying spells of bad form. It had been fun and he could remember England team-mates such as Hedley Verity and Ken Farnes who had not survived the War. Denis had come through it, so how could he bemoan the fact that nature had decided to make a thirty-nine-year-old limp like a pensioner?

Since his retirement, he has watched innumerable Tests in his capacity first as television commentator, and then as newspaper columnist. Bombast is not part of his make-up, and he insists that he would still go down the pitch to the fast men if he played today – 'Imran Khan wouldn't know where to bowl if you gave him the charge', he told me as we watched the Pakistan captain make the English batsman duck and weave. He feels there is too much emphasis on training and net practice: 'If you have the basic ability, all you need is the feel of the bat on ball just before the start of play. I only had a long net before the season began.' Of all his performances, he singles out two where he feels he could not have played any better – at Lord's in 1938 when he made 76 not out for England on a damp pitch against Australia, and the match at Lord's in 1947 when Kent asked Middlesex to get 395 at more than ninety an hour. Denis made 168 and his duel with Doug Wright was a thrilling, challenging highlight of that dazzling summer. Middlesex lost by 75 runs, but the game of cricket was even more triumphant.

He laughs resignedly about his running between the wickets and agrees that he never really knew how to judge singles. Bill Edrich feels Denis was unjustly criticised and points out that he merely forgot where the good fielders were stationed: 'He would play one straight to Neil

Harvey, call for one and then suddenly remember that Neil was a great fielder. It all stemmed from Denis's attitude that every ball had the potential of at least one run.' Nevertheless, Denis did run out his brother Leslie in his benefit match – not the most fraternal of actions, and one about which he still winces. Fred Titmus was another casualty of the 'yes,no' Compton style that day and he recalls the pressure he felt when he partnered Denis: 'You'd get keyed up because he was such a great player and you knew you mustn't run him out, even if it was his own fault. There was no malice about it, he was just forgetful.'

It seems that the legendary stories about Denis's forgetfulness are also deeply rooted in fact – he did often forget his gear, borrow a bat and go out to make a hundred with it. He invariably forgot his passport when going on overseas tours with England and his living quarters on tour were a perennial shambles and a nightmare for the cleaners. He did turn up half-an-hour late for a Test once because he had forgotten that play started earlier on the last day: it was the 1949 Oval Test and he was sitting in a traffic queue in London when a taxi driver leaned out of his cab and shouted to him: 'Ere, Denis, the radio says England are just going out on the field. What's going on?', a question echoed by his captain, Freddie Brown later that morning. Bill Edrich also has cause to recall the famous Compton mental torpor; the game was the Bank Holiday fixture with Sussex at Hove. Edrich declared Denis in his side before the captains tossed for innings, even though there was no sign of him. After over an hour's play, he came running onto the field, easing himself into his sweater (not his own, of course) and spluttering: 'I'm terribly sorry, it was my wedding anniversary last night and the telephone people forgot to ring me!' Edrich, shaking his head with due solemnity, put Denis on to bowl as a punishment – and he grabbed three wickets before lunch. Typical Denis.

I know of no other player held in greater affection by his former playing colleagues than Denis Compton. Not one person I interviewed uttered a breath of criticism of him as a person and all were united in their admiration at his brilliance as a player. Here are just a few random reflections on Denis . . .

Alec Bedser: 'I can't think of anyone of such class who enjoyed himself more in the game and got away with so much.'

'Roley' Jenkins: 'I toured South Africa with him and Denis, the star, was wonderful to Jenkins, the novice. If I were the spectator, he'd be the man I would want to watch above all.'

Joe Hardstaff: 'Such a lovely, unaffected bloke. He'd shun the limelight and just be one of the boys.'

Godfrey Evans: 'I've never seen a man go down the wicket so far to the fast bowlers. He played cricket for fun and made it look fun.'

B.D.('Bomber') Wells: 'He got to 99 in an hour against Gloucestershire and I bowled him, when he cut a high full toss onto his off-stump. He laughed his head off as he walked away. It was a privilege to play against him. He was a hero to me.'

Alf Gover: 'I caught and bowled him for 99 after a rare old battle of wits, and as he walked past me he said, "Well bowled, Alf – I enjoyed that!" No word about getting out for 99.'

Bill Edrich: 'His tremendous sense of adventure rubbed off on me. He would have played cricket for nothing if necessary, he loved it so much.'

Perhaps the most impressive tribute to Denis comes from G.O.Allen, the grand old man of cricket, who batted with him on his first appearance for Middlesex. Denis was picked against Sussex as a slow bowler who batted number eleven, and Allen had to shepherd him through some testing overs from Maurice Tate. The composure of Denis impressed everyone and although he made just 14, Allen's prognosis that Middlesex had unearthed a great player was soon confirmed. 'Gubby' Allen – England captain, chairman of the selectors and influential administrator – is not the man to toss eulogies around for no real purpose, yet he says that if he had the chance to see just one batsman again, it would be Denis. 'He had this capacity to entertain. He was an authentic genius – once Walter Robins told Denis at tea-time that he had never seen him hit a straight six. Denis said, "Watch the third ball after tea." Well, he took two steps up the wicket, hit a long, straight six and turned and waved to Robins. I call that genius.' This from the man who captained Hammond, played against Bradman and McCabe, selected May and Cowdrey for England teams, bowled against Jack Hobbs and saw Frank Woolley make those two immortal nineties against Armstrong's Australians in 1921.

The statistics of Compton, D.C.S., cannot compare with the pleasure he gave in such generous portions, but they will certainly act as an impressive adjunct to a glorious career. Tenth in the list of centurions with 123 hundreds, including 17 in Tests, a batting average of nearly 52, and the fastest triple century in history – 181 minutes. If he had possessed two good knees after the age of thirty and a greedier attitude to batting, then those figures would have been much more impressive – yet the scorebook was never the gazetteer of a Compton innings. Denis traded in shining faces, sore palms and unread newspapers. If he had his way, every year would be like 1947.

15

Tom Graveney

'He would never have been out of an Australian side
during *my* Test career.' (Richie Benaud)

Tom Graveney of Gloucestershire and Worcestershire. There, that looks
and sounds right, as fitting as Frank Woolley of Kent and Geoffrey
Boycott of Yorkshire. I could never really visualise Tom Graveney
plying his elegant trade for twenty years under the soccer floodlights at
that utilitarian ground in Northampton, or caressing those sumptous
cover drives around the vast wastes of the Oval. Both the man and his
batting were made for that lovely Cheltenham ground, where the tents
blend with the Cotswold stone of the college during Festival Week, or
Worcester, with that picture postcard setting dominated by the most
famous cathedral known to cricket lovers.

Tom Graveney summed up all the aesthetic delights of cricket; even
his name seemed to fit the image. A name that conjured up visions of
tributaries winding gently into the main river of batsmanship, where all
the artists of different eras merge into a cornucopia of quality. Graveney
is in that exclusive river by right: he had to swim against the tide of
functionalism for most of his career, to learn how to play with elegance
against inswingers and balls that whip in off the seam, making batsmen
hop about on green wickets, thankful to jab it through the packed
cordon of fielders close in on the legside. Men like Les Jackson and Brian
Statham and off-spinners such as Jim Laker, Roy Tattersall and Don
Shepherd gave Graveney precious little opportunity to indulge in his
beautiful offside play. When he started just after the War, the absence of
quick bowlers and the abundance of top-class spin bowling meant he
could concentrate on the offside, to the delight of himself and his many
admirers. During his twenty years in the game, the angle of attack
changed drastically: batsmen in the 1950s and 1960s prospered if they
could play off middle and leg. Peter May was the best English batsman
of that decade, partly through his own supreme ability, but also because

his on-side play was prodigious. It is to the great credit of Tom Graveney that he learned how to play the 'bread and butter' shots on the legside, to 'milk' the ball off middle stump through midwicket, or ease a leg-stump yorker past square leg's left hand. He did not jettison his easy elegance in the learning process and his batting had a bloom that was never surpassed in postwar England. May, Cowdrey and Dexter were equally delightful in their differing styles, but they had the good fortune to hone their skills on good University wickets. Tom Graveney learned how to bat on the slow, low wickets of Bristol, where the ball turned sharply and offside indulgences were limited to the occasional punishment of a bad ball before returning to the grind of chiselling out runs by the use of a strong right hand. Arthur Milton grew up with Graveney at Bristol and pays tribute to his work on those wickets: 'Those pitches produced poor players. They were so bad that you were out of form for half the season. Tom's attitude was far better than mine; he'd graft away, whereas I would shrug my shoulders and complain about the ball not coming onto the bat.'

Graveney always looked a cricketer – tanned, smiling, relaxed. His critics in the early days thought he was too convivial with the fielders and contrasted the taciturnity of the great Hammond when he batted. Len Hutton could never get on his wavelength when he captained him for England, unsurprisingly when you consider their different backgrounds and attitudes to the game. Graveney's high backlift allowed him to bat elegantly and he would be deluged with praise when he played well; if he was dismissed early, it would be judged carelessness and the fault of that ridiculously extravagant pick-up of the bat. The implication that he played cricket for fun did not help, either; he did not believe in parading his misery after a bad day, preferring to enjoy a few pints with both colleagues and opposition. Did he not realise that cricket was a serious business?

Yes he did; but it was not the fulcrum of his life. He could have played golf for a living and he was naturally talented at all sports. He had drifted into county cricket and did not play for the first team until he was twenty-one. Young men of his age were thankful to be alive in the immediate postwar years, and so the rigours of professional cricket could easily be held at bay with the right attitude. Graveney was lucky: natural talent, allied to a recommendation from his elder brother, who was already on the Gloucestershire staff, brought him to Bristol. He was on leave from his Army job as a physical training officer in the Middle East and he turned out in a few benefit matches for Gloucestershire players in and around the Cotswolds. He recalls: 'No one wanted to open those games, so I went in first. I got about thirty against the new ball in one game and thought I'd done rather well. Billy Neale, the batsman at the other end, was still on Gloucestershire's books and he put a good word in for me. I still had no thoughts of playing cricket for a living – I loved the life in the Army.'

His early matches for Gloucestershire did nothing to wean him away from his fondness for the Army. He made nought on his first-class debut and scraped together about 250 runs in his first 25 innings. He was dropped from the first team and, in despair, turned to golf – the committee had earlier warned him off golf, fearing that it would distort his batting style. He was resigned to the sack when Don Bradman played a crucial part. With England being swept away by Bradman's Australians, the England selectors turned in desperation to the Gloucestershire batsmen, George Emmett and Jack Crapp. At that time, Gloucestershire had just twelve professionals and a handful of amateurs. They had to turn to this young chancer Graveney again. In his first game back in the side, he made an impressive forty on a turning wicket against Hampshire; in the month of August, he made over 600 runs and he was soon established as the most promising young batsman in the land.

Comparisons with Hammond were made. Apart from the silkiness of Graveney's off-driving, it is difficult to see any similarity; Hammond was equally awesome off the back foot, whereas Graveney played forward almost constantly to combat the low bounce of the wickets in Gloucestershire. Hammond was a glorious medium-pace bowler in his youth – Graveney bowled occasional leg-breaks that sometimes pitched. The arguments about their respective merits raged for years, but Graveney never took them seriously: 'I had such a bad start to my career that I could never be judged in Hammond's class, quite apart from the fact that we batted differently. I relied on timing, he combined power with timing. I saw him bat once and that was enough – he was magnificent.'

Nevertheless, Hammond's former team-mates who were still in the Gloucestershire side realised that young Graveney could become a major batsman, a man who would score 2,000 runs a season for the county for the next twenty years if handled properly. Graveney acknowledges the help he got from those elder players, as he struggled to come to terms with challenges that were foreign to his affable temperament. 'I remember the first time we played Kent. I had never seen Doug Wright bowl and he frightened me out of my wits as he bounded in off his long run and bowled unplayable fast leg-breaks. Jack Crapp was batting with me and said: "Just stay up the other end, watch him bowl and then play a few shots when you feel comfortable." That's the way to encourage a youngster – no waffle, just solid common sense.'

He longed for such encouragement when he first played for England. A succession of beautiful innings had whetted the public's appetite for a new batting star; the comparisons with Hammond would not go away, even through Graveney remained unperturbed by them. He was more concerned about the inferiority complex he felt when batting for England: 'I'd sit in the dressing-room, look around at Compton, Hutton and May and think – what the hell am I doing here? I'll never be as good as them! I don't think Len Hutton believed I was up to much, he couldn't understand my attitude. As far as I was concerned, I played no differently in a Test than I did in a county match. I was a poor man's Compton – enjoy the game, have a laugh with the fielders and a drink with them afterwards. Len couldn't believe it.'

A partnership with Hutton at Lord's in 1953 hardened the captain's mind over Graveney. He was bowled in the first over of the morning by a Lindwall yorker. On the previous day, he and Hutton had added 168 with batting of the highest pedigree and Graveney – on 78 – was expected to coast home to his hundred. Hutton (of course) went to his century but he had been bitterly disappointed at Graveney's early dismissal. Richie Benaud, who was on the field that day, told me that not enough credit has been given to the bowler and that Graveney had unluckily deflected the ball onto his stumps. No matter – the dismissal had confirmed Hutton's view that Graveney lacked substance and an incident in their partnership confirmed that feeling, as Graveney recounts: 'I'd scored about thirty when Bill Johnston bowled one to me that was fairly well up. It swung across me and I followed it and flat-batted it square to the boundary. I laughed out loud at my good fortune, thinking it was going to be my day – but Len, at the other end, frowned and looked at me as if I was off my rocker.'

Graveney also blotted his copybook with F.R.Brown, the chairman of selectors. Brown, who was playing in that Lord's Test, was very pleased with Graveney's unbeaten innings and he told him to be at the ground early on the following morning for a net. Brown – like Hutton – had a long memory of Australian dominance and this was England's chance to grind away for a victory. The next morning, Graveney was late and Brown was furious: 'He turned up just in time to pad up. He told me that he'd taken his wife shopping and he got a rocket for that. So he goes out and gets dismissed in the first over with his mind not attuned to the job. That was typical of Tom in his early days with England – all the ease and grace, but he never got stuck in.'

That opinion was echoed by G.O.Allen, who succeeded F.R.Brown as chairman of the selectors. He told me: 'Of course Graveney was very graceful, but you know, elegance can hide faults. His record for England wasn't really all that good in those early years.' Yet inferior players kept him out on several occasions. Jim Laker remembered: 'They said he wasn't as good as Hammond, because he averaged forty to Hammond's sixty – then they'd pick someone who averaged 25! It didn't make sense to me – Tom Graveney was class and should've been in the side as a regular.' He did not achieve that until 1957 and in the meantime, he was shuffled up and down the batting order and jettisoned intermittently. May and Cowdrey justifiably held the prime batting positions but it does seem that Graveney never enjoyed the confidence of the selectors during that period in the mid-1950s. He missed the 1956–7 tour to South Africa, despite topping the averages in the 1956 season; his place was taken by the likeable Alan Oakman, a man not remotely in Graveney's class. Jim Parks – a fine, free batsman, even though inconsistent – also went on that trip. Graveney feels the reason why he missed out stemmed from the Old Trafford Test – Laker's Match – when he pulled out with a damaged hand. Oakman played instead and caught some brilliant catches in the leg-trap. The following week Graveney had recovered and played one of the greatest innings of his career – 200 out of 298 all out on a turning wicket at Newport against the spin of the splendid Don Shepherd. As Graveney walked back to the pavilion, he heard a comment from the Glamorgan captain, Wilf Wooller: 'That's the worst double hundred I've seen in my life.' Wooller was also an England selector at that time. Players who saw that innings tell me Wooller could not possibly have meant what he said, and Graveney thinks that Wooller was merely articulating the disapproval of the selectors at his withdrawal from the Old Trafford Test.

For a couple of years, Graveney gained a foothold in the England team but after the disastrous tour to Australia in 1958–9, he was cast aside, along with Evans and Bailey. He assumed his England career had finished at the age of thirty-two and his detractors rested on their laurels: they agreed his hundred in the Sydney Test of 1955 had been dazzling, but pointed out that Graveney had not played well when it mattered, when the rubber was at stake. They dismissed his 258 against the West

Indies in 1957 as a cosy innings on a dead wicket, but they had more trouble over his 164 at the Oval in the same series, on a turning wicket that later saw the West Indies bowled out for 89 and 86.

The blossoming of Tom Graveney into a mature technician would probably never have happened without the unwitting help of the Gloucestershire committee. When they sacked him from the county captaincy in 1960, Graveney packed his bags and walked out on the club in much the same way as W.G.Grace in 1899. Graveney insists it was not caused by the loss of the captaincy – 'I wasn't all that good at the job, I was too close to the players I'd grown up with. I had an unbalanced attack with three class off-spinners jostling with each other, and I wasn't a great disciplinarian.' What upset him was the way the matter was handled and that his successor, the Old Etonian Tom Pugh, was not worth his place in the side, as a career batting average of 23 from 1,300 runs confirmed. Graveney was accused of being a bad loser and attitudes hardened on both sides. He gratefully transferred allegiance to Worcestershire and his former county obdurately insisted on him serving a one-year qualification period before he could play county cricket.

Graveney was nearly thirty-five before he played a championship match for his new team. It proved to be the best thing he ever did in his career – 'the challenge was just what I had needed. I had become stale at Bristol and the year out of the game put some steel into my soul. I came back refreshed and determined to make Gloucestershire sorry.' He was treated with respect at Worcester and he responded to the different environment. It made clear to him that his job was to score a lot of runs on wickets that favoured the county's strong bowling attack; as the best player in the side, his responsibility was to play major innings. There was an extra incentive – Worcestershire were genuine championship contenders and Graveney desperately wanted to win something after all the years of dilettante enjoyment.

In his first season, Worcestershire just missed out on the championship, but secured it in 1964 and in the following year. Graveney made 2,385 runs and 1,768 runs in those two seasons, in the process playing some innings of majestic certainty on bad wickets. The one that gave him greatest pleasure was at Cheltenham in 1965 against his former county. On a spiteful wicket Worcestershire needed 130 to win against the highly professional off-spin of David Allen and John Mortimore; they lost three wickets before the score had reached twenty and, with a long tail, Worcestershire looked finished. Graveney and Basil D'Oliveira proceeded to play with astonishing assurance in their different styles: D'Oliveira played everything off the back foot, while Graveney moved forward at every opportunity to hit Allen and Mortimore back over their heads. They both made unbeaten fifties to win the match. D'Oliveira modestly told me that Graveney's innings was the greatest he has seen while Norman Gifford, who watched the stand from the players' balcony, called it the most fascinating piece of cricket he has witnessed in his career.

D'Oliveira's presence in the Worcestershire side also acted as a spur to Graveney; he knew that the remarkable South African was determined to prove himself the best player at the club and Graveney had to keep nudging ahead of him. 'Basil was great for me. I loved batting with him and he brought out a competitive streak in me that I didn't know I possessed. I was very annoyed, though, that he was better-looking than me, I couldn't do much about that!'

No one was more pleased than Graveney at the selection of D'Oliveira for the England team against the 1966 West Indians; little did he realise that he too was about to enter a final, productive period in Test cricket. Graveney is convinced that if M.J.K.Smith had won the toss at Old Trafford in the first Test, then he would have played out the rest of his career exclusively with Worcestershire. The ball turned sharply for Lance Gibbs on the third day at Old Trafford, and when England lost by an innings, the captain was dropped and a vacancy in the middle order appeared. Graveney was selected for Lord's, made 96 in his usual, unhurried manner and he stayed in the side until 1969. The reception at Lord's as he walked out to bat was moving and unnerving: 'I was frightened stiff – they started clapping me as I came through the Long Room! In the circumstances, that was one of my best innings. Hall and Griffith didn't exactly say "welcome back" to me!'

At last Graveney was a reassuring fixture in the England side at the age of thirty-nine. His batting had reached a well-rounded maturity and he felt content: 'It was so much better for me when May, Hutton and the others had gone. I then felt I could compete on equal terms with the rest!' As Graveney began the 1969 series against the West Indies, there seemed no reason why he should not be good enough for another season or two; the limited-overs game was causing him some technical problems and a few stiff limbs, but he was ideally equipped for the longer Test Match game. He made an accomplished 75 in the first innings at Old Trafford to underline his suitability for the series, but then took a conscious decision to end his England career. Graveney had told the selectors that he wanted to play in a match at Luton on the Sunday – it was his benefit season and he had been promised £1,000 if he played. He advised Alec Bedser, the chairman, about the Luton offer before the Test team was picked, so when he was selected, Graveney assumed that he was going to be allowed to go to Luton on the rest day of the Test. Bedser told him he could not go after the end of the first day at Old Trafford, but Graveney went ahead with the game at Luton. He was banned for the next four Tests, which effectively meant the end of his Test career. As Keith Fletcher, John Hampshire, Mike Denness and Peter Parfitt shuffled in and out of Graveney's place for the rest of that summer, lovers of class batsmanship cursed the benefit system, and berated the intransigence that did not trust a mature professional to keep out of the way of physical danger during a Sunday beer match at Luton.

Graveney accepts his share of the blame and says he knew what he was doing. Within a year, he was lost to English first-class cricket, terrified that his powers might possibly be on the wane. 'I didn't want to hear the kids saying: "Why is he still in the side?" and I was finding the Sunday League hard going. Looking back on it now, I packed up two seasons early.' In his last season, he was second in the national averages (62.66), with only Sobers ahead of him.

Now he presides benevolently over business at his pub near the race-course at Cheltenham and ventures forth to the golf course and the TV commentary box from his delightful cottage at Winchcombe. Graveney of Winchcombe – a happy case of onomatopoeia. As he watches batsmen ducking and diving against the short-pitched line of attack, he shudders and wonders how he avoided getting killed when he batted with such a pronounced forward emphasis. He concludes that his head must have been in the right position and confirms that Lindwall, Miller, Adcock, Heine, Hall and Griffith were every bit as hostile as the present breed of fast bowlers. Alan Knott and Dennis Amiss – who both played for England with Graveney – feel that he would be forced onto the back foot today, and that his front foot style would be his undoing. I wonder. Wickets have got even slower in England since Graveney's retirement and most batsmen play forward to avoid lbw decisions against deliveries that keep low. David Brown, the former England fast bowler, agrees: 'Tom was always pretty good at getting out of the way of the short-pitched stuff. His head position was marvellous – he wouldn't take his eye off the ball, as some current England batsmen do. He never seemed to miss much around his legs when I bowled at him and those wristy, late dabs were very productive. They'd have to pitch it up eventually, because they'd get fed up with Tom swaying out of harm's way. If they pitched it up, he would drive them on both sides of the wicket without any problems at all.'

The modern batsmen would be surprised at the amount of net practice Graveney took – only Geoffrey Boycott has emulated him since he retired. With Graveney, it was an article of faith to have a net every day at Worcester; he would arrive at the ground early, and take his practice very seriously. Len Coldwell and Jack Flavell would take the new ball against him and Norman Gifford always aimed for Graveney's net: 'You could bowl properly at Tom in the nets, because he would bat properly – no slogging, just a sensible attitude to finding his touch. He treated a net like an innings in a match and you could learn to bowl accordingly. At the end, he'd walk out with the sweat pouring off him – last night's beer! He had great pride in his performance at Worcester; even today, if he had to play in a charity match he'd pop down to the nets and get the feel of the bat in his hands.'

A strange paradox in some ways, Tom Graveney. A dedicated practiser, even though he played with refreshing freedom of expression and sense of enjoyment. A man of immense natural talent, yet highly superstitious – he always sat in the same seat on the Worcester balcony when waiting to bat and he would use the same piece of chewing gum throughout his innings, placing it neatly on top of his bat handle at close of play and then popping it in his mouth when he resumed the next morning. When fielding, he always wanted to touch the ball; if the wicket-keeper missed him out at slip, he would fret as the ball made its way back to the bowler. A chivalrous opponent, delighted to chat about the achievements of others, yet his memory of his own performances smacks of Boycott. His recall of precise dates, locations, appropriate bowlers and the state of the wicket is as precise as his memory of his exact score at any stage in his career. Not surprisingly, the match which saw him reach a hundred hundreds is easily recalled – Worcestershire against Northants at Worcester in 1964. He reminded me that he got 132 – correct – and went on: 'David Larter bowled me a bouncer, I tried to hook it, got a bottom edge and it plopped just over short leg's head for a single. Achieved in the grand manner!'

An articulate talker on the technique of batsmanship, he can remember the occasions when he worked out how to play certain shots – that little push on the bounce through the offside that got so many 'bread and butter' runs, the half-cock stroke on the front foot that allowed him to defend so skilfully on turning wickets. His weight distribution was always excellent; even though he played almost everything off the front foot – including the hook – he never seemed off-balance. As Tony Brown, a colleague at Bristol, recalls, 'Tom never seemed at odds with his game. If he was dismissed, we would assume it was a very good ball. He never had a bad run in my experience, his technique and timing were so good.' Fred Titmus told me that Graveney was the best player of off-spin he ever saw: 'He was always so far over the ball that you couldn't get him off balance. He would work you away on the legside, then if you bowled a little outside the line of middle and leg, out would come that superb cover-drive!'

He must have missed out on around thirty England caps. He should have gone to South Africa in 1956–7 and again in 1964–5, and to Australia the following winter. Although recalled in 1966, he was just as good in 1964, when his batting prowess – five hundreds, sixteen fifties – put him in a class of his own, fully twenty runs an innings ahead of the next batsman in the side. He was considered good enough for the Rest of the World side in Barbados in 1967, yet not for England until the previous season. Richie Benaud told me that the Australians could never believe that Graveney was not rated highly enough by England's selectors in successive years: 'We never sung Tom's praises unless we were asked and then we said he should be in the England team. A lot of people thought that was a double-bluff, a piece of Australian sharp practice, so Tom missed out a lot. There was a definite prejudice against his style of batting. He would never have been out of an Australian side during *my* Test career.'

Graveney has no regrets about the way he batted. 'I couldn't help being a front-foot player, nor playing the game in a certain way. I feel sorry for David Gower at the moment, he's going through the same wall of criticism that I faced. If he plays a lovely shot, he gets all the praise but if a stump goes out of the ground, they say "what a terrible shot", without giving any credit to the bowler. You simply have to play the way that suits you as a person and as a batsman.'

We can only be grateful for Graveney's independence of mind, for he gave pleasure consistently for twenty years. Those who accuse him of inconsistency should know that he scored more runs in the 1950s than anyone, that his Test average was 44 and that he scored more runs than Cowdrey, Hayward and Hutton. Since Frank Woolley's death, he is the heaviest scorer among living cricketers. A reasonable effort from a man who did not play serious cricket till he was twenty-one, a batsman who was a bit of a dasher until he was thirty-five. How he would have flourished in the pre-1914 era! The very thought of Wilfred Rhodes bowling at Tom Graveney with seven men on the offside makes me long for a time machine.

16

Colin Cowdrey

'When Colin was in that sort of mood,
you could take your pads off for the rest of the day'
(M.J.K.Smith)

The career of Colin Cowdrey is cogent proof of the maxim that cricket is a matter of inches – those between your ears. When his mind was clear, he was peerless: an effortless timer of the ball, a batsman with so much time to spare that he made the game look a case of men against boys. He would caress the fastest bowlers around the field with the paternal air of an indulgent father amusing his brood on the beach. The contrast in Cowdrey on his introspective days was striking and sad to anyone who admires class – he would scratch away diffidently against bowlers who should never have troubled him, the penalty of all 'touch' players, those who rely on instinctive timing. Jim Laker neatly summed up the enigma of Colin Cowdrey when he told me: 'I always felt you could bowl a maiden over at him when he'd scored 120'. M.J.K.Smith – a contemporary at Oxford and former England colleague who captained Cowdrey – assessed him equally succinctly: 'The word to describe Colin's batting is frustration.'

Before delving too deeply into the Freudian and estimating why Colin Cowdrey sometimes complicated the game to his own detriment, it is important to emphasise his class and record as a batsman. For twenty-five years his name was synonymous with grace and charm, yet he was also an extremely prolific batsman – only Grace and Woolley have surpassed his tally of a thousand runs in a season (27), he is eleventh in the list of run-scorers (42,719), the fourth highest scorer in Tests and only Sobers, Greg Chappell, Bradman and Gavaskar made more Test hundreds (22). He also scored 107 first-class hundreds and in doing so, left indelible memories of a glorious batsman who possessed every shot, and the tactical intelligence to alter his style to the prevailing trends of the game. He is also acknowledged as a chivalrous opponent, an unselfish team-mate and one of the most impressive representatives of the game.

153

And yet, and yet; both Les Ames and Doug Wright think he should have scored two hundred centuries, opinions based on the prodigious natural talent he displayed when those two veterans first played with him for Kent. Fred Trueman pitches his estimate a little lower – around 150 hundreds. M.J.K.Smith's tribute is impressive: 'He made batting look easier than anyone I've ever seen', and F.R.Brown, a man associated with first-class cricket for over fifty years, says: 'If I had to assemble a coaching film on the art of batting, the man I would choose from my time would be Colin Cowdrey.' Jim Laker considered he had more natural ability than his great partner, Peter May, and Ray Illingworth judges him the nearest technical equivalent to his hero, Sir Leonard Hutton.

Cowdrey was the ideal number four, a man capable of playing on any wicket against all varieties of bowling, yet such was his vast ability that he performed superbly as an opener. He hated opening – 'I used to dread getting out early and having no further part to play for the rest of the day' – but he had a wonderful tour of the West Indies in 1959–60, when his hooking of Wes Hall was masterful. Cowdrey, acknowledging that some of his best innings were played on that tour, recognises the anomaly that they were made from a batting position he did not like; yet his adaptability was one of his greatest assets and the brave, composed way he stood up to Lillee and Thompson at the age of forty-two in wholly disconcerting circumstances crystallised his enduring talent.

Perhaps his choice of Hutton as his mentor when young gives a clue to Cowdrey's occasional batting schizophrenia. Cowdrey, a keen cricket historian, had imbued himself with knowledge of Hutton's deeds before meeting him on the cricket field: then he fell under the spell of Hutton's poise and perfection of style. It seemed that Hutton batted like a master every time Cowdrey saw him in his early days as a first-class cricketer. Cowdrey admits that he became a committed disciple of the Hutton style and temperament. Crashing the ball to the boundary fence was 'infra dig'; the ball had had to be persuaded away, with just enough speed on it to beat the pursuing fielder. When Cowdrey first toured Australia under Hutton's captaincy, he was deeply impressed by his tactical grasp, his beautiful batting art, and the kind, thoughtful way he helped the young man recover from the shock of his father's death. Hutton had told Cowdrey Senior: 'I'll look after him,' on the day the England team left for Australia; when they arrived in Perth to learn of the bereavement, Hutton was as good as his word. That made a deep impression on Cowdrey, and may partly explain why he has been such a kind counsellor and sympathetic friend to so many young cricketers in the past thirty years. To return to the influence on him of Hutton's batting: there can have been no finer mentor to copy at that stage, yet something of Hutton's innate caution must have rubbed off on him. 'You've got to think it out,' Hutton would say – and perhaps Cowdrey did too much of that in subsequent years.

Cowdrey admits he used to fret during an innings if he thought he had lost the thread of consistent timing that was crucial to him. He had made a conscious decision not to rely on strength, to play like Hutton and not May or Dexter, and therefore he needed to feel 'in touch': certain wickets do not favour the effortless strokemaker who likes to use the pace of the ball, to open the bat's face and glide a delivery away with deceptive speed and certainty. Cowdrey needed pace in the wicket to be at his best and would watch with a certain amount of admiration someone like M.J.K.Smith, a scourge of off-spinners on slow wickets, who used a strong right hand to punch the ball with the spin through the legside. Smith never compared with Cowdrey as an all-round batsman, nor in his ability to play the fast bowlers, but there is no doubt that during their careers, many slow wickets favoured the Smith pragmatism rather than the Cowdrey delicacy. When Cowdrey went out to bat, he had attuned his mind and body to the exigencies of the situation – the wicket, the appropriate bowlers and the tactical needs. He admits he could be thrown off course by an inspired bowling spell or his inability to stroke a half-volley to the boundary; he would enjoy the need to delve into his store of temperament and technical ability to combat the bowler, but he would worry more about the placement of his shots. Why was he hitting a half-volley straight at mid-off, rather than five yards to his left? On such days he would seemingly potter around after racing to a fluent fifty and take stock of his game, wondering whether to tinker a little with the system. 'Batting always fascinated me,' he says. 'Life becomes a bore if you've nothing left to prove, if you're not stretched. I relished the challenge of surviving at the wicket, of trying a few experiments.' He is inordinately proud of developing the 'paddle' shot – that curious sweep he played from an almost erect position which sent the ball to the wicket-keeper's left, at a very fine angle. Cowdrey perfected that shot to thwart the legside line which Richie Benaud once used to tie him down: 'The next time England played Australia, I was ready for him. It proved that I was not just an offside player, but more importantly that I was justified in thinking about my game to an exact degree. I had kept pace with an evolving tactic of a bowler.'

Such a capacity for a technical adaptability led to periods when a new method was in the gestation stage; at such times, Cowdrey could be maddeningly passive. Even though an excellent judge of a run, he occasionally allowed himself to be subjugated by bowlers whose only merit was nagging accuracy. Many of his former team-mates could not understand the depth of technical conundra that swirled around in his brain; several of them have told me that if Cowdrey's ability could have been fused with the ruthlessness of Peter May, then the game of cricket would have seen the perfect batsman. Godfrey Evans said: 'Colin had all these heroes – but why couldn't he just bat like himself? That would have been world-class.'

At Melbourne in 1966, Cowdrey was caught at the wicket off the bowling of Doug Walters for a lovely 79. He returned to the dressing-room, acknowledged the congratulations and sympathies with his customary modesty and admitted the dismissal was his own fault: 'I knew as soon as he let go of the ball that I could have hit it past cover's left hand, but I thought I'd run it down through the slips for four instead.' Cowdrey could not understand why that remark was greeted with such mirth by less talented, but more realistic team-mates; he was enjoying the battle so much that he had reached the stage where he could play two shots to each delivery. Such a range of options is only available to batsmen of the highest class, yet his unconscious attempt to over-complicate a simple matter of stroke selection had got him out.

Fred Titmus recalls occasions when Cowdrey would amuse the fielders at certain stages of the game with virtuoso displays of mastery: 'Sometimes if a game was drifting to a draw, we'd say, "come on, play us some shots," and John Murray behind the stumps would nominate a particular stoke and he'd play it whatever the delivery. Amazing talent, done without showing off – he was just amusing himself.' Dennis Amiss remembers being captivated by a duel between Cowdrey and Tom Cartwright on a green wicket at Gravesend; at that time, Cartwright was supreme on green wickets with his subtle medium pace and Amiss admits that he could not be certain about Cartwright's delivery from his position at slip. 'Colin had no such problems – he kept going down the pitch to Tom, saying, "I can read you from the hand, now Tom." No one else could lay a bat on him. In the second innings, he got a brilliant hundred against seam and spin with the wicket changed in character. His versatility was amazing.'

In the Oval Test of 1960, Cowdrey was opening the batting with Geoff Pullar, against South Africa's Neil Adcock, a splendidly hostile, genuinely fast bowler. Cowdrey calmly announced: 'I'm going to go out there and play him as if the ball isn't moving at all.' Adcock's first delivery was stroked through cover by Cowdrey and he went on to make 175 as England, following on, easily avoided defeat. Mike Smith was due to bat number five that day but recalls: 'When Colin was in that sort of mood, you could take your pads off for the rest of the day.' Adcock had already dismissed Cowdrey five times that series, and he had returned a string of low scores, but once he worked out the technical answer, he exuded an aura of omnipotence that day at the Oval.

Yet there were times when Cowdrey could not unlock the technical door, when he would retreat into his shell in the manner of a southern Hutton. On the 1956–7 tour of South Africa, Peter May, the captain and his manager, F.R.Brown, spent a long time trying to persuade Cowdrey to attack that splendid off-spinner, Hugh Tayfield. They felt that Cowdrey's range of strokes and nimble footwork were the right answer to Tayfield's wiles and with May out of luck in the Tests, it was becoming an urgent matter. Brown remembers vividly the Durban Test: 'Colin went in with our instructions ringing in his ears, and soon he hit Tayfield for an effortless six over long-on. The next ball was played in the direction of mid-off, who made a great stop, but couldn't prevent the batsmen running three. After that, Colin hardly played a shot at Tayfield for the next ten overs and eventually got out. I said "What happened, you had him!" He replied: "I was dropped and felt I had to stay in." Tayfield, who couldn't bowl at him, was allowed to get back on top.' He took 8 for 69, and 37 wickets in the series.

Ten years earlier, life must have seemed much less complicated to Colin Cowdrey, as the small, rotund schoolboy impressed the harshest judges. He was marked down early for greatness; at the age of thirteen, he stood out at Alf Gover's cricket school and he dominated cricket at Tonbridge School for five years. At seventeen, he was in the Kent side, two years later he was capped (the youngest in the county's history) and at twenty-one an England player. Trevor Bailey saw him score a hundred for the Gentlemen against the Players at eighteen and judged that he looked more like a thirty-year-old craftsman than a mere boy. In 1953, he played two innings of remarkable maturity against Surrey on an Oval wicket that was ideal for Laker and Lock's diverse spinning talents. Cowdrey made 154 out of 270 and 34 out of 63, and Jim Laker – eight wickets in the match – told me: 'He played me better than any young player did at any time in my career. I was certain he was an England batsman for the next twenty years.'

An innings of grandeur in the Melbourne Test eighteen months later added to his glittering reputation. Keith Miller, bowling with inspiration on an unreliable pitch, had reduced England to 41 for 4: Cowdrey scored a sumptuous 102 out of 191 and the crowd of 63,000 forgot their impartiality to roar him home to the pavilion at its end. Only three other batsmen reached double figures and Cowdrey, while at the crease, scored 100 out of 158. Bill O'Reilly described it as the finest innings he had seen in a Test match and whether or not that was Irish hyperbole, it did not matter: O'Reilly knew a high-class innings when he saw one. At twenty-two years of age, Cowdrey had proved himself at the highest level and seemed set fair for greatness.

That matchless performance became an albatross around the neck of his career. During his uninspired efforts, his critics would call on Melbourne as proof that he had the quality, but not the vital spark of consistency. If he could do it once, he should be able to repeat the dosage at will, they said. Cowdrey is well aware that his great innings raised expectations too early – 'After that, I was judged by a different yardstick, even though circumstances change so often from day to day. At Melbourne, everything went right – I had some luck, and also played to my full capacity – but that was something people took for granted. I feel sorry for David Gower today: he has looked a class player since he was 21 at Test level, yet people expect him to turn in great innings irrespective of the quality of the bowlers and the wicket.'

The England captaincy cannot have helped Cowdrey's peace of mind: at various stages, he lost it to Dexter, Close, Illingworth and May. The selection of Ray Illingworth to captain the England tour to Australia in 1970–1 caused Cowdrey some heartache; he hesitated before accepting the vice-captaincy and he never did himself justice on that trip. Cowdrey insists that the distractions of the England captaincy never consciously affected him, but the general feeling among his contemporaries is that he was indecisive and lacked sufficient dynamism. His many kindnesses are acknowledged – particularly by Basil D'Oliveira during his traumatic times in 1968 – but his fondness for cricketers seems to have militated against a course of action that would possibly upset anyone. He did manage to cast aside the air of diffidence on the tour of West Indies in 1967–8, when he won the series by a mixture of team spirit, tough out-cricket that did not baulk at slow over-rates, a generous declaration by Gary Sobers, batting depth and excellent fast bowling by John Snow. Cowdrey batted magnificently on that tour and his innings of 71 that won the Test at Port of Spain was a masterpiece of calm, controlled batting. Even then, the old diffidence reappeared; at tea on the final day, John Edrich and Tom Graveney had to take their captain into a corner and persuade him the match was there for the taking.

No matter who was captain, Cowdrey served England loyally. Halfway through his career, he learned to battle it out at the crease, to graft for his runs even though they were not coming with their usual facility. Edgbaston 1957 was a turning point in his development as a major batsman, the first time he had scored a Test hundred by occupation of the crease, rather than strokeplay. The situation of the game demanded that Cowdrey stay in with Peter May, but they both realised that they also had to quell the menace of Sonny Ramadhin for the series. They dominated the little leg-spinner in differing ways – May stroked the ball cleanly while Cowdrey played forward, padding the ball away for ever after. Ramadhin appealed himself hoarse, but on a slow wicket with little bounce, he had no chance of an lbw decision with Cowdrey a long way down the pitch. It was not pretty batting from one of the game's great stylists, but it worked. May and Cowdrey added 411 and Ramadhin was never the same bowler again. Cowdrey's success with the pad/bat method was to be imitated by a generation of less talented English batsmen, with distressing results, but he had proved that he had the stomach for the fight underneath the veneer of elegance.

Alan Knott, who played for a decade with Cowdrey, likens him to Ken Barrington in the way he would pick up runs by unostentatious shots. 'He would accumulate like Kenny – a tickle off his legs early in the innings or a little dab down to third man, just to judge the pace of the wicket. Of course, when he established himself, he was a much more fluent player then Kenny, but he really got stuck in during my time with him. He would be really disappointed at getting dismissed cheaply. He may not have looked it, but Colin was a real competitor.'

The competitive instinct led him to accept an invitation which he instinctively knew he should refuse. It came one morning in December 1974 when his morning ablutions at home were rudely shattered by a phone call from Mike Denness in Australia. The England captain explained that injuries had disrupted his tour party and that he wanted Colin to fly out to join them. As a batsman. At forty-two years of age. Against Lillee and Thomson. On lightning fast, unreliable wickets that had reduced the English batsmen to nervous wrecks. Cowdrey forgot about his disappointment at not being originally selected after a fine season, and agreed to go. Five days later he was playing in the Perth

Test, on the fastest wicket in Australia, against bowlers who had broken one of Amiss's thumbs and one of Edrich's hands. At Perth, he was sent in first wicket down and then in the second innings, he had to open after Brian Luckhurst broke a hand. Cowdrey made 22 and 41 and gave an astonishing display of defensive batting. Dennis Amiss, one of the men who suffered most on that horrific tour, told me: 'It gave us so much confidence to see how fast bowling could be played. Colin would drop his wrists to anything short of a length, and take his bat down and across his body, away from the ball. That casual sway of the head while the rest of us were all arms and legs and undignified scuttling – a wonderful technical effort.' Unfortunately, Cowdrey had to opt for survival. Very few deliveries were pitched in an area that favoured his front-foot driving, even if he had acclimatised himself to the bounce. Bob Willis remembers feeling desperately sorry for Cowdrey: 'He could survive through his wonderful technique but he couldn't score runs. He'd battle away to get twelve in an hour-and-a-half, then watch Tony Greig come in at the other end and carve three boundaries over the slips in an over. But the fact that we wanted him out there is a great tribute to the guy'.

Six months later, on a balmy June evening, Cowdrey paid back some of the dues to the Australians, when an innings of 151 not out steered Kent – chasing 354 – to a four-wicket victory. Ian Chappell, with his usual tact, had ordered the coach driver to be ready to take the Australians off to Southampton at four o'clock; they arrived at midnight after a thrashing from a master. Brian Luckhurst, the Kent captain that day, still smiles at that innings: 'He was absolutely in control as he tore Lillee apart. After the battering I had taken in the previous winter, it was a delight to beat them by a vintage Cowdrey innings. At the age of forty-three, he was hooking Lillee in front of square!' It was a wonderful way to end Cowdrey's career; he had already decided to retire at the end of the 1975 season and he longed for one more good innings at Canterbury, the ground he loved. Now, another ambition fulfilled, he was content to leave the stage to others.

More than a decade after his retirement, he tells me he still misses the game desperately. He has regrets – that he was not fit enough to do himself justice on his final Australian tour, that he waited until halfway through his career before realising the need to adapt and improvise. He wishes he could have played more against the spinners – 'That part of cricket was always special to me. In my early days, I would happily watch Hutton and Compton playing the spinners in their different ways. It was wonderful to be in the same side as a man like Doug Wright, such an inspirational leg-spinner.' Perhaps Cowdrey would bat differently if he played today – 'Yes, I think I'd smash it a bit more now. I was coming to terms with that in the one-day games towards the end. Perhaps I overdid the delicacies a little, but that was my style, the way I was brought up to play.' Gently, he takes issue with the modern fad of net practice: 'Roger Bannister wouldn't have run the four-minute mile if he'd trained that morning. I never wanted to lose what I had within me, I wanted to bring out everything in the middle.'

Fred Titmus believes Cowdrey would have been an even greater player if he had not been an amateur: 'If he had to earn his money as a pro, Colin would've been more practical and got rid of all the theory. He could afford to experiment, because his job didn't depend on it.' There may be some truth in that – Cowdrey admits he played the game for fun. The influence of his father was profound; he insisted young Colin's initials would be MCC and one night in March 1938, he ensured his son would be hooked on the game for the rest of his life. The Cowdrey family was sailing back from India to England and six-year-old Colin was dragged from his bunk by his father to observe a ship passing three miles away. Reverentially, Cowdrey Senior told his son: 'Don Bradman is on board that ship. He's bringing the Australian team to try to beat England.' Thereafter cricket fired the imagination of young Cowdrey and even now – after a goodly crop of personal disappointments – he inclines towards an optimistic, romantic, opinion on cricket, refreshingly free from the jaundiced, unsentimental stance of many former players.

He is properly proud of scoring a hundred hundreds, and pays due homage to the keenness of Asif Iqbal to scamper the necessary single from a push to cover in the Surrey match at Maidstone in 1973. He modestly suggests that he had a pretty good temperament to play first-class cricket for twenty-five years and to surmount reverses such as a broken arm and a snapped achilles tendon that ruined his chances of captaining an England tour to Australia. Strange how an ambition like that should be rooted in such a modest man, a player who never courted the England captaincy; yet the choice of Illingworth for the 1970–1 tour remains one of his greatest disappointments.

Equations like 'May's steel plus Cowdrey's natural ability plus Botham's self-belief equal a great player' are, in the end, self-defeating. Cowdrey's batting was like the man: charming, prone to self-doubt, civilised and human. We should be grateful for the privilege of watching him unravel the complexities of a game that fascinated him. He was rare value when the jig-saw fitted.

17

Geoffrey Boycott

'I wish he'd opened when I played for England.
We would have won a few more Tests!'
(Jim Laker)

I shall start with Geoffrey Boycott's batting record. He would approve of that – 'judge me by what I've done, not what some people say about me,' he would say. Very well – he is ninth in the list of run-scorers and just four batsmen have bettered his number of centuries. He has made more runs and scores of over fifty than any other Test batsman.

It is a record of which he can justifiably be proud. It has been achieved by technical skill and dedication of the highest order and none of Boycott's many detractors should forget how much of himself he has given to the game. He has performed wonders on short rations, on a frugal diet of strokeplay; a hundred by Boycott is a triumph of will-power, when a lonely man can find freedom of expression in the way that suits his own character. For most of his career, he has prospered through a defensive technique of great class and a quiver of about five shots. Whether or not he has been capable of playing more shots is a matter for conjecture – he has not wished to, and he should therefore be judged on the means he has chosen to reach his goals.

Boycott is one of the few batsmen who still subscribes to the axiom that 'it's a sideways-on game': he plays beautifully straight with an initial 'back and across' movement that gives him time to decide whether to play forward or get back on his heels. Alan Knott, an expert on the physical attributes needed for cricket, points out that Boycott has a very flexible, supple body, which enables him to get his elbow pointing up at the sky when he plays a defensive stroke. Says Knott: 'This helps him get on top of the bouncing ball, simply because he can get his bat so high that he can bring it down a long way. His superb fitness is geared to making him a better batsman.' Boycott's head and feet positioning has been faultless, apart from a traumatic tour of Australia in 1978–9, and his placement of strokes is shrewdly productive. His best shots are the cover drive, the on-drive to the left of mid-wicket and a back-foot force square on the offside which brings his strong right hand into play. He does not hook any more, after a brief flirtation with the stroke in the early 1970s – it got him out a number of times, because he played it in the air. His footwork against the spinners is excellent and his forward defensive shot, with the hands loose on the handle, is exemplary. Mike Brearley, who opened for England with Boycott, is a great admirer of his defensive technique: 'He holds the bat so loose when playing defensively that the ball would drop short of the slips if he got an edge. I take my hat off to him for his survival instincts – perhaps he'd be in trouble with the bouncer but next ball, he'd be back in line, still battling away.'

Geoffrey Boycott's most admirable quality is that he has made himself into an opening batsman from the top drawer. I make the distinction about his place in the batting order, because his obsession with occupying the crease has served Yorkshire and England well due to his being an opener. He has played in a succession of weak batting sides and his view that he had to stay in the middle was generally compatible with the needs of his side. Differences of opinion have arisen when something other than the anchor role has been needed. Boycott's reluctance to go up several gears disqualifies him, in my opinion, for batting greatness – I say 'reluctance' because I do not believe he suffers from an inability to force the pace. He is a product of an environment that values efficiency and achievement. Fancy cameo innings are regarded with deep suspicion by the good folk of Yorkshire, especially when they feel that a batsman could have done better for himself with a little more backbone and professionalism. Mike Brearley appreciates the difference in attitudes to batting, compared with southern counties: 'At a place like Hove, they love to see the ball crashed through the covers. The Yorkshireman likes to see things done correctly – the full face of the bat, playing "through the V", the bent knee in forward defensive strokes, etc etc. To play a correct defensive innings is admirable to them, as it is to Geoff Boycott.'

I believe that Boycott would have scored many more runs in a more attractive style if he had contrived to play his cricket for a southern county. Yorkshire to the marrow, his many batting virtues are essentially those that stem from his upbringing, but life is easier for a batsman in the south of England. The wickets are faster, the boundaries shorter and spin bowlers are more readily used, a style of bowling against which Boycott is a master; in Yorkshire, the wickets are greener and they seam and lift for the quicker bowlers. You have to graft for your runs on Yorkshire wickets, a point acknowledged by a man from that county, Barry Wood: 'Boycott has really had to work hard up there. He would have got about twenty per cent more runs if he'd played in the south.' Bob Willis estimates the difference to be about fifteen per cent. Whatever the figure, there is a genuine admiration in the game for the scope of Boycott's achievements in the light of his lack of outstanding natural ability. Norman Gifford told me: 'You can say to a youngster "now look at Boycott, just see what he's done with himself" and to that extent Boycott's been good for the game. There's nothing wrong with working hard to better yourself.' Ray Illingworth remembers his reaction when he saw the young Boycott twenty years ago: 'I wasn't very impressed. He couldn't seem to hit the ball off the square, I thought someone like Titmus would just bottle him up all day. He worked and worked at his game and he deserves tremendous credit for achieving so much.'

Boycott was a late developer, compared to other Yorkshire players with more natural talent. He was twenty before establishing himself in the Yorkshire colts side and played his earliest Championship matches in his twenty-second year. He had practised and practised for years before that: his uncle Albert and the former Somerset leg-spinner, Johnny Lawrence, were the two props on which the bespectacled introvert leaned. They consoled him on the many occasions when the Yorkshire Club reacted non-committally to his advance as a batsman in league cricket. Boycott stuck at his clerical job with the Ministry of Pensions throughout the frustrating years of his youth: where he came from, a living wage was a bonus compared with fancy notions of becoming a Yorkshire cricketer. One of Boycott's favourite sayings to any querulous team-mate is 'it's better than being down the pit', and there is no doubt that his early struggles amid that close-knit mining community of South Yorkshire toughened him mentally for the challenges ahead. He might fail through lack of top-class ability, but no one would chide him for not trying. His relentless ambition and self-absorption astonished the first-team players at Yorkshire in his early days and led to innumerable personality clashes; more than one established player was run out by the intense young man immersed in his struggle for survival and self-respect. He was determined to make up for lost time; John Hampshire, who came into the first team at about the same time, may have looked the freer, more impressive batsman but Boycott would outshine him in the end. Boycott's style of batting was bound to cause tension in a team that prided itself on an unselfish attitude towards scoring quick runs, a side captained by Brian Close in a daring, imaginative manner. Close solved the problem by suggesting to the young man that he should open the batting, rather than bat in the middle order. Close told me: 'There was no room for him down below because of his attitude to occupying the crease. As a restricted player, that was the best place for him.'

Boycott's first appearance for Yorkshire at Lord's revealed the self-imposed tensions from which he suffered. On a rain-affected wicket, he scored a magnificent 90 out of an all-out 144; it was the innings of a mature player, ended only by an unplayable delivery from Alan Moss that he was good enough to follow and touch. It was not good enough for Boycott; as he rushed blindly past well-wishers at the top of the pavillion stairs, he ignored a 'well played, lad' from a slight, silver-haired gentleman, walked into the dressing-room, put a towel over his head and wept. He had desperately wanted a hundred in his first game at Lord's. The man who had tried to congratulate him was Sir Leonard Hutton.

Don Mosey, the BBC radio cricket commentator, vividly recalls the pressure that the young Boycott piled upon himself. At that time, Mosey was a cricket writer on the *Daily Mail* and his brief was to cover Yorkshire's matches; he used to drive Boycott to the various games in those early days. Mosey described him as shy, intense and very conscious of the fact that he was having to battle for everything in his life. He remembers stumbling upon a weeping Boycott in the Bradford dressing-room in 1962. 'I said to him "whatever's the matter, lad?" and he sobbed, "They've left me out, Mr Mosey. The day will come when I decide who gets left out." Some senior players had properly been brought back into the first team and he had to drop out. He couldn't understand the reasoning.'

The Yorkshire captain, Brian Close, says he treated Boycott with a mixture of tolerance and discipline in those days: 'In some respects, he was immature, which stemmed from this burning desire for success. He would ask me where I was eating that night, so he could join me and discuss cricket. I was impressed by his keenness to learn, but he had some funny ways'.

Boycott impressively made up for lost time. Within a year of being capped by his county, he was scoring a Test hundred – the first of 22 – against Australia. On successive tours to South Africa and Australia, he alienated some England colleagues by his running between the wickets, an inclination to hog the strike even though a more talented strokeplayer was fretting at the other end, and his tendency to say the first thing that came into his head, no matter how justified or ill-advised the sentiments. Boycott at least was clear-sighted in his objectives: to be the most consistent, heaviest run-scorer in the side. No one could ever accuse Geoffrey Boycott of duplicity; he felt that his interests and those of his team ran concurrently. His job was to stay in as long as possible and to present himself for cricket in a supremely fit, mentally clear state. Within these constraints, his career has been a model of consistency.

By 1970, Boycott was the best opener in the world. The England batting order of the late 1960s – including Cowdrey, Edrich, Graveney, D'Oliveira, Barrington – was strong enough to make up for any dilatoriness on his part. On the 1970–1 tour to Australia, he batted magnificently, playing some fine shots on good wickets. Ray Illingworth, his captain on that tour, feels he got closer to him than at any subsequent stage: 'Geoff respects ability in others, as long as they try to the utmost. What he can't stand is incompetence or someone who doesn't do himself justice through his own fault. We came from similar backgrounds and, on that tour, talked the same language.'

At the height of Boycott's eminence on that trip, a decision was taken 12,000 miles away that gave him initial pleasure but ultimate sadness. Brian Close was sacked from the Yorkshire captaincy and Boycott was appointed successor. On the face of it, that was a tremendous compliment to a man who had crammed so much experience into a short career: after all, Close had played for England at eighteen, an age which saw Boycott still at the Ministry of Pensions, still grafting away in league cricket. The affairs of Yorkshire County Cricket club since Boycott's appointment as captain have taken on a quality that would be recognised by Lucretia Borgia, and it would be remiss of someone like myself to try to unravel its complexities, treacheries and heady moments of farce. More than one eminent cricketer has been handed a loaded revolver and ushered towards cricket's equivalent of a forest; lawyers have prospered as writs, extraordinary meetings and press statements have fluttered in the air like ticker-tape. The rumour machine has picked up many a productivity bonus as claim and counter-claim have permeated committee rooms, bars and dressing-rooms. For more than a decade Yorkshire County Cricket Club has been a laughing-stock in the game, a matter of sadness to those of us who believe that the club's basic principles on cricket are sound.

Since the intriguing began in the first year of Boycott's captaincy, one man has remained in the eye of the hurricane: Geoffrey Boycott.

Committee chairmen may come and go, other captains may dip in and out of controversies, but Yorkshire's best batsman is a constant presence. If you accept that premise, then Boycott must bear some responsibility for the shambles. Other major batsmen in cricket history have had a highly-developed sense of their own importance, but how many have also been insecure? Boycott's prickly, self-justifying persona partly stems from his hard upbringing, partly a reaction to those dissemblers who have falsified the facts, and partly a feeling that some influential people were out to get him. His ambivalence to the media is typical: he will lose no opportunity for castigating the media for fanning the flames of controversy, yet blithely appear on the Michael Parkinson Show to indulge in an orgy of recrimination that was ultimately self-defeating. No one is more adept at backing reluctantly into the spotlight, then discovering that the water of publicity is not that chilling to the toes. He is a splendidly articulate framer of his own point of view; no one in my journalistic experience has said 'no comment' so often without meaning it. The views that have been readily coaxed from him have not been the doings of the dastardly media, they represent the willing involvement of Geoffrey Boycott in situations he feels demand some good, honest, Yorkshire plain speaking. He has a flair for self-destruction that makes a moth near a flame seem a canny investor: in January 1982, upon his controversial early return from the Indian tour, he allowed himself to be interviewed by David Coleman on BBC Grandstand and, in doing so, did his cause no favour. Clearly he was not himself – but his rambling, disparate remarks smacked of a persecution complex. He had been badly advised: just once, he should have kept his own counsel and tried to recover his health.

Boycott's willing excursions into publicity in the 1970s harmed Yorkshire CCC. The supporters, accustomed to success, needed a hero in the absence of a team to admire and laud; Boycott was happy to oblige. The individual became bigger than the team by dint of supreme individual cricket ability and the media's complicity in building up Boycott as a cult figure, the 'good guy' boxed in by the machinations of jealous team-mates and administrators with long memories. The 'them and us' syndrome will always enjoy a healthy run in Yorkshire and Geoffrey Boycott was as skilful as his opponents in drawing up his battalions. His playing prestige inevitably attracted some sycophants who just wanted to be seen in his corner of the ring, while others joined him after being bruised by other bouts of in-fighting. Reform Groups flourished, players' polls were bandied about and the activities of one batsman seemed more important than the fortunes of a great cricketing county. John Hampshire, a proud Yorkshireman, was so sickened by events that he did the unthinkable – he walked out and joined Derbyshire. Anyone who knows the fierce pride of John Hampshire in following his father into the Yorkshire eleven will appreciate the depths to which the farce had sunk. John Hampshire still finds it painful to talk about the tensions and the factions that drove him from Yorkshire. He accepts that Boycott's personality was just one of many contributory factors, and stresses that at no stage would he align himself with groups either for or against Boycott. Hampshire blames the people who put Boycott on a pedestal, rather than the man himself – 'Geoff just wasn't suited for the job of captain when he was appointed,' Hampshire told me. 'He was completely absorbed in his cricket. He could never, it seemed, relax for a moment and somehow he couldn't really talk to us except on his own terms.'

Hampshire says Boycott was at his best during his years in exile from the England team: he encouraged the players to bring their wives to Yorkshire's matches and he appeared more outgoing in every way. When he returned to the England fold in 1977, Boycott reverted back to his old ways, according to Hampshire: 'His conversation was all about Test cricket, money, records and the England captaincy. The more pressing matters at hand seemed to have no real place in his thoughts.'

Hampshire blames Boycott for much of the melodrama at Scarborough at the end of the 1981 season which precipitated his move to Derbyshire. Boycott had been suspended by Ray Illingworth for making allegedly unauthorised comments to the media and the atmosphere at the ground was charged with tension, as the various pressure groups made their vociferous presence felt. John Hampshire, an undemonstrative, disciplined person, was appalled to see Boycott linger on the ground after being told to go home: 'He stood there, signing autographs and generally holding court while signatures calling for Illingworth's sacking were being collected alongside him. Out in the middle, Yorkshire were trying to play a county championship match. I was sick to the depths of my soul.' Hampshire could take no more of the squalid personality clashes and this proudest of Yorkshiremen left. He took to Derbyshire painful memories of, in his own words, 'supporters torn apart by a cult which regarded one man as greater than the club and even the game itself, and of a committee that made a terrible mistake and didn't try to put things right until it was too late.'

Ray Illingworth, who stepped into the hornets' nest on being appointed team manager in 1978, feels the various pressure groups have caused untold damage to the club's prestige and to Boycott: 'Because of his cult following, it's harder for him with Yorkshire than it was with England. He just has to succeed. A team should be the first priority for the supporters, not an individual. If Geoff Boycott had played for another county, there would've been none of this fuss, but in Yorkshire, cricket's a religion and everyone's got a positive view about Geoff Boycott.'

Illingworth believes that Boycott should have been given the captaincy a decade after the sacking of Close. He wishes that Boycott had been appointed vice-captain for the 1970–1 Australian tour, so that he could have started cutting his teeth on responsibility for players and the differing ways of handling them. One can see that he would have learned much from Illingworth, an acknowledged expert at fostering team spirit at the expense of individual ambition. Jim Laker believed that Boycott did a good job as Yorkshire's captain: 'not even Brian Sellers would've won anything with that lot, they weren't good enough.' In eight seasons under Boycott's captaincy, they finished twice in the top four, yet never won a trophy. Since 1978, they have won just one trophy – the John Player Special League.

Boycott also allowed himself to be side-tracked by the issue of the England captaincy as his eminence as a Test batsman increased. Ray Illingworth tells me that he phoned Boycott to tell him that Mike Denness had been chosen England captain after Illingworth's sacking in 1973: 'Geoff was very disappointed, I think he really thought he would get it after me.' When Boycott pulled out of the 1974–5 trip to Australia, he cited personal reasons that did not equip him for the pressures of Test cricket – he was embroiled in his benefit season, his mother's illness was a worry, the intrigues at Yorkshire were ticking over at a merry pace, and he had been embarrassed at being dismissed several times in May and June by the innocuous Indian left-arm seamer, Eknath Solkar.

Boycott went into purdah for the next three years, concentrating his energies on Yorkshire cricket. Alec Bedser – great cricketer, uncomplicated patriot who would have played for England on one leg if necessary – had to keep the lines of communication open in his capacity as chairman of selectors. He knew that an England team containing Boycott was automatically a more difficult one to beat, but he had to indulge in an extraordinary amount of wooing before the Yorkshireman graciously allowed himself to be selected in 1977. He returned to play two innings of immense character and guts in the Trent Bridge Test against the Australians – running out the local hero, Derek Randall, and remaining strokeless and prone to self-doubt for three hours, before Alan Knott galvanised him to play some fine strokes. In the following Test, he scored his hundredth hundred – the first man to achieve it in a Test (Zaheer was the second). For good measure, it came on his home ground, and the crowd euphoria moved him greatly. He had proved overwhelmingly that he was still a major batsman at Test level and he proceeded to do so until his exile in 1982 after going to South Africa to play in a series of 'unofficial' Tests.

Boycott played some splendid innings for England from 1977 to 1982, but I think he was at his most impressive in Australia in 1979–80 and against the West Indies in two series a year later. He went to Australia with a score to settle: in the previous year, he had played badly under the weight of losing the Yorkshire captaincy and the death of his mother. This time, he reverted to his orthodox stance and played staunchly in the Tests and excellently in the one-day internationals against Australia and West Indies. Mike Brearley, his captain on that tour, is full of admiration for the way Boycott coped: 'We dropped him from one of the early one-day games and told him he had to step up the tempo. He was a revelation – playing the West Indian quickies off the back foot through the covers and going down the wicket to hit people like Max Walker over the top. All this, plus his immense skill at placing the ball, and getting twos instead of ones.'

Against the West Indies, his wicket was always the most prized one: Graham Gooch was the most exciting player, but Boycott sold his wicket dearly against a quartet of intimidating fast bowlers, who were allowed to pitch short by weak umpires. In the summer of 1980 and the winter of 1981, Boycott triumphantly doused the slurs of Tony Greig that he did not fancy quick bowlers – a reference to his non-availability for the 1974–5 tour. Boycott showed his character and tenacity in the Antigua Test with an unbeaten hundred, a stark contrast to his innings of 0 and 1 in the previous Test at Bridgetown. Michael Holding clean-bowled him at the end of an opening over that has become a legend: the first five deliveries reared steeply and sharply off a length and there was Boycott – firmly in line – dropping the wrists on them. The sixth ball was too fast even for Boycott, taking out his off-stump. Graham Gooch, watching from the other end, says it was the fastest and best over he has seen. Clive Lloyd, the West Indies captain, told me that Holding's over was exactly what he had ordered: 'I made Michael get warmed up in the nets just before the innings began. I wanted him to steam in at Boycott right from the first ball, rather than just ease himself in gently. The result was the best over from a fast bowler I've ever seen.' In its own way, it was a great compliment to Boycott and that night, after watching endless re-runs of that historic over on the BBC's video machine, Boycott pronounced himself satisfied that he could have done nothing about the delivery which bowled him. A fortnight later, he scored 104 not out in the Third Test, and, as the West Indies players applauded Boycott's century, Viv Richards paid him a generous and well-deserved tribute. He turned to Clive Lloyd in the slips and said:'You've got to hand it to this guy, he never gives it away.'

How right Richards was. Boycott would settle for that as a memorial to his career. He has triumphed remarkably over his limitations of ability and eyesight – only Zaheer has scored a hundred hundreds with such poor eyesight. Mike Brearley says that he found Boycott's batting at its most fascinating when the conditions were against him: 'I wouldn't want to watch him on a slow wicket against a second-rate attack, but he is excellent when keeping out Lillee if the wicket is helping the bowler. They say attacking batsmen win you matches, but so does Boycott if he scores 100 out of 220, when you could have been bowled out for 120.' Dennis Amiss, who partnered Boycott many times for England, pays tribute to his judgment of when to leave the ball that starts near the off-stump and moves away: 'Some of us would nibble at them, but he always knew where his stumps were.' John Edrich, another of Boycott's illustrious partners, recalls how he would regularly draw comfort from watching him play properly, and with confidence. Jim Laker's praise is heartfelt: 'I wish he'd opened when I played for England. We would have won a few more Tests!' Sunil Gavaskar, the Indian captain in Boycott's last series, rates him very highly. He told me: 'In India, we are still temperamentally suited to Test cricket, rather than the one-day slogging and that is why we respect Boycott so much. He is the best defensive batsman in the world, who has adapted brilliantly to the different bowling strategies of his career.' One statistic from Boycott's Test career summarises his excellent defence: he has been bowled only thirty times in 193 innings, a percentage of 17.65, compared with the average of 22.

He must be proud of the respect of his fellow-professionals and the public awareness that he was in the top flight of opening batsmen. The occasions when his behaviour embarrassed his colleagues will fade into the mists of time, they will be embroidered in the telling and therefore lose their impact. Here is just one anecdote and it comes from a man I consider speaks the truth just as easily as Geoffrey Boycott, albeit in a more personable manner. Dennis Amiss partnered Boycott in the opening Test of the 1973 summer against New Zealand with the words of his county captain, Mike Smith, ringing in his ears – 'there are enough ways of getting out, so don't be run out by Boycott.' In the second innings, Amiss and Boycott had an early misunderstanding: Amiss, unlike previous openers, was not to be overawed by his senior partner and he made good his ground. Boycott was run out for one and Amiss compounded the felony in his eyes by scoring 138 not out. Amiss told me: 'Boycott thought I'd done it on purpose and wouldn't speak to me for the rest of the game. I met him in the lift at our hotel, said "good morning" and he ignored me. It wasn't until our team talk on the eve of the Lord's Test that Ray Illingworth got us both talking again. Boycott fired off at me, but Ray was very fair and told him that unless he sorted it out, we'd both be dropped.' In that Lord's Test, Boycott and Amiss put on 112, but the relationship was still uneasy. In subsequent Tests, Amiss – always conscious that his senior partner would want to lead the way out of the pavilion gate – would wish him 'good luck' as they reached the middle, only to be told sniffily, 'it's not luck that matters, it's ability.' Dennis Amiss had enough of the latter quality to secure his place in the England side and to prosper as Boycott's batting partner. In the Trinidad Test of 1974, as Boycott and Amiss tried to shore up the England innings, Amiss was given another insight into the Yorkshireman's character. 'He suddenly said to me; "I've just realised that you're not trying to run me out." He had finally accepted me, even if it meant deluding himself that I was after him in the early days.'

Such vignettes would fill the whole of this book if I recounted every one I have unearthed. I am fully conscious of Boycott's fondness for litigation – he must be the James Goldsmith of cricket – so I shall forbear. Ultimately, it matters not one jot whether Brian Close really did bully him to play that wonderful Gillette Cup final innings in 1965 or if Boycott was responsible for it himself. They are both former England captains with detailed differing knowledge of the circumstances and one can only guess whether Boycott deserves all the credit for that knock, or whether Close did effect the transformation with a few well-chosen words when he joined him at the wicket. Everyone seems to have a story about Boycott, an inevitable corollary to his prolific record over twenty years in the game, the fame that he has enjoyed and the chip on the shoulder beloved of so many Yorkshiremen. I agree with Mike Brearley, the son of a Yorkshireman, but a different animal from Boycott, when he says: 'It really is extraordinary how anything to do with him is inflated out of all proportion.' It is equally strange to me that a 'percentage player' like Geoffrey Boycott is such a crowd-puller – a man like John Edrich had an equally good record over the same period, yet he never appeared on chat shows or fended off journalists anxious for his side of the latest story. I suppose there is a part in all of us that enjoys hearing the old emotive stuff about 'old school tie', 'public school cronies' and 'enemies in high places' – good knockabout rhetoric that never fails to sell papers or strike a chord in disaffected breasts. Bob Willis remembers Boycott once telling him: 'They want my runs, not me,' and this sense of alienation seems central to Boycott's character. 'The public understands,' he seems to be saying, 'they've been sold down the river in their lives. They can identify with me.'

I would have welcomed the chance to discuss Geoffrey Boycott's career with him, but that proved impossible. I spent six months waiting for the right moment that suited him, but it never came. At his request, I sent him a list of questions for his perusal, but he never acknowledged their receipt. I enlisted the support of Don Mosey and Don Oslear, that fine umpire – to no avail. I drove from Birmingham to Grimsby to chair a sports forum which involved Boycott; he had given an undertaking that he would grant me an audience, but it was not forthcoming. He was excellent value on the sports forum, incidentally – happily signing innumerable autographs, talking great commonsense on a host of cricketing topics and, with true populist flair, tossing in the ritual amount of sneers about Cambridge graduates who should not play for England. Jibes about Mike Brearley's batting are always good for an easy laugh in the north of England.

Perhaps I am an effete southerner in Boycott's eyes. No matter: I admire what he has achieved although I wish he had been better advised by some of his Praetorian Guard. There is plenty of mileage left in Geoffrey Boycott's cricketing tank. Both Graham Gooch and Ray Illingworth thought he was fit and able enough to open again for England when his ban was removed in 1985. He was forty-five years of age then, and if he had managed that, my admiration for him would have been sincere and profound. Boycott also passed Herbert Sutcliffe's record of centuries, to leave him the most prolific Yorkshire batsman of all time. What he will do when he reluctantly leaves the goldfish bowl of constant publicity is his problem – perhaps the media whose practices he apparently deplores will offer sanctuary. For the moment, I believe he will be content with this verdict on his career from

Ray Illingworth: 'I reckon Geoff's epitaph should be that he would always do you a solid, professional job. You can't ask for more than that.'

18

John Edrich

'It's not the hundredth one that counts,
it's the previous 99'

A month before Geoffrey Boycott.had reached the milestone of a hundred hundreds amid the emotion of a Test Match, the feat had been quietly reached by an unassuming left-hander in front of the metaphorical three men and a dog. John Edrich of Surrey made it at the fag-end of a fairly meaningless last day in the Derbyshire match at the Oval. If the event lacked the stage-managed qualities of the Boycott spectacular, that was wholly in keeping with the career of the admirable Edrich.

Edrich had got used to second billing. Indeed, a place on the poster was sufficient for him throughout most of his time in first-class cricket. Unheralded and reticent, he was greatly admired by his fellow-professionals. Like Boycott, he was a limited player; unlike Boycott, he went about his business with the minimum of fuss. Of his 103 centuries, twelve were made in Tests and seven against Australia – only Hobbs, Hammond and Sutcliffe scored more against the traditional enemy. His average of nearly 49 against Australia was four points better than his career average, the kind of statistic appreciated by Herbert Sutcliffe, the man Edrich resembled most in terms of temperament. Edrich was one of the most unflappable batsmen ever seen in the Test Match arena; his ability to forget about the previous delivery and concentrate instead on the next one, was priceless. In the tightest of situations, the sturdy figure of John Edrich would steadfastly bend to the task – no matter how tight the bowling, how difficult the wicket, Edrich would sell his soul dearly. Fred Titmus neatly encapsulated the frustrations bowlers experienced at the hands of Edrich: 'I got fed up conceding eight runs in an over after beating him four times in it. He was the best hitter of the slightly bad ball I can remember.'

At the end of his career, Edrich would have won no prizes for displaying the aesthetic delights of batting. He was an even worse sight twenty years earlier. One day, a member of the Surrey first team encouraged the rest of the squad to walk over to the nets where the second team were practising. He said: 'Come and look at this bloke, I can't make out whether he's supposed to be a bowler or a wicket-keeper. He's certainly not a batsman.' John Edrich was in that net, trying his utmost to do himself justice: he looked stiff and mechanical, his footwork was minimal and he seemed to follow the ball hypnotically. The Surrey first-teamers had a quiet snigger at him for about a quarter of an hour, then the voice of the highly-respected Bernie Constable interrupted the levity: 'I don't know what you're all sniggering at, he hasn't missed a ball yet.' For the rest of his career, Edrich continued to confound his critics.

He was lucky enough to be born into a famous cricketing family. His cousin, Bill, had played with great distinction for Middlesex and England and cousins Geoff, Eric and Brian had all played county cricket. Bill remembers bowling at young John when he was about eleven, but apart from that, the illustrious quartet played no real part in his development. John's father was the early influence; he bowled at him on a concrete pitch on the family farm in Norfolk, in between the back-breaking stints of pulling up sugar beet that toughened up John's impressive physique. John was very disappointed that Norfolk was not a first-class county and he set out to prove himself elsewhere. Cousin Bill had suggested he try his luck with Middlesex, but John sensibly opted for Surrey, not least of all to duck allegations of nepotism at Lord's.

Andrew Sandham takes the major credit for Edrich's development once he arrived at the Oval. Sandham knew enough about batting to realise that the youngster's determination was of priceless value – he would tell him, 'you can't get hundreds sitting in the pavilion,' and the sturdy young man would take it all in. Today Edrich speaks with great fondness about Sandham: 'We had just one little skirmish early on when he threw down his cap in frustration at my efforts in the nets. I told him I had to work things out my own way and after that he was marvellous. He was very good at the mental side of batting – he told me it didn't matter how I got my runs, just to get them. Once I got to forty, I had to go on to get a hundred,' Sandham, an unselfish partner for the great Jack Hobbs, also instilled in Edrich the importance of team spirit, of playing for the side: 'He said I had to make things happen, to learn to judge quick singles to keep the score ticking over. At no stage must I play exclusively for myself.' One of the features of Edrich's career was his unselfishness – his readiness to take the strike against dangerous bowling or to support a free-scoring partner. He also learned how to increase the tempo at strategic moments, especially in limited-overs cricket. It is a happy coincidence that, of the four Surrey batsmen to score a hundred hundreds, two of them should play such important roles in the success of the others – Tom Hayward for Jack Hobbs and Andrew Sandham with John Edrich.

Under Sandham's guidance, Edrich made impressive strides, even if he was never to win any garlands for elegance. Edrich was happy with runs in the book and in his first game as an opener for Surrey, he scored a hundred in each innings at the start of the 1959 season. In the same summer, he came up against Fred Trueman and Frank Tyson, who both managed to break an Edrich finger in the space of a couple of months. An orthopaedic surgeon solved the problem during that winter by grafting a piece of leg bone into his hand to strengthen him against buffeting from fast bowlers. It was the start of Edrich's association with the pain barrier; no player in recent years has gone deeper into that barrier without flinching. For the rest of his career his name was synonymous with bravery and no fast bowler could rattle him. When Peter Pollock hit him a sickening blow on the head in 1965, he was back in the middle a week later, battling away against Les Jackson on a dangerous seamers' wicket, steeling himself to get in line. On the 1974–5 Australian tour, Edrich broke a hand on the unreliable Brisbane wicket, then picked up two broken ribs at Sydney. After being patched up, he insisted on going out again to bat, and remained unbeaten on 33 as England were swept aside. It was ten days before Edrich discovered he had broken two ribs; he felt discomfort sleeping and found difficulty in bending down in the gully. Many other players would have been only too pleased to accept they were badly injured to avoid facing Lillee and Thomson in that series. Edrich's attitude to pain was as simple and uncomplicated as his batting: 'I was brought up not to show pain. We'd be out in all weathers, working long hours at harvest time and, for me, playing cricket in the sunshine for my country was a huge bonus after working on a farm. That's what I call hard work.'

Hard work never frightened John Edrich. He grafted away in the nets to work out his selection of shots and settled on his armoury of strokes very early. He says he often got confused with the theorising of the older players. 'Far too many cricketers try to do the things they can't manage, they go out of their depth. I reckoned I could get away with about three main shots, plus the knack of being able to pick up ones and twos here and there. I learned how to use the pace of the ball against the quick bowlers, to glide it away off the face of the bat.' When Edrich reached 30,000 runs in his career, his colleague Robin Jackman kidded him that 28,000 of them had come through the third man area!

There was far more to his batting than just guiding the ball easily through the gap between gully and the slips. Those strong forearms enabled him to punch the ball from a short backlift; when established in his innings, Edrich was not averse to lofting a few sixes. He was a splendid driver square on the offside, from front and back foot. He was adroit at slackening the grip on his bat if the ball found the edge, so that it would invariably drop in front of the close fielders behind the wicket. For a fairly short man, he played the quick bowlers in front of his face remarkably well. Alan Knott modelled his defensive technique on Edrich: 'We were about the same height and I'd always admired the way he'd got his bat up so high to play the short-pitched stuff down at his feet. It might be heading for his chin, but he'd get the middle of the bat to it.' Against the spin bowlers, Edrich would advance a couple of paces and loft the ball over mid-on with a fully extended swing of the bat. Norman Gifford bowled for many years at Edrich and cannot remember ever thinking he would get him out: 'He was such a good worker of the ball. He would slide it away off a slightly open face and if I bowled at middle and leg, he'd find the gaps on the leg-side. On slow wickets, his enormous strength of forearm would help him play forcing shots.'

As a left-hander, he was vulnerable to the ball slanted across him by the right-arm bowler coming over the wicket, but Edrich worked out a method to combat the late swing. He played wicket to wicket, ignoring the slant of the ball if he was set to play defensively. If the ball was straight, then he would hit it; if he missed it, he would do so by a long way. Edrich only followed the ball that slanted away if he was either out of form and unsure of his position, or seeing the ball so well that he could afford to estimate the amount of late swing. David Brown opened the bowling for Warwickshire, to be frustrated regularly by the method of Edrich: 'Quite simply, he would play it if it was a bad ball; if it was a good ball, he'd contrive to miss it. It was all a matter of nerve. He had stacks of that, and he'd stand his ground and play down one line, instead of hopping around to follow the ball.'

Thus Edrich was an extremely frustrating man to bowl at, because he always looked as if you had a chance with him. Yet he played and missed so often that it could not just be a matter of luck; he had worked out the mechanics of batting with precision. His serene temperament allowed him to ignore the gestures and imprecations of the long-suffering bowler.

'I saw it as a direct challenge between me and the bowler. Cricket is like any other walk of life in that you are faced with a series of challenges. I relished them. Being brought up on a farm, I enjoyed being out in the sunshine, rather than sitting in the pavilion, feeling sorry for myself. I was lucky because I saw things in perspective, I learned that every day is a new day and that you can do absolutely nothing about what's gone before – either the previous day or the ball you've just missed.' Edrich learned to conceal his doubts under a façade of unflappability, but I learned from his former opening partner, Micky Stewart, that he was not always so phlegmatic. 'Sometimes, he'd come up to me at the end of the over and whisper, "What the bloody hell's going on?" He never let the bowler know he was worried.' Dennis Amiss, who opened for England with Edrich, remembers that he used to enjoy a little moan before getting down to the business of the day: 'He was a bit of a Job's Comforter. On tour he'd say something like: "Oh hell, we've got so-and-so tomorrow and he's really quick." On the way out to bat, he'd jib a little about something or other, but I think that was just to get it out of his system. Some players talk themselves out of an innings once they get out there, but John would love a scrap.'

Robin Jackman used to enjoy Edrich's phlegmatic attitude just before he went out to bat: 'We'd all be in the dressing-room and he'd have a little dig about something like the dark clouds, or that he didn't fancy a particular bowler. It would be a green wicket and we'd lost the toss and had to bat, with immense pressure obviously on John. As he went out, I'd say "good luck", and he'd smile and say, "We'll see what happens." He always seemed to be in charge mentally, he didn't appear to be frightened of failure, as most of us are.'

One innings at Headingly in 1965 demonstrated Edrich's rock-like temperament. He scored 310 not out against New Zealand in a truly remarkable manner; on average, he played and missed at one ball an over, but never lost an opportunity to hit the bad ball to the boundary. One could not imagine England making 300 on that pitch, never mind one batsman scoring that amount – it was grassy and every time the ball pitched, it left a lush green mark. New Zealand were well equipped with good seamers – Motz, Collinge and Taylor – and they all moved the ball around over two days. Batsmen of the class of Barber and Cowdrey were nonplussed by the tricky conditions, but Edrich kept banging the bowlers over long-on, thrashing them through the covers and whacking them past midwicket. Edrich whimsically points out that he stopped playing and missing after he passed the 200 mark, but agrees that he gave the bowlers heart failure. 'They obviously thought I'd get a touch eventually, but they didn't realise I was having a great season. I had played on excellent wickets in South Africa during the previous winter and I returned to England, bang in form. I had decided to hit the medium pacers straight back over their heads and I hit a lot of sixes that season. That day at Leeds, I never thought I'd get out.' That triple hundred was part of a sequence of scores by Edrich that were positively Bradmanesque: in nine innings, containing three not-outs, he scored 1,311 runs at an average of 218.5.

The following winter, Edrich scored two hundreds against Australia, to add to the one he made against them on his debut in 1964 at Lord's. David Brown recalls with a smile how baffled the Australian journalists were at Edrich's style of batting: 'The papers were full of opinions that Edrich must be dropped through lack of form, yet he was averaging sixty at the time. The Aussie players learned quicker than their writers that Edrich didn't worry too much about style.' Like a good team man, Edrich also agreed to bat number three to allow the dashing Bob Barber to partner Boycott; on his next tour of Australia, Edrich agreed to do the same because Brian Luckhurst was unhappy waiting to go into bat. Edrich typically made no fuss; 'I wasn't a great waiter either, but I reckoned I was lucky to get a game for England.' When Edrich partnered Boycott, they were an impressive pairing for England, averaging 55 for the first wicket.

By the time the Australians visited England in 1968, Edrich was at last an automatic choice after several disappointments. A series of brave innings in the West Indies against Hall and Griffith had cemented his place in the side; 554 runs in the 1968 series confirmed his worth and 648 runs on Illingworth's tour was further proof of his fondness for the Australian bowling. After that triumphant effort for Illingworth, things went rather flat for Edrich for the next three seasons. He was a little jaded after several English tours, the captaincy of Surrey distracted him somewhat and he took a little time to adapt to the demands of the Sunday League. He slipped into some bad habits in the three-day games that he picked up on Sunday and his record declined for a couple of seasons. By 1974, he was rejuvenated and the England selectors, mindful of his excellent temperament and the imminent tour of Australia, brought him back for the India series. At thirty-seven, he was appointed vice-captain of the Australian tour party and although the trip was a painful one for England, he achieved one personal ambition by captaining the side in the Fourth Test when Mike Denness stood down because of his poor form. Edrich averaged 43 in that series of broken limbs and ribs – a great effort against fast bowlers who were allowed to bowl up to four bouncers an over on dangerously uneven wickets.

With Boycott in exile, and Amiss in eclipse, Edrich was again invaluable for England. He made 175 against Australia in the Lord's Test of 1975 and this gave him greater pleasure than any of his other innings – 'It was great to see Lillee on his knees after the hammering we had taken from him a few months earlier.'

A year later and Edrich had become sickened of Test cricket. For some time, he had been concerned at the latitude allowed fast bowlers, as they intimidated batsmen with short-pitched deliveries which remained unchecked. One hour of batting in the Old Trafford Test against the West Indies convinced Edrich that it was time to go: he and Brian Close were subjected to a most vicious barrage of bouncers by Michael Holding, Andy Roberts and Wayne Daniel. It was a tribute to the remarkable courage of Close and Edrich that they survived on that Saturday night, but Edrich knew he was playing in his last Test: 'I wasn't scared, just frustrated that blatant intimidation was not curbed by the umpires. I couldn't see the point in standing out there for hours, waiting to get my head knocked off and wondering if I'd ever get a chance to score. I calculated that the amount of short-pitched bowling allowed me about six deliveries an hour to have a chance of runs. I was fed up of being a target man, with no hope of taking the fight to the bowlers. It was the last straw, after the way Lillee and Thomson had been allowed to bowl.'

Even though England needed his example and guts, Edrich would not be swayed from his decision; to him, cricket had to have some sort of purpose and he could see no sign of an overdue crackdown on intimidation. Such was his bravery and sheer competence that no one could impugn his motives. John Edrich never walked out on a fair challenge within the spirit of the game. At the age of thirty-nine, he saw no reason why he should waste his time doing something that bored him.

Two years later he was through with first-class cricket: it was important to him to go before he was pushed. A profitable business career loomed, so one chapter of his life closed with no regrets or sentimental rhetoric. 'I have to have challenge in life and cricket was no longer providing too many of them. You have to make the best of your life, rather than sitting around expecting things to happen to you.'

His contemporaries with Surrey and England speak of Edrich with immense respect. Robin Jackman praises his fielding: 'He'd try like a demon in the field if he was having a bad run with the bat. He had such strong hands – he took some blinding catches in the gully.' Jackman admires the way he'd graft for his runs: 'I've watched him score a hundred and that night, I couldn't remember a shot he'd played. But the runs were in the book, and he hadn't taken all day getting them.' Bob Willis calls Edrich 'my kind of batsman – brave, unselfish, he knew his limitations. And he didn't get out.' Derek Underwood says Edrich was more respected by the Australian players than Boycott, while Fred Titmus observes with amusement: 'All the quick bowlers fancied their chances against him – yet he got a hundred hundreds, most of them as an opener. It's a funny game, isn't it?' M.J.K.Smith says he was a less predictable player than Boycott, and therefore more value in limited-overs cricket, and David Brown positively drools at his solidity: 'If he came back today with a runner, he'd be better than the present lot who open for England. And he wouldn't wear the helmet.' Norman Gifford sums up the Edrich unflappability thus: 'He didn't play and miss – we bowlers didn't hit his bat.'

Edrich is perfectly happy to be just an occasional visitor now to first-class cricket. With a flourishing business and a secure family life, he is likely to lose touch with the game, apart from a few innings a year with the Old England XI. He chuckles at the memory of his hundredth century against Derbyshire – 'Eddie Barlow said he liked a glass of champers now and again, and he didn't mind staying on the field. The game was as dead as a doornail, you know.' He assesses the achievement shrewdly: 'It's not the hundredth one that counts, it's the previous 99.' Edrich is content to be in illustrious company and thinks fondly of Andrew Sandham, the kindly little coach who died in 1982. 'He and I soon realised I was no Cowdrey. I set out to be more like a Barrington. I realised that to play for England, I would need to perform to the absolute limit of my capabilities and Andrew helped me achieve that.'

Lovers of cricket genealogy will be interested to know that the Edrich production line which produced five county cricketers has not completely dried up. John's son, Jonathan, is impressing a few good judges at Millfield School. Like his father, he is a left-hand batsman. John wants him to learn from someone else, a role currently being fulfilled by the headmaster, Colin Atkinson, a good leg-spinner with Somerset in the 1960s. The thought of Edrich Junior handing out the same punishment to Atkinson's bowling as his father did in the past is a comforting one.

19

Glenn Turner

'I realised just in time that unless I put bat to ball
I'd have to change in another dressing room!'

In one way, Glenn Turner is unique among the batsmen in this book. He started as a stonewaller and then halfway through his career he became a dashing strokemaker. Others such as Hobbs, Hammond and Graveney learned to curb their aggression while remaining masterful all-round players, but Turner took a conscious decision to enjoy himself, to lose the tag of being 'New Zealand's Boycott' and play shots that he did not really know he possessed. The last fifty of his hundreds have been glorious, flowing affairs: if you walked on the ground at lunchtime, and discovered that Turner was undefeated, then he would certainly be near, or past the hundred mark. In recent years, only Vivian Richards and Ian Botham have rivalled him for destructive strokeplay, but, unlike the two Somerset batsmen, Turner had to contend with the new ball as an opening batsman.

At the end of the 1982 season, he left Worcestershire and county cricket for good, to return to New Zealand. The education of his children was becoming more and more important, and Turner wanted to consolidate his business interests and put down roots back home. He left behind warm memories of his uninhibited batting in recent years and an impressive list of achievements. He was the second non-English player to score a hundred hundreds, the first to reach that landmark with a triple century and, with 24,562 runs in the 1970s, he was the most prolific batsman in that decade. He is also the only batsman to score a thousand runs in May since the Second World War.

It was typical of Turner that he would become the first batsman to reach a century of centuries by scoring a hundred before lunch. He went on to make 311 not out that day against Warwickshire, and it could have been 400, such was his cool mastery of the bowling. That innings had all the hallmarks of the Turner of the last few seasons – calculated belligerence, perfect timing and a calm certainty that made him look invulnerable. His fellow New Zealander, Richard Hadlee, calls him 'the run-a-ball man', and one can understand what he means; when Turner was in the mood, it seemed impossible to set a field to thwart his variety of strokeplay. He won countless matches for Worcestershire by cool supervision of the run-chase. His ability to pace an innings was matchless. All this with a slight physique totally unsuited to buffeting from fast bowlers and long days in the middle; Turner amply demonstrated the value of timing to those who lacked the muscular stature of a Botham.

He was even more physically unimpressive almost twenty years ago when striving painfully to get a toehold on first-class cricket back home. He played for Otago while still at school, and all he had to offer was a good defence and a huge inferiority complex. In his first game, he opened the batting against Dick Motz, the experienced international seamer, and Turner remembers his embarrassment: 'He couldn't get me out and I didn't understand why. I was just a schoolboy, petrified at the occasion and he was bouncing me and I kept blocking him. I thought to myself, "Surely these guys are so much better than me, what am I doing here?" But they still couldn't get me out.' Motz was the first of many bowlers to know that feeling. Turner's immaculate defence had been the one thing to impress his school coach, Billy Ibadulla, the former Warwickshire player who was coaching that winter in New Zealand. Ibadulla recalls his first impressions: 'I watched this pale skinny little lad getting behind the line of the ball, trying desperately hard. All he could do was block it, but he wanted to do well, and that's half the battle. I thought that things could be grafted on to his immaculate defence. Above all, he wanted to learn, he asked intelligent questions.'

Ibadulla believed Turner could prosper in county cricket and he recommended him to his old county, Warwickshire. They asked him over for a trial, but then Turner came up against a slight problem – he had no money. With the determination that became a characteristic of his batting, he set out to earn his air fare. He worked on the night-shift at a bakery for the next eighteen months and scraped enough together for a one-way ticket. A couple of days before he left for England, he received a letter from Warwickshire, informing him that the club now had its quota of overseas players, and that he would be wasting his time coming over. Other teenagers would have cut their losses, shrugged their shoulders and blown the money on a week of hedonism somewhere. Not Turner:

he got on the plane, went to Birmingham and asked Warwickshire to arrange trials for him with other counties.

Turner's impact when he appeared in the Edgbaston nets was extraordinary. He batted against the Warwickshire first team and he stunned them by his reluctance to do anything but block the ball. David Brown – at that time an England opening bowler – recalls: 'All he did was hit the ball back to me. Mentally, he was on the back foot – defence was everything. I thought he hadn't a hope of playing county cricket.' Worcestershire must have seen something extra, because they were sufficiently impressed to take him on the staff. He made his debut for them in 1967 and proceeded to play a succession of dull, careworn innings that contrasted with the elegance of Graveney, the aggression of D'Oliveira and the dash of Headley. Yet he stayed in: Turner had to be prised out. He demonstrated that limpet tenacity for his country on the 1969 tour to England, carrying his bat for 43 at Lord's as Underwood devastated the rest in an all-out total of 131.

He was beginning to earn respect in the county game for an iron will, impenetrable defence and rocklike temperament, but no more than that. There seemed no reason to doubt that, in a couple more years, Glenn Turner would slip back to the mediocrity of New Zealand cricket, having earned nothing but the ire of countless, bored spectators. He was saved by the John Player League, that bane of classical batsmanship, the home of the slogger. Initially, Turner could not adapt to its forty-over demands: hard hitters like D'Oliveira would sit fretting in the dressing-room, waiting to get in while Turner studiously played the ball to mid-off and the fielding side hoped fondly he would not get out. The turning point came after one match against Northamptonshire when Turner took 34 overs to make 40, an incredible effort in hindsight. The Worcestershire players doled out a few home truths in a locked dressing-room: he was heading for oblivion unless he played some shots. The following Sunday, he made 60 against Essex, including five boundaries back over the bowler's head. Tom Graveney, his captain that day, recalls the turning point; 'He knew what was needed, yet after seven overs, we were seven for nought! He saw me pacing up and down, looking furious, and he made fifty in the next ten·overs, an amazing transformation. Before then everything about his batting had been basically right, but all he needed to do was unlock the key. After that he was a brilliant player in the Sunday League.' Turner remains the only man to top 6,000 runs in John Player cricket.

If Turner had discovered the secret of Sunday cricket, such freedom still eluded him in the longer games. In the West Indies on the 1971–2 tour, he scored four double hundreds – including two in Tests – but he became frustrated by the attrition of the performances. He says: 'At that time, New Zealand looked on a draw as a bonus, and my job was just to stay there and wear the bowlers down. I was beginning to realise there was more to batting than a watertight defence.' The strain of carrying a weak batting side began to tell on him during that tour: after a long innings, he found it almost impossible to sleep.

Turner decided to get his relaxation from the game itself. From 1973 onwards, he started to play with great freedom and an increasing amount of risk. Cricket became a pleasure, rather than a chore. On the 1973 New Zealand tour of England, he scored a thousand runs in May: he says he was lucky to bat against some friendly bowling on good wickets in favourable weather, but it remains a staggering effort from a man with a reputation as a stonewaller. To score a thousand runs in May you need to be a fast scorer as well as a fine player. Glenn Turner was now both. Typically, he thought little of the record, until he got near to it: 'I've never really bothered about statistical achievements, but in the end, everyone else was so wound up about it that I tried hard to do it. I reacted to the outside influences on me.' That season began and ended magnificently for Turner but, in between, he suffered failure in the three-Test series, averaging just 23. If he had made a reasonable contribution to the Trent Bridge Test, New Zealand would have triumphed, instead of going down by 38 runs – Turner made 20 in the match. He just could not get going; Geoff Arnold, his *bête noire*, troubled him as usual. Derek Underwood remembers Arnold's dominance over Turner in Tests: 'Geoff was the best new-ball opener in the world at that time, and Glenn was good enough to get a touch to his late swing.'

That Test series left its mark on Turner. It was not enough to average 62 for the overall tour, or 74 for Worcestershire at the season's end: he had failed in the vital games. Despite his great performances on tour, his reputation dipped in New Zealand; the whisper was that Turner had lost his old steel after deciding to enjoy his batting. That was the start of the downward spiral in his relationship with the New Zealand Board – Turner eventually became captain and resented having no say in the selection of the side. An articulate man with a clear, hard mind, Turner ruffled some feathers in the New Zealand dressing-room by dispensing a few lectures about the inferiority complexes. By 1977, he was disenchanted with the administrators in New Zealand. He decided to stay in Worcester during the winter of 1977 to prepare for his benefit season, thereby ruling himself out of three Tests against England. Turner was disenchanted with the new harshness creeping into Test cricket and he deplored the 'sledging' tactics of Ian Chappell's Australian team. A proud man, he felt a prophet without honour in his own country and wondered what he had to do to instil a sense of professionalism into the make-up of the Test side. He was also tired of continuous cricket throughout the year. 'I reasoned that I would make more money by playing county cricket for a fair amount of time, rather than burn myself out all the year round. I felt I owed it to Worcestershire to return fresh and eager every season and I could only do that by resting for a few months and getting away from cricket.' He confined himself to radio and television commentaries on New Zealand's home Tests, a decision that rankled with several players and officials. Not for the first time, Turner would not be swayed from a course of action he had mapped out.

Turner's absence from the Test arena in his last five years is the main reason why some of his opponents refuse to recognise him as a great player. Alan Knott told me: 'It's much easier taking on an overseas fast bowler in county cricket, when you can get runs at the other end. It's a different game when you have to battle through against four of them at the same time. Test cricket has changed drastically in the last few years – there are hardly any spinners and it's all about quick bowlers.' Bob Willis agrees and points out that Turner only scored one hundred against England. Willis feels that Turner had a bit of an obsession about fast bowlers taking an unfair advantage by indulging in too much short-pitched bowling, and concludes: 'There were few better players when the ball's not deviating off the wicket.' Sunil Gavaskar, on the other hand, feels that Turner would have been as prolific a Test run-scorer as himself and Geoffrey Boycott if he had stayed around.

For the last five seasons of his career in England, Turner had to live with the jibes that 'he doesn't fancy the quicks'. His short answer to that was that nobody does, that some batsmen show it and others do not. Turner's remarkable way of playing quick bowlers may have contributed to the generalisation – he perfected the knack of stepping away from his stumps and steering the ball over the slips, or smashing it through square cover with a flat bat. He decided to play championship matches like the John Player League. 'I was fed up of getting into line, playing correctly, taking the knocks and getting hardly any runs. Umpires have allowed quick bowlers to get away with murder in recent years, and I found the only way to combat the short-pitched stuff was to step back and take a free swing at it. Does that mean I'm scared? I've gone out and taken apart all the top fast bowlers at some stage in recent years – sometimes on wickets nowhere near as good as Test tracks – yet some feel I don't fancy it. I thought the early part of my career had proved I could stand and take the knocks.' There is no doubt that the protective helmet helped Turner's confidence; in common with most modern professionals, he had become increasingly worried about the uneven bounce on English wickets.

If Turner's method of combating the fast bowlers has been unique among modern batsmen, so was his grip on the bat. He wrapped his left hand round the top of the handle, so that the back of the left hand faced the bowler. That high grip enabled him to bring the bat down straight; the top hand guided and the bottom hand eased it through the shots. He used a very heavy bat and concentrated on a free flow of it with a powerful follow-through. The bat came up and down straight like a pendulum, which gave him great power from such a slight physique. He stroked the ball through a very wide arc and the variety of shots at his disposal enabled him to play a series of unpredictable strokes to areas containing no fielders. He had two shots that carried the Turner trademark – the 'flat bat' and the 'chip'. The first one was played off the front foot to a ball of any length that was in his driving area; he hit it square with an uninhibited swing of that heavy bat. It was a shot that drove slow left-arm bowlers to distraction, as he waited for the precise moment, then smashed it away with amazing power. Turner's mastery of the 'chip' shot was a boon in a run-chase when several fielders were positioned on the boundary. He would advance down the wicket, chip the ball over the inner ring and run two while the ball landed safely some way from the deep fielders. Other players would either be caught on the boundary or get frustrated as they smashed the ball direct to the inner ring: Turner's gift of timing was so sharp that he could play the shot as if he was chipping out of a bunker on the golf course. Norman Gifford remembers how the Turner of later years would approach early-season nets after his lay-off: 'All he worried about was getting his hands working properly on the bat. Lesser players would have to worry about timing and footwork but Glenn had those naturally. He worked at keeping his bottom hand out of his game, so that he followed through correctly and played straight. A light bat would wander in his hands and the heavier versions helped him with that swing like a pendulum.' Alan Ormrod, Turner's opening partner for many years at Worcester, had the fascination of observing his unique technique at close quarters:

'I've never known a player hit the ball so consistently in the drive area of the bat. That's why he hit so many boundaries. Unlike other great batsmen, he didn't need to pinch the strike with quick singles, he got enough boundaries to score quickly.'

That point was amply demonstrated at Swansea in 1977, when Turner's ability to score at will enabled him to create a new world record for monopolising a complete innings. He scored 141 not out in Worcestershire's total of 169 – 83.4% of the total score. No other player reached double figures and the other ten batsmen made fourteen scoring shots between them. Norman Gifford, second top scorer with seven, helped Turner add 57 for the ninth wicket – he remembers being staggered at the way Turner would play the ball and call for a run in the same instant. 'He was so much in command that he knew not only where the ball was going, but that no fielder was there. We'd got used to his dominance in recent years, but this was the first time he'd done it all the way through an innings.' Turner, with characteristic candour, says he had got drunk the night before with an old friend from New Zealand, and, as far as he was concerned, he was still a little groggy at the start of play. 'I concentrated harder as a result and soon the top order had gone and I was left with the tail. We had to avoid the follow-on, so the lower order just played for me and blocked it. The wicket wasn't a bad one and although I played well, the circumstances created the record.'

The circumstances were equally propitious on that sunlit Saturday in May 1982 when Turner reached his century of centuries in great style. He had long developed a fondness for the Warwickshire bowling – eleven championship hundreds in all – which partly stemmed from the disappointments of 1967, and the slow wicket for the Bank Holiday match at Worcester was ideal for him. He was due a big innings – his previous six knocks had totalled 45 runs – and he was getting fed up with everyone talking about the missing hundred. The day before the Warwickshire match, I reminded him that he averaged 71 against them in first-class cricket; he said he would try to get another 29 as well. The first ball of the innings – a short one from Willis – was pulled to the square leg boundary and in the next over he hit Gladstone Small for six over long-on. He reached his century in 114 minutes with a legside flick for three and celebrated with a gin and tonic at the wicket. Fittingly, the man who brought out the drink was Billy Ibadulla, his old coach, now a first-class umpire but without a game that day. Turner did not stop there; in 342 minutes, he made 311 not out and the declaration robbed him of the chance of toppling Macartney's record of 345 in a day in England. Not that Turner knew of the record, or even cared: 'I was pleased to reach the target stylishly, in fine weather, in front of my home crowd in a local derby. Somehow it all felt right.' Alan Ormrod who helped Turner add 291 that day, thought he was looking for a big score: 'He had that look in his eyes early on. I wasn't at all surprised that he made 300. Glenn's a very aggressive thinker and he can be very determined.' Dennis Amiss was sufficiently impressed by Turner's mastery that he sidled up to him after half-an-hour's batting and whispered, 'Bet you can't get 300 in a day.' Turner smiled and carried on looking at the pitch. Amiss says: 'Our lads weren't too pleased with me when I said that, but I didn't think he would carry on in the same vein. He just battered us to death, taking a fresh guard when he reached the next fifty. Eventually he was just coasting along.'

It is true that Warwickshire bowled badly that day on a flat wicket, but that cannot really detract from Turner's display. The only surprise is that he did not reach his hundred with a boundary. Turner pronounces himself 'fairly pleased' at attaining the landmark reached by just twenty other batsmen. A touch of the old inferiority complex surfaces when he says, 'It's one of the few ways a New Zealander can be compared to the top batsmen from other countries. Rugby will always be the sporting religion back home, so I had to gain some prestige elsewhere in the world. I suppose I was most pleased by the way I got the latter half of my hundreds, once I decided to stop boring the pants off myself and the spectators.'

By the 1982 season, Glenn Turner had worked out his game and his aspirations to precision. He still loved a challenge – he was disappointed that an appendix operation robbed him of scoring 2,000 runs, or bowing out with an average of over a hundred – but no longer was cricket the dominating force in his life. 'I used to hate getting out, I'd mope and sulk for hours. Suddenly I realised it was time to change the way I played, to cram more enjoyment into a shorter stay at the crease. I was cheesed off with my style of batting, so heaven knows about the poor spectators. It dawned on me that there were other things to do – write some letters, read a book, broaden my mind. Occupation of the crease for the sake of it is self-destructive, you end up knowing nothing but cricket.' Conversations I have enjoyed with Turner over the years confirm his diverse mind: he sets out to acquire an understanding of a topic and only then will he speak on it with authority and clarity of thought. I find his self-deprecating humour amusing – he still laughs at the comment of a Dunedin taxi-driver to a friend of his during the 1976 series against

India: 'That guy Turner, he's boring to watch!' First impressions take a long time to die. His appendix operation during the summer of 1982 gave Turner further comic potential – he was being whisked to the operating theatre at high speed and just before he passed out, the porter asked him for his autograph. 'Perhaps he thought he would be the last guy to get it before I snuffed it!' smiles Turner. 'It seemed a funny time to ask for my autograph.'

He has no time for negative cricket any more, a whimsical volte-face for anyone who saw him bat more than a decade ago. Turner feels that English county captains are killing the game by negative tactics and that Test cricket is even more spartan. He agreed to return to the Test fold in Australia early in 1983, but admitted the attraction of night cricket was the magnet. 'I can't have one or the other, so I played Test cricket to try something different. Playing under the lights in front of an emotional crowd was exciting.'

Glenn Turner is not the most popular man in cricket for a variety of reasons, some of them reflecting no credit on his detractors. He is very much his own man and will not compromise when he feels he is right – in this, he resembles another prolific opener who went into voluntary exile from the Test arena for a time in the 1970s. When Turner feels he has been wronged, he is not slow to say so, as the New Zealand Cricket Board have discovered. When Ian Chappell disconcerted him with a string of abuse during the Christchurch Test of 1974, Turner demanded a public apology: it never came. Turner's sense of fair play was also outraged by the West Indies team that came to New Zealand in 1980. From his seat in the commentary box, he was disgusted at the boorish behaviour of some of the West Indians as they crashed to defeat in the Dunedin Test. He also felt that they behaved unsportingly at certain post-match social functions. When Turner batted against them a few months later at Worcester, he tried to teach them a lesson in a bizarre way. He cross-batted every ball, made 45 off 24 deliveries, then deliberately sat on his wicket after playing a shot to mid-off. The West Indies team and the Worcester crowd were bewildered at Turner's antics, but he says he did it to show his contempt for cricketers who cannot take defeat in the proper manner, or handle themselves with dignity in public. 'I didn't want them to get any pleasure at all from my dismissal. I know it seems childish to everyone else, but I made my protest in the best way I knew.'

Glenn Turner is nothing if not positive, even when registering disapproval. His strength of character has seen him through enough

191

disappointments to hamper lesser men, while his strong beliefs have rubbed more than one influential person up the wrong way. Yet he was generally popular with the players because he stopped taking himself seriously; when dismissed, he would walk calmly back to the dressing-room and switch on to some other interest almost immediately. Cricket was only a part of his life and we can be grateful that he saw the advantages of enjoying his game: 'I realised just in time that unless I put bat to ball, I'd have to change in another dressing-room!'

Was he a great player? Was he too unorthodox to be ranked in the top bracket? That maverick streak offends the fastidious side of Mike Brearley's nature: 'I'd much rather see him fight it out like Boycott and show the youngsters how to play properly, rather than slogging it around.' John Emburey feels he was a great player – 'the best timer of the ball I've ever bowled at, and perfectly happy against the fast bowlers. He saw the ball so quickly from the hand, the sign of a great player.' Richard Hadlee, Turner's compatriot, makes the valid point that he was lucky to bat on good wickets at Worcester, but concedes that he could see off the new ball in about five overs, thereby altering the shape of an innings. David Brown, the Warwickshire manager, thinks he was unique – 'I've never seen anyone play so fluently with such an amazing grip. They way he picked up the ball was fantastic.'

When Tom Graveney retired at Worcester in 1970, he forecast in his farewell speech that Glenn Turner would be the batsman of the 1970s. Statistically, he was – but just seven Test centuries with an average of 45 does not suggest greatness. I believe he was a great player because of his adaptability – he turned his game upside down and worked out a unique method of batting against top-class bowlers from all over the world. A man who can play an innings like the Swansea one in 1977, a batsman who toyed with county attacks in recent years and dominated defensive field placings in limited-overs cricket – such a player should not have feared batting on a flat wicket in an Edgbaston Test or churning out the hundreds in Pakistan and India. He should not be denied his eminence just because he was brave enough to say that he found Test cricket boring. The challenge in Glenn Turner's batting marks him out for greatness. One of the qualifications of a great batsman is that on his day, the bowlers are helpless to stem the tide of fast runs. In recent years Turner always went out to bat with that aim in mind and he consistently succeeded. When necessary, his bat was as straight as Boycott's: the spectators who came to relish him must be delighted his aspirations went much higher than that.

20

Zaheer Abbas

'If only I could bat all the time'

If the year 1982 remains a memorable one for Glenn Turner, it will linger equally long in the memory of Zaheer Abbas. For Zaheer became the third non-English batsman to reach the target of a hundred centuries and, to his great delight, he managed it during a Test.

Earlier in the year, he had told me how much he envied Geoffrey Boycott's achievement of making his hundredth hundred in a Test Match; Zaheer admitted his sights were set on getting there in a Test against England, the opponents for whom he had the greatest respect. He cautiously agreed, too, that the Lord's Test would be perfect, as appropriate for Zaheer as Headingley was for Boycott in 1977. It was not to be. Zaheer had to wait until December, but at least he got there in a Test Match and – even more typically – with a double century.

He had started the Pakistan season on 96 hundreds, still fretting over missing out during the English summer. Due to a combination of illness, lack of opportunity and good English bowling during the Test series, Zaheer had managed only six first-class centuries during the 1982 English season. He was quickly into his stride in Pakistan: a hundred in each innings for the eighth time put him one ahead of Hammond and he came to Lahore and the First Test against India on 99 centuries. On a typically slow wicket, with only Kapil Dev bowling above medium pace, Zaheer resumed his love affair with the Indian bowlers. He had slaughtered them in 1978 and continued the carnage throughout this latest six-Test series, scoring three more hundreds.

Just after lunch on the second day, Zaheer came to his hundred. At the other end, the equally graceful Mohsin Khan had been comprehensively overshadowed by his dominant partner. Madan Lal provided the delivery that sent Zaheer into the record books for the umpteenth time and the stroke was one of his specialities – a flick off his pads through midwicket for three runs. Typically, he took a fresh guard and went on to score 215.

Such was his hunger for runs and fondness for batting records that he was on course for a hundred hundreds for several years – all of them made with charm and distinction. Zaheer was that precious commodity: an unashamed seeker of records, yet a lovely player incapable of being dull. Spectators of differing loyalties shelved their partiality when Zaheer Abbas came in to bat – they wanted him to stay in almost as much as he did.

He was the first Asian to reach the target, an achievement that meant a great deal to him: 'I have always wanted to be respected in the cricket world and by its historians in later years. I want to be like Don Bradman and Jack Hobbs, to be talked about long after I've finished.' Zaheer combined the typical Asian batting subtleties with the mental approach of a Boycott – he was a wristy, elegant player who flourished the bat on the follow-through. His on-side play was almost faultless and his driving square on the off-side a joy. Slow left-arm bowlers were meat and drink to him. Sunil Gavaskar remembers how he continually pierced Bishen Bedi's field of six men on the offside and Derek Underwood remembers suffering the same treatment with seven men on the off. Says Underwood: 'He's so wristy that he deflects the ball at the moment of impact and guides it into places where there are no fielders.' Underwood needs no reminding that Zaheer averaged 81 against Kent.

He was unashamedly a big-innings man, cashing in on flat wickets because he knew that on the next day the bowler would have the advantages and that his defence was not his strong point. He made 274 and 240 in Tests in England and if the wicket was lifeless on both occasions, nevertheless Zaheer batted charmingly. He made a conscious effort to carry on past the hundred mark, and admired Boycott for the same approach. Ten years of county cricket tightened up his technique; when he first played for Gloucestershire, he played away from his body rather too often and kept the slips and wicket-keepers occupied up and down the land when the ball seamed around. In recent years he got closer to the ball, and he could play down off his toes to gully with practised ease.

His fondness for long innings put a strain on his slight physique: during his two centuries at the Oval in 1976, he lay on the floor during the intervals to harbour his resources and then screwed himself up to a pitch of concentration just before going out again to the middle. It seemed to work – he scored 372 without being dimissed in the game. In an English summer, Zaheer will eat porridge and drink Guinness to build up his strength, in the process laying himself open to some ribald comments in the Gloucestershire dressing-room.

A friendly, soft-spoken man, Zaheer is grateful to his father for fuelling his ambition: 'One day he took me to the railway station at Karachi and pointed to all the sweating masses in the overcrowded third-class compartments. He then showed me the air-conditioned first-class compartments and told me that would be my reward if I worked hard. He didn't realise that I would get there by playing cricket!' He promised his father that he would give up cricket if he failed on the 1971 tour of England, but an innings of 274 in the First Test silenced the paternal doubts.

Since that day in June, 1971, Zaheer has scored six more hundreds for Pakistan, a poor return for such a prolific, talented player. His Test average (44) compares unfavourably with his overall one of 52; he averages just 17 against the West Indians, who have usually managed to rattle him with fast bowling. Zaheer agrees his Test record is a little disappointing and suggests that it is harder to score hundreds in Test cricket because of the predominance of fast bowling: 'It's very difficult to score against men like Holding, Croft and Willis. The standard of batting is deteriorating because of the quality of quick bowling.' Certainly Zaheer is at his weakest against authentic quick bowling, as Bob Willis agrees: 'On bouncy wickets, the place to bowl at him is his nose – he doesn't fancy that at all.' David Graveney, Zaheer's county captain, says he noticed a change in his attitude to fast men after he returned from two years with World Series Cricket: 'He had been subjected to high pace aimed purely at his body. His courage was tested and he had to learn to stick it out. As a result, certain bad habits have stayed – he showed more of his chest to the fast bowler in order to get quickly into a hooking position. Before Packer came along, he was never out of position between 1975 and 1977.'

If the wicket did not favour the fast bowlers, Zaheer was a very difficult man to contain. The England bowlers did very well to restrict him during the 1982 series on wickets that would normally suit Zaheer's style. The England captain, Bob Willis, worked out a way to block his shots: 'We had a square cover and a normal cover, just ten yards apart, to combat that wristy stroke of his that goes square. The place to bowl at him is about a foot outside his off-stump to encourage him to play his strokes. He rarely hits you to mid-off, he prefers to take his right leg back towards leg stump and work you squarer. He murders you if you bowl straight – he'll just whip you away through legside.' The plan worked and a frustrated Zaheer never got past 75, despite majestic displays in the county games.

It seems Zaheer Abbas will never achieve greatness. He still remains a slightly 'iffy' player: if batting was just a matter of playing slow bowlers and seamers, he would be supreme. Against sheer speed, he will always give the bowler a chance. For all that, he remains a splendid batsman, a man who thankfully eschewed the bored attitude of someone like Barry Richards and who never got tired of charming runs out of tired bowling. He tells me with feeling: 'If only I could bat all the time! You know, I hate fielding – someone once said to me, "we've come here to see you bat and not field", as I stood at third man. I couldn't help agreeing with him!' There speaks a batsman with the right priorities.

21

Dennis Amiss

'Once he gets in, he doesn't get out'
(Alan Knott)

When the gods were handing out unspectacular qualities like guts and determination they lingered long at the door of Dennis Leslie Amiss. If ever a man embodied the strength of character needed to score a hundred hundreds it is the affable Amiss. This is not to decry Amiss's talent: few contemporary English players can match his ability to churn out big scores elegantly and masterfully. Unlike Geoffrey Boycott, Amiss has always been an aesthetic pleasure, the master craftsman, at home in any form of cricket – technically adept to graft through troubled waters and yet ready to hit over the top in limited-overs games. Yet Dennis Amiss would never have lasted as long in the game if he had not abundantly possessed the ability to grit his teeth and fight his way through a host of crises.

On at least five occasions in his career, Dennis Amiss has considered packing up the game that he still loves deeply. He once had to face the wounding fact that his county did not wish to retain his services because of his association with Kerry Packer, and he has never really mastered the demands of short-pitched fast bowling. At no time could Amiss ever be considered the supreme batsmen in the Warwickshire side, with the likes of Rohan Kanhai and Alvin Kallicharran alongside him. He did not crave for pre-eminence at any stage: all he has ever wanted was to play cricket for Warwickshire, and for more than a quarter of a century he has been an object lesson in how to utilize natural ability. Dennis Amiss has been one of the supreme profession-als of cricket since the war and his stature has increased as the laurel wreaths have been modestly accepted.

Dennis was too diffident ever to dream of a century of centuries. As a boy, he set his ambitions at nothing higher than a place in the War-wickshire team. Born and bred in Birmingham, his father Vic was a good club cricketer and very supportive of his son's ambitions. The talent was obvious very early on, a fact confirmed by M.J.K.Smith, who was then Warwickshire's captain: 'He was always around the indoor nets at Edgbaston at the age of fourteen or so – and he looked a class above the other boys of his age. I never had any doubt that we would be taking him on the staff.' David Brown, Warwickshire's fast bowler and later the cricket manager, recalls the promise of the tyro: 'Even as a kid he looked a complete player. He used to score millions, even though he was tiny.'

Dennis was taken on the staff at Edgbaston at the age of fifteen, the youngest player ever to be chosen for the county. Initially he was out of his depth – a shy lad, ill at ease with the worldly elders on the staff. But thirty years on, Dennis agrees that those painful early days were typical of later challenges: 'I've never been at my best in a new situation. I need to come to terms with changes. Throughout my cricket career I've had to get used to reverses and come back with my teeth gritted.' Those are not chip-on-the-shoulder sentiments, more an acknowledgement of nerves from a man who is still naturally shy and modest. His achievements are more admirable because he admits to psychological defects. Some outstanding batsmen need to create an aura of invincibility, to let the bowler think his dismissal was simply and aberration. Not Amiss: his steely resolution does not preclude a gracious acceptance that he has been worked over by good bowling.

That mental strength was fostered early on at Edgbaston by one of the legendary figures in Warwickshire cricket, E.J.('Tiger')Smith. Now 'Tiger' had been the quintessential old-style professional cricketer: tough, independent-minded, with exacting standards of behaviour on and off the pitch. He recognized the talent of the young Amiss and proceeded to drum home the basics: 'He always told me that you learn to bat once you're past the century mark. 'Tiger' was great on mental attitude and making the best of your resources. I remember how he had me in tears when I couldn't play the ball off my legs, but he sorted me out.' In doing so, 'Tiger' contributed to a scene that has become part of Edgbaston folklore. Despairing of Dennis's attempts to play the ball off his legs, he took his bat and proceeded to order two bowlers to bowl at him. The first delivery was played beautifully away and Dennis was impressed. 'Tiger' then ordered the two bowlers (Roley Thompson and Jack Bannister, two fast-medium bowlers) to bowl at their fastest. They did not protest that 'Tiger' had no pads on, that he was over seventy and should beware the curse of failing eyesight and slowing reactions – they knew the old boy too well. The next ball cracked him on the shin and he went down like a sack of potatoes. Waving away the ministrations of Amiss, he got to his feet and rasped; 'It doesn't matter about hitting the ball – that's the way to play the shot.' Dennis still chuckles affectionately about 'Tiger' when he tells that story, but admits that the shot which has become his trademark – the clip through midwicket – was honed and perfected under the baleful eye of that hard old taskmaster.

Despite his obvious promise, things did not run too smoothly for Amiss during his apprenticeship. Those who have suffered at the hands of his erratic calling will not be surprised to learn that on his debut for the second team, he was run out without facing a ball and the same fate befell him in 1960, when he first batted for Warwickshire in a championship match. As Dennis struggled to establish himself in the harsh, unyielding world of county cricket, he developed a bit of a 'drawbridge mentality' about running between the wickets. Instinctively he would protect himself, with the result that on several occasions, senior players were run out when they should have been leading the chase for batting bonus points. More than once Dennis was involved in heated arguments in the dressing-room and the calming influence of M.J.K.Smith was vital. Smith also took the youngster's side as he grafted out in the middle, accumulating twenties and thirties when a more positive attitude was needed; the captain's view that 'He's got to learn somewhere', and Smith's standing in the side was such that grumblings among the senior players were at least muted.

Although Dennis was shedding his shyness layer by layer as the seasons slipped by, he did not feel fulfilled. He was not doing himself justice in county cricket, even though he drank in every morsel of advice that was offered, and toughened up mentally. By 1965, he was a capped player at the age of 22, yet the runs were not coming in any impressive amount. The lure of the family tyre business became stronger and stronger as his batting marked time. Dennis worked for his father's firm every winter (humping around enough tyres to develop those massive forearms that have benefitted his batting so much), and he had enough self-respect to get out of first-class cricket if he felt he could go no further. Then came a surprising development: he was picked for England. Today, it seems astonishing that a young man of little statistical prowess should be picked to bat against Hall, Griffith, Sobers and Gibbs when the likes of Cowdrey, Barrington, Mike Smith, Eric Russell and Jim Parks had been found wanting. Moreover, Amiss had never scored a championship hundred and his tally of first-class wickets (five) outnumbered his first-class hundreds (three). When former Test players decry modern batsmen from the comfort of the commentary box, they might care to ponder the case of Dennis Amiss in 1966. Predictably, the occasion was too much for Dennis – he was lbw to Wes Hall for 17 after batting 43 minutes, and with England winning by an innings, a second chance to impress had gone.

At least the selectors kept faith with him for a time. He was sent to Pakistan in the winter of 1966 with the England Under-25 side, averaging 61 and returning with a growing self-belief. Five hundreds and 1,850 runs in 1967 indicated his quality, but he could never get started whenever the call came from England. A total of 108 in five innings against India and Pakistan in the summer of 1967 suggested he was out of his depth. He was. 'I was just like Mike Gatting in later years,' he recalls, 'I chose all sorts of daft ways to get out, and underneath I felt completely overawed with all these famous players in the side. I didn't feel I belonged at all.' When Ken Barrington came down the wicket for a chat in the final Test against Pakistan, that was the first time Amiss had ever received any help from an England colleague. Worse was to follow in 1968: the dreaded 'pair' in the Old Trafford Test against Australia. He was close to tears as he walked back up the pavilion steps past unsympathetic members. 'My frame of mind contributed to my downfall. I just couldn't come to terms with the special pressures of Test cricket.' At the age of 25, it seemed that the tag 'former England player' would soon be used by the Fleet Street scribes.

He went back to county cricket to re-learn his trade, experimenting with his technique, steeling himself to churn out the big hundreds that would make the selectors notice him again. In 1971, he played in four Tests against Pakistan and India, with little success. At the twelfth time of asking he finally passed fifty in Tests, but there was no tangible evidence that Amiss had worked out how to play the game at the highest level. Every generation sees a talented batsman who dominates county cricket, but cannot go up a vital gear in Tests. Amiss seemed the latest contender for that stereotype.

In 1972, his cup of misery overflowed. He was dropped from the Warwickshire side. At that time the team oozed batting class. John Jameson, that punishing striker of the ball, opened the batting with John Whitehouse, elected Young Cricketer of the Year in 1971. The great Rohan Kanhai was first wicket down, followed by Alvin Kallicharran, the latest West Indian sensation: at number five, Mike

Smith, later to play for England again in 1972. The winter signing of Kallicharran meant there was no room for Amiss in the top five and the capture of Derryck Murray as wicket-keeper also stiffened the middle order. This would allow Warwickshire to select five bowlers and strengthen their push for the championship, which had faltered by just one point the previous year. Amiss could not be fitted in and Alan Smith, the captain that year, remembers the dilemma. 'Mike Smith, Rohan Kanhai and I sat in my car at Northampton debating who to drop for an important Benson and Hedges match. As the windows steamed up, it was clear it could only be Amiss. We needed the extra bowler.' Amiss was hurt and worried. He was now in his thirtieth year, with a wife and young daughter to support. Nine caps for England meant nothing when languishing in the second eleven. A prolonged spell of second eleven cricket would ruin him. A move to another county seemed the only solution. Then the gods smiled on him and frowned on John Whitehouse; the man in possession completely lost his touch and Amiss realized he could get back in the side if he volunteered to open. 'I had always thought of myself as a number four, but if it meant I could play for the first team again, I'd be happy to open. With so much limited-overs cricket around, there was always a good chance for the openers to get among the runs. I thought my technique would be good enough against the moving ball and I would battle through against the bouncers.' Warwickshire agreed to give it a trial: in his first innings as opener, Amiss scored 151 not out and Middlesex were beaten by ten wickets. Amiss stayed as opener for the rest of the season and made five hundreds, with an average of 55. Warwickshire won the county championship and a superb opening pair came together. John Jameson was the belligerent cavalier, Amiss the majestic strokemaker, with the patience to play second fiddle whenever the Muse of inspiration was upon Jameson. They were marvellous value for the next four seasons and today Jameson says, 'We just gelled together, as simple as that. Our basic differences as batsmen meant the bowlers always had to alter their line. As for running between the wickets, we tried to deal in boundaries and avoid too much anguish. We had known each other for years, so that there were no problems in getting used to each other as blokes.'

Amiss's new lease of life was noticed by the England selectors and they picked him for the Prudential one-day series against Australia at the end of the summer. A hundred at Old Trafford – partly exorcising the spectre of the 'pair' in 1968 – saw him selected for the England tour of India and Pakistan that winter. Tony Lewis, the captain, had no qualms about selecting Amiss, despite the vicissitudes of his career. 'I always thought he was a high-class player,' says Lewis. 'He got in ahead of me at the Oval in 1966, but I knew he was a better batsman than me and I could accept that. It's amusing to recall that Brian Close picked him ahead of me because he thought Dennis to be the better fielder! It wasn't exactly a clash of the giants in that department.' Certainly Dennis was never a fleet-footed athlete in the field (a slipped disc in his early days at Egbaston restricted his mobility), but he set his stall out to score heavily on that 1972–3 tour. Yet again he had to show his determination after a nightmare series in India. He averaged just fifteen against their great spinners and Tony Lewis had to drop him. 'Poor chap, he was in a dreadful state against Bedi, Chandra and co. I should have shown more courage and stuck with him, but I found myself wondering if I had only seen him play well at Edgbaston on flat wickets.' Characteristically Amiss practised his way back into the groove. At the deserted Brabourne Stadium in Bombay, he took a net against Bishen Bedi, Venkat and Abid Ali and asked them to simulate match conditions and to appeal every time they thought they had him. To the eternal credit of the Indian bowlers, they did just that and Amiss learned how to combat the turning ball. When he returned four years later to India, he showed his gratitude by averaging 52 in the series!

When the Pakistan leg of the tour started, Amiss was far happier. On the flat wickets, he scored two hundreds and a 99 in three Tests. 'At long last, I felt I had arrived. I'd come through the torments and honestly believed I could bat at Test level.' He was almost thirty before he scored his first Test hundred, but he was right: he was now an England player and the next eighteen months were golden ones for him. Back home in 1973, he showed his soaring self-confidence by running out one Geoffrey Boycott. It came in the Trent Bridge Test against New Zealand, when Amiss sent back Boycott after a mix-up over a second run. Boycott hurled a few expletives in Amiss's direction and stalked back to the pavilion. Amiss made 138 not out and Boycott did not speak to him for the rest of the game. When the sides reassembled for the next Test, the England opening batsmen were still ignoring each other and it took the good offices of the England captain Ray Illingworth to heal the rift. Amiss smiles at the memory of the day when he turned his back on Boycott. 'When I went off to the Test, Mike Smith told me there were many ways I could get out, but getting run out by Boycott shouldn't be one of them. I wasn't going to be the sacrificial lamb, especially as I shouted 'No!' to the second run and he kept on coming.' Boycott had met his match in the self-preservation stakes, and they settled down to a rewarding year as England openers.

They were among the few successes on England's tour to the West Indies in 1973–4, a series that England somehow managed to square, even though outplayed for much of the time. With three hundreds in the series, Amiss was outstanding. At Sabina Park he played the innings that all his England contemporaries refer to within five minutes of his name being mentioned. England had to bat the best part of two days in enervating heat and humidity to avoid defeat – it was as simple, or as daunting, as that. Dennis Amiss managed to do just that, batting 9½ hours for 262 not out. He was just the man for the situation; by this time, he loved the tensions associated with Test cricket and his confidence enabled him to take on the West Indians on equal terms. Yet he might not have lasted so long if his running between the wickets had been sounder. By the end of the penultimate day, England were 258 for 6, just 28 runs ahead. Amiss was unbeaten with a hundred, but he had also run out Frank Hayes and Alan Knott. 'I was at fault each time and I dreaded the reception from the dressing-room when I got back. I realised it was now my responsibility to stay there the next day.' Alan Knott, his room-mate, woke him up the next morning with, 'Come on, you've got to bat all day!' and he did not let him down. John Jameson recalls, 'He came in at tea-time with his eyes sunken in his cheeks, looking totally drained. We poured a brandy down his throat, pointed to the middle and pushed him out there again. Even in that state, he was keen to keep batting.' The Test was saved and back home in Birmingham, the *Evening Mail* reflected the current general election fever with pardonable parochial pride with the headline, 'Amiss for Prime Minister!'

By the time Dennis arrived in Australia later that year, he was acknowledged to be one of the world's best batsmen. He was to finish just short of the record for Test runs in a calendar year and, in the absence of Boycott, the Amiss scalp was the prized one for the Australians. Every one of the English batsmen was scarred by subsequent events, as they ran into Lillee and Thomson bowling frighteningly fast on green, under-prepared pitches. The series was lost 4–1 and Amiss found it a traumatic experience. He was stunned to receive a volley of foul-mouthed abuse from Lillee after steering him through the slips and admits that Lillee established a psychological stranglehold over him. 'All the sledging would not have bothered me if I had been playing well, but I wasn't. I kept worrying about my technique – why was he getting me out? It all got to me and I was totally unbalanced.' Lillee dismissed him three times in a row for nought – including two in the first over at Adelaide – and Amiss's decline was pathetic to watch. 'I got to the situation where I walked out to the middle, knowing it was virtually a waste of time carrying a bat. The physical and verbal intimidation wore me down.' Later Dennis came to appreciate that he was undone by fast bowling of the highest class. Lillee subsequently paid tribute to Amiss, saying that he was a good enough player to get a touch to some devastating deliveries, and the wicket-keeper Rodney Marsh said: 'We never gave him a chance, everything he touched we caught.' Alan Knott was on that tour and remembers how Amiss was scarred. 'He shouldn't have let it get to him, because he was our best player and the Aussies bowled wonderfully well at him.' Reasonably, Knott points out that great players like Denis Compton (Australia 1950–51) and Peter May (South Africa 1956–7) had nightmare series, but came back impressively – whereas Amiss was written off far too soon after such a frightening experience. Derek Underwood agrees: 'He just seemed to play a little half-cock – neither back nor forward – and the late movement and bounce did for him. But it was only a phase, he would have come through it. Dennis always did, you know.'

The Australians still had the upper hand on Amiss in 1975, when they toured England: a total of 19 runs in four innings meant it was kinder to send him back to county cricket for a rehabilitatory spell. He was beginning to look more and more uneasy against the short-pitched ball, and when Michael Holding hit him on the head in May 1976, it looked as if he would have to bow out of a game that was becoming increasingly harder. 'Today it isn't unusual to see someone hit on the head because we all wear helmets, but ten years ago, it was very embarrassing. What made it worse was that I had turned my head away from the delivery and it hit me on the back of the head. I've still got the lump today to remind me of my lowest ebb.' There was no question of Amiss's suitability to combat the pace of the West Indians; even in county cricket he looked terrible. David Brown, Warwickshire's captain at that time, says, 'He was bobbing and weaving against medium-pacers like Ken Higgs. He couldn't stand still and fight it out by orthodox means. His nerve had gone.' Amiss acknowledges that if he had not survived that awful period, he would have retired that season, at the age of thirty-three. Always the theorist, he worked out a two-eyed stance to enable him to combat the pace bowlers by keeping his eyes on the ball. He tried the new stance against Sussex and heard Tony Greig shout to his fast bowler, John Snow: 'Okay Snowy, let him have it!' Amiss withstood the bouncers and got a brave eighty. Greig – by now the captain of England – was impressed and decided he wanted Amiss back in the England team. He rang Jill, Dennis's wife, and asked about his frame of mind. Could he fight it out again with the quicks aiming for the upper parts of his body, not the stumps? The pace barrage that summer had even worn down the likes of John Edrich and Brian Close. When Amiss was contacted, he said he could do it: the new stance gave him time to get onto the back foot and watch the ball. He wanted to play.

If Sabina Park showed Amiss's superb concentration, then the Oval 1976 demonstrated the man's guts. He knew he looked very odd as he moved onto the back foot from an exaggerated two-eyed stance. He knew that in moving across his wicket, he was leaving his leg stump exposed. He admits he was very lucky early on, as Andy Roberts beat him with some superb outswingers. Yet he stuck it out, and scored 203 of the bravest runs imaginable, as England was swept away by some remarkable bowling from Michael Holding. 'I never thought I'd get out, once I got through that tricky early stage. From a professional point of view I was delighted to make such a good comeback, and it restored some of my confidence against the quicks. But I wished I'd scored that double hundred by playing properly, using my normal technique.' There speaks a craftsman.

With his Test career re-established, Dennis then took the decision that effectively ended it at the age of 34. He signed for Kerry Packer's World Series Cricket in the summer of 1977, a brand of cricket that set itself on an inevitable collision course with the established version. Dennis's involvement was a more rational one than the early crop of signatories: he had an extra month in which he watched the ferment raging in the game and heard about all the grim penalties facing the Packer players. Finally he signed during the one-day international series against the Australians. 'It was my own decision. When I came home and told Jill, she said, "Are you sure about this?" She was more cautious than me about it, but I was a little disillusioned. I felt we deserved better rewards for the incredible pressures of Test cricket. There was a lot of talk about Boycott coming back for England and I thought "he's after my place". Apart from all that, there was my ego. When I first looked at the list, I thought, "Why haven't they asked me, aren't I good enough?" I wanted to be considered among the élite. And

I was also attracted by the promise that the wives of Packer players could come on the tour with them.'

That decision plunged Dennis into the unhappiest period of his life. It lasted two years and the divisions at Edgbaston hurt him deeply. He accepts that passions were bound to be fanned at a county club which was an acknowledged supporter of the Establishment line at Lord's. He always understood that his England career would be in abeyance during the Packer period, but could not see why Warwickshire felt they could dispense with his services. That was the decision reached by the club in 1978: he would not be retained because of his involvement with World Series Cricket. This despite Amiss's continuing prowess with the bat – he was the only man to score 2,000 first-class runs that summer. The Warwickshire dressing-room was not a harmonious place in 1978: for good or ill, the rest of the players were toeing the traditionalist line that Packer was harming Test and county cricket, while Amiss had given up trying to change their minds. On my visits to the dressing-room that summer, a sad sight would greet me – Amiss on his own, writing letters on World Series notepaper while the rest of the team watched the game at the far end of the viewing area. The previous summer, the captain David Brown had taken the unprecedented step of moving Alvin Kallicharran into his home in the Worcestershire countryside to get away from the threat of Packer. Kallicharran had originally signed for Packer, then changed his mind, much to Warwickshire's relief. One day, Packer rang the Warwickshire dressing-room at Chesterfield and asked to speak to Dennis Amiss. He told Amiss that he wanted to talk to Kallicharran and Amiss conveyed that message. The rest of the players construed that as harassment by Amiss on behalf of Packer, and that led to the ridiculous sight of the little West Indian being escorted by hulking Warwickshire fast bowlers whenever he stepped out of the dressing-room. Amiss says, 'It was ridiculous to suggest that I was hassling Kalli. All I ever did was pass on the message from Kerry Packer. The whole thing was blown hopelessly out of context and I kept out of everyone's way after that.'

Yet the mythology of Chesterfield lingered on and, the following summer, the Warwickshire players stated in August that they felt Amiss should go in the wider interests of the game. The club then announced that Amiss was playing his last season. For a time affairs at Edgbaston resembled Yorkshire during one of its periodic bouts of blood-letting. There were calls for a special general meeting and assurances from the club that the decision was in the best interests of English cricket. Meanwhile Dennis Amiss soldiered on at the wicket: 'I realized the best thing to do was stay out there as long as possible, to get away from all the squabbling. It was coming all the way down from Lord's to the players and I was very hurt at their attitude.'

Today David Brown admits he and the players over-reacted. 'I was also chairman of the Cricketers' Association at that time and that body felt it was vital to preserve Test cricket, because that is where a good proportion of the average county player gets his wages from. Dennis was also very stubborn – I remember a big shouting match at his house. It was a very sad time.' Luckily the Cricketers' Association played a crucial part in the discussions that enabled Amiss to return to Warwickshire in 1979. The Association Executive talked to Lynton Taylor of World Series Cricket, who confirmed that Packer would be disposed to settle his dispute with the International Cricket Conference if Amiss was offered a new contract. In the eyes of Packer, Amiss had been the only player victimised by his county club and he had always promised to protect his players. At the same time Warwickshire had learned that an accommodation was imminent between WSC and ICC and when the tape of Taylor's phone conversation was played to some Edgbaston officials, it was clear that a rapprochement between club and player was possible. Over Easter, Amiss announced he would accept a new contract and he paid tribute to the Association's role in the peace formula – but it was a very close run thing. 'I just wasn't sure the slate could be wiped clean after all the trouble of the previous two years. I was on the point of packing it all in. I only wanted to play for Warwickshire. I even took up golf as a substitute in case I wasn't going to play cricket any more.'

Many of Dennis's friends in the game are convinced that his Packer involvement thwarted his chances of an England return once everybody was available for selection again in 1979. Certainly England caps have gone to inferior players and his fielding no doubt told against him. Alan Knott says, 'Around the county circuit, the pros all say that Dennis should have played a hundred Tests.' Mike Smith, hardly a Packer disciple, agrees: 'I've no idea why he didn't play after Packer's peace, he was in a class above several other selections.' Keith Fletcher fought hard for Dennis's inclusion on the 1981–2 tour to India that he captained – he was outvoted because the average age of the tour party would have risen. Derek Underwood went on that tour and says, 'Dennis would have made a stack of runs out there, and in good time as well. He was as much in his pomp around that time as anyone.' Bob

Willis would certainly have asked for Amiss if he had been England captain before 1982, by which time he had been banned again from Test cricket. The South African Breweries tour was an obvious attraction to Amiss, even though he knew a Test ban would follow. 'I hadn't been picked since 1977 for various reasons and I had nothing to lose. It was a much simpler equation than signing for Packer.'

So Dennis Amiss has not been seen on a Test pitch since the day in July 1977 when he cracked a ball from Kerry O'Keefe to the offside boundary to earn England a nine-wicket victory at Old Trafford. As he anticipated, Geoffrey Boycott deigned to return to the fray at Trent Bridge and out went Amiss. An average of 46 underlines his class at Test level, despite those dreadful early forays. His biggest regret is his record against Australia – an average of 15 in eleven Tests, compared with one of 70 in ten Tests against the West Indians. 'Great players don't have the kind of problems I had against the Aussies' he says – and it is hard to disagree. He was unlucky to come up against Lillee, Thomson and Walker in their prime, on wickets that did not suit an essentially front foot player like Amiss. He does not favour the hook or the pull shots and his cut is more of a dab than an authentic rasping shot. The glory of his offside play was never likely to flourish against fast bowlers intent on intimidation on unreliable pitches. Yet the Australians rated him highly; they thought he should have been spared the new ball and batted at number three or four. Alan Knott agrees: 'There was always the chance that Dennis would be done by a great delivery with the new ball and he was too good a player to sacrifice early on. When the score is 200 for 2 and Dennis walks in, you think, "Oh dear, we're in for some hard work".' As Derek Underwood puts it, 'He's the gaffer when he gets in. He just loves to churn out the big scores. He's the greatest thinker and theorist on the game I've known. And no Englishman today plays me better on a wicket that's helping me.' The match at Gravesend in 1970 convinced Underwood of Amiss's talent on a bad wicket. He took 14 wickets in the match and Amiss made a superb 91 until Underwood stuck out a hand to an Amiss drive and was astonished to see the ball lodge there! 'Dennis plays so late that he doesn't commit himself on bad wickets,' says Underwood. 'He's a wonderful leaver of the ball, with enormous concentration. Those big forearms are handy when he wants to ping you away if you over-pitch slightly. If there's a bloke I'd pick to bat for my life, it's Dennis.' Alan Smith, former captain of Warwickshire and now a Test selector, points out that Amiss's manipulation of the bat is very deft for such a powerful man. 'He's the best I've seen for adjusting his hands with smallish movements to combat the turning ball. He is a model for any young batsman.'

Dennis admits he has been very lucky to play at Edgbaston: 'When you're in a bad trot, it's not a bad place to come back to, and sort out what's wrong.' He agrees that his constant fiddling around with his technique has driven his team-mates to despair over the years, 'especially as I always come back to the original format after the experiments. But it motivates me to fiddle around, it keeps me interested in the game. Apart from batting, I have been a pretty ordinary cricketer. It's the one thing I do well, so I keep telling myself to get more than nought, then the target is fifty and after that, a hundred.' Significantly, eight of his eleven Test hundreds were 150 and more: Amiss has always been a big innings man. His technique is so sound that he can score very fast in limited-overs matches, without slogging. Unlike many modern batsman, he does not try to play 'inside out'; he adopts his normal, sound method and plays 'through the V', with a penchant for skimming sixes. The years spent lugging around tyres in the sixties helped him dominate by sheer power when slow pitches frustrated the 'touch' players. Many players of Dennis's experience do not like the limited-over games – all that dashing around, those frantic finishes – but he loves it. 'There's nothing better than hitting it over the top and nudging quick singles to disconcert the bowler.' His team-mates would say that his calling for singles disconcerts everyone in his own dressing-room rather than the bowler and the grapevine is full of Amiss stories. When he ran out Gordon Lord for 199 against Yorkshire in 1985, it seemed he had lost none of his touch. 'It was my fault, I know. I called him for a quick single behind square leg and he was run out at the bowler's end. Gordon hesitated when I called, and I admit it was a sharp run. The trouble is, I can see a single, but I'm not sure about my partners.' It is a tribute to Dennis's genial nature that none of his colleagues ever believe he runs people out deliberately. His popularity has survived sterner tests than that.

I first alerted Dennis to the possibility of a century of centuries around 1980. At that stage he had made about 75 hundreds and he said there wasn't a hope of it. I could tell, however, that he was intrigued by the prospect, and by 1983, he had changed his attitude to 'Perhaps if they let me bat with a runner all the time!' By 1984, he was sufficiently committed to be annoyed at a baffling sequence of innings that ended in the eighties rather than past the century mark. A testimonial season in

1985 gave him a further incentive to keep going – a considerable feat for a man in his forties, in a sport where athleticism gets more important – and he approached the 1986 season with a degree of self-denial that astonished his friends and team-mates. Dennis has always liked a sociable drink and an enjoyable meal, yet with the new season more than a month away, he was to be found sipping Perrier water – and contemplating where he could find another four centuries.

Dennis's professionalism was soon rewarded when he made his 97th century at the end of April against Essex. By mid-June he had added two more – both splendid efforts against Gloucestershire and Glamorgan. He was playing so fluently that another century seemed imminent: yet he had to wait a further six weeks and fifteen innings. The runs had not dried up – he made three 50s and averaged 31 between the 99th and the 100th hundred – yet he was starting to fret as the weeks slipped away.

Finally, on July 29th, in front of his home crowd, Dennis got there. He had Clive Lloyd to thank. The match against Lancashire was drifting to a draw when Amiss (not out 64) asked the opposition captain to stay out in the middle a while longer. Dennis promised that he would slog the runs and – the clincher – that copious bottles of champagne were available if the deed were done. In the next five overs he made 37. John Abrahams, plying his occasional off-spin, told him when he reached 99, 'short outside the off-stump and it's yours', and a delicate dab backward of point brought him two precious runs.

Dennis viewed his membership of the club of 21 with typical modesty: 'There are many great players in that list and I'm pleased to know I'm now in the supporting cast.' It sums up the man. Dennis Amiss has always loved the game too much to over-estimate his own importance.

Bibliography

Books

Amiss, Dennis: *In Search of Runs* (Stanley Paul, 1976)
Arlott, John: *Cricket: The Great Ones* (Pelham, 1968)
Arlott, John: *Jack Hobbs* (John Murray, 1981)
Bailey, Trevor: *The Greatest of My Time* (Eyre and Spottiswoode, 1968)
Barker, Ralph: *The Cricketing Family Edrich* (Pelham, 1976)
Barker, Ralph: *Innings of a Lifetime* (Collins, 1982)
Bedser, Alec: *Cricket Choice* (Pelham, 1981)
Boycott, Geoffrey: *Opening Up* (Arthur Baker, 1980)
Callaghan, John: *Boycott: A Cricketing Legend* (Pelham, 1982)
Cardus, Neville: *Cardus on Cricket* (Souvenir Press, 1977)
Cardus, Neville: *Cardus in the Covers* (Souvenir Press, 1978)
Cardus, Neville: *Play Resumed with Cardus* (Souvenir Press, 1979)
Cardus, Neville: *A Fourth Innings With Cardus* (Souvenir Press, 1981)
Close, Brian: *I Don't Bruise Easily* (Macdonald and Janes, 1978)
Compton, Denis; Edrich, Bill: *Cricket and All That* (Pelham, 1978)
Compton, Denis: *Compton on Cricketers Past and Present* (Cassell, 1980)
Cowdrey, Colin: *M.C.C.: The Autobiography of a Cricketer* (Hodder & Stoughton, 1976)
Dexter, Ted: *From Bradman to Boycott* (Queen Anne Press, 1981)
Fingleton, Jack: *Fingleton on Cricket* (Collins, 1973)
Fingleton, Jack: *Batting From Memory* (Collins, 1981)
Foot, David: *From Grace to Botham* (Redcliffe Press, 1980)
Frith, David: *The Golden Age of Cricket* (Lutterworth Press, 1978)
Gibson, Alan: *The Cricket Captains of England* (Cassell, 1978)
Grace, W.G: *Cricketing Reminiscences and Personal Recollections* (Hambledon Press, 1980)
Leveson-Gower, Sir Henry: *Off and on the Field* (Stanley Paul, 1953)
Martin-Jenkins, Christopher: *The Complete Who's Who of Test Cricketers* (Orbis, 1980)
Mason, Ronald: *Batsman's Paradise* (Hollis and Carter, 1955)
Mason, Ronald: *Walter Hammond* (Hollis and Carter, 1968)
Mason, Ronald: *Jack Hobbs* (Hollis and Carter, 1960)
Phelps, Gilbert: Editor *Arlott and Trueman on Cricket* (BBC, 1977)
Peebles, Ian: *Spinner's Yarn* (Collins, 1973)

Peebles, Ian: *Patsy Hendren: The Cricketer and his Times* (Macmillan, 1968)

Peebles, Ian: *Frank Woolley: The Pride of Kent* (Hutchinson, 1968)

Robertson-Glasgow, R.C: *46 Not Out* (Hollis & Carter, 1947)

Root, Fred: *A Cricket Pro's Lot* (Arnold, 1937)

Rose, Gordon: *The Surrey Story* (Stanley Paul, 1957)

Rosenwater, Irving: *Sir Donald Bradman* (Batsford, 1978)

Sewell, E.H.D: *Well Hit Sir!* (Stanley Paul, 1947)

Streeton, Richard: *P.G.H.Fender – a Biography* (Faber & Faber, 1981)

Sutcliffe, Herbert: *For England and Yorkshire* (Arnold, 1931)

Thompson, A.A: *Cricket: The Golden Ages* (Stanley Paul, 1961)

Walker, Peter: *Cricket Conversations* (Pelham, 1978)

Warner, Oliver: *Frank Woolley* (Phoenix House, 1962)

Journals

Wisden Cricketer's Almanack
Playfair Cricket Monthly
The Cricketer
Wisden Cricket Monthly

Statistical Appendix

BY ROBERT BROOKE

Association of Cricket Statisticians

(These statistics go up to the end of the 1985 English season, with the exception of Denis Amiss, whose career record is taken up to his hundredth hundred.)

THE INNINGS NEEDED

D.G.Bradman	295
D.C.S.Compton	552
L.Hutton	619
G.Boycott	645
Zaheer Abbas	658
W.R.Hammond	679
H.Sutcliffe	700
E.H.Hendren	740
G.M.Turner	779
J.B.Hobbs	821
A.Sandham	871
C.P.Mead	892
L.E.G.Ames	915
G.E.Tyldesley	919
T.W.Graveney	940
J.H.Edrich	945
F.E.Woolley	1,031
M.C.Cowdrey	1,035
T.W.Hayward	1,076
D.L.Amiss	1,081
W.G.Grace	1,113

The career figures for W.G.Grace are still a matter of dispute. The Association of Cricket Statisticians maintains that certain matches in which Grace played cannot be regarded as first-class – the runs and wickets from the games were not included in the first-class career records of any other players, either at the time or subsequently.

Having studied again this question closely I feel there is no justification to delete the matches previously deleted by the ACS which reduce W.G.Grace's total number of centuries. The games in question were:

ELEVEN GENTLEMEN WHO VISITED CANADA –v– 14 GENTLEMEN OF MCC, Lord's, July 1873. The first named team consisted of players who had toured Canada during 1872; all were of 'first-class' standing in contemporary cricket. The opposition were also first-class players though not so distinguished as the other team. It was not uncommon to try and even up two teams by giving one side extra players and it happened in subsequent seasons in matches accepted by everyone (even ACS diehards) as 'first-class'. So there are precedents which can be quoted. Grace scored 152 and 5 in this match, which was widely reported in the contemporary press and in Annuals and given *more* importance than many other obviously first-class matches.

GLOUCESTERSHIRE –v– SOMERSET at Clifton, August 11, 12, 1879. Although Somerset were not generally playing against first-class opposition at this time their side seems as strong on paper as it was in the early 1880s when they were accepted into the first-class ranks. In *Wisden* the game was treated with as much importance as any of Gloucestershire's inter-county matches against accepted first-class sides and there seems no reason whatsoever that it cannot be included. Grace scored 113 in his only innings.

A third game for which I can now find no justification for its omission is Gloucestershire v MCC at Lord's in 1868. Neither team was particularly strong but Gloucestershire did include W.G., E.M. and G.F.Grace and it seems to have been played under first-class conditions. W.G.Grace scored 24 and 13.

These additions bring Grace's career total of centuries back to the figure which was accepted for many years and restore to their old glory and relevance the celebrations in 1895 when W.G. scored his 288 v Somerset to complete his 100th century.

William Gilbert Grace

Born Downend, Bristol 18.7.1848; Died Mottingham, Kent 23.10.1915.

1st 100: 224* England –v– Surrey, The Oval 1866: Age 18 years, 12 days

100th: 288 Gloucs –v– Somerset, Bristol 1895: Age 46 years, 304 days

CAREER RECORD AT TIME OF COMPLETING 100TH HUNDRED

1,113 Innings   41,863 Runs   40.68 Average

SOME STATISTICAL FEATS

First batsman to score 100 centuries in a first-class career. First batsman to score 20,000, 30,000, 40,000 and 50,000 first-class runs. Highest score 344, MCC –v– Kent, Canterbury 1876; First first-class score of 300: Remained best first-class until A.C.MacLaren's 424 in 1895: Still the highest against Kent, and the highest for MCC.

Two scores of over 300 in 1876 – still unequalled in an English season. 318* –v– Yorkshire at Cheltenham in 1876: still best score for Gloucs. 301 for Gloucs –v– Sussex, Bristol 1896. Age 48 years, 17 days. Remains the oldest player to score triple century.

1,000 Runs in season 28 times – record until equalled by F.E.Woolley in 1938. 2,739 runs in 1871: First aggregate of more than 2,000 runs in an English season. Remained a record until 1896. Average of 78.26 in 1871 – first of more than 70 for a first-class season. 1,000 runs in May 1895 – first instance; reached it on May 30, a record until 1927 when beaten by W.R.Hammond: 1,024 runs in August 1871 – first instance of 1,000 runs in a single month: 1,278 in August 1876 – the best for any month until W.R.Hammond scored 1,281 in August 1936.

Ten centuries in 1871 – a record until R.Abel's 12 in 1900.

Scored 130 & 102* for South of the Thames –v– North of the Thames at Canterbury 1868: First batsman to score two hundreds in a match since W.Lambert in 1817. 116* at lunch on first day, MCC –v– Kent, Canterbury 1869. First recorded hundred before lunch on the first morning of a first-class match.

First-class career lasted from 1865 until 1908 – a record span of 43 years.

OTHER FEATS

In 1874 the first player to record the double of 1,000 runs and 100 wickets. In 1876 the first to score 2,000 runs and take 100 wickets in one season. Altogether performed the double 7 times. Took 100 wickets 9 times. For MCC –v– Oxford University at Oxford 1886 performed unique match double of century and 10 wickets in an innings.

RECORD IN TEST CRICKET

Tests	Inns	n.o.	Runs	H.S.	Av'ge	100s	50s
22	36	2	1,098	170	32.29	2	5

SEASON-BY-SEASON: FIRST-CLASS MATCHES ONLY

Season	Matches	Inns	n.o.	Runs	H.S.	Av'ge	100s
1865	5	8	1	189	48	27.00	–
1866	8	13	2	581	224*	52.82	2
1867	4	6	1	154	75	30.80	–
1868	8	13	2	625	134*	56.82	3
1869	15	24	1	1,320	180	57.39	6
1870	21	38	5	1,808	215	54.79	5
1871	25	39	4	2,739	268	78.26	10
1872	20	29	3	1,485	170*	57.12	6
1873	21	34	7	1,962	192*	72.67	7
1874	21	32	0	1,664	179	52.00	8
1875	26	48	2	1,498	152	32.57	3
1876	26	46	4	2,622	344	62.43	7
1877	24	40	3	1,474	261	39.84	2
1878	24	42	2	1,151	116	28.78	1
1879	19	29	3	993	123	38.19	3
1880	16	27	3	951	152	39.63	2
1881	13	22	1	792	182	37.71	2
1882	22	37	0	975	88	26.35	–
1883	22	41	2	1,352	112	34.67	1
1884	26	45	5	1,361	116*	34.03	3
1885	25	42	3	1,688	221*	43.28	4
1886	33	55	3	1,846	170	35.50	4
1887	24	46	8	2,062	183*	54.26	6
1888	33	59	1	1,886	215	32.52	4
1889	24	45	2	1,396	154	32.47	3
1890	30	55	3	1,476	109*	28.39	1
1891	24	40	1	771	72*	19.77	–
1891–2	8	11	1	448	159*	44.80	1
1892	21	37	3	1,055	99	31.03	–
1893	28	50	5	1,609	128	35.76	1
1894	27	45	1	1,293	196	29.39	3
1895	29	48	2	2,346	288	51.00	9
1896	30	54	4	2,135	301	42.70	4
1897	25	41	2	1,532	131	39.28	4
1898	26	41	5	1,513	168	42.03	3
1899	13	23	1	515	78	23.41	–
1900	18	31	1	1,277	126	42.57	3
1901	19	32	1	1,007	132	32.48	1
1902	22	35	3	1,187	131	37.09	2
1903	16	27	1	593	150	22.81	1

SEASON-BY-SEASON: FIRST-CLASS MATCHES ONLY

Season	Matches	Inns	n.o.	Runs	H.S.	Av'ge	100s
1904	15	26	1	637	166	25.48	1
1905	9	13	0	250	71	19.23	–
1906	5	10	1	241	74	26.78	–
1907	1	2	0	19	16	9.50	–
1908	1	2	0	40	25	20.00	–
	872	1,483	104	54,518	344	39.54	126

Thomas Walter Hayward

Born Cambridge 29.3.1871; Died Cambridge 19.7.1939.
Father Daniel Hayward played first-class cricket for Cambridgeshire;
uncle Thomas Hayward senior was the leading batsman in England in
1850s and 1860s.

1st 100:   112 Surrey –v– Kent, The Oval 1893: Age 22 years, 129 days
100th: 139 Surrey –v– Lancs, The Oval 1913: Age 42 years, 90 days

CAREER RECORD AT TIME OF COMPLETING 100TH HUNDRED

1,076 Innings   41,534 Runs   42.34 Average

SOME STATISTICAL FEATS

HS 315* Surrey –v– Lancs, The Oval 1898: at the time the highest score
for Surrey in the County Championship, to be beaten next season by
R.Abel (357). Still the highest score against Lancashire in a first-class
match. A hundred in each innings three times, including twice in
consecutive matches during the same week. D.W.Hookes equalled the
first part of the feat during 1976–7, but performing them in the same
week remains unique. The details of the record are: 144* &
100 –v– Notts., Trent Bridge 4, 5, 6 June 1906; 143 & 125 –v– Leics,
Leicester 7, 8, 9 June 1906.

These hundreds were part of a run of 9 consecutive fifties – a record until
beaten by Ernest Tyldesley in 1926.

In 1906 Hayward scored 3,518 runs (66.38). A record until beaten by
D.C.S.Compton & W.J.Edrich in 1947.

In 1906 Hayward also scored 13 centuries, equalling the record of
C.B.Fry in 1901 and remaining unbeaten until J.B.Hobbs scored 16 in
1925. In 1906 Hayward reached 2,000 runs on 5 July, 3,000 on 20
August. Both remain records though W.R.Hammond equalled the date
for 3,000 runs in 1937. In 1900 Hayward scored 1,000 runs before the
end of May, the second to do so.

In 1899 Hayward added 448 for the 4th wicket with R.Abel,
Surrey –v– Yorkshire at The Oval. This remained an English 4th wicket
record until 1982. In 1907 Hayward and Hobbs added more than 100

for the Surrey first wicket four times in the same week – a unique feat. The details were: 106 & 125 –v– Cambridge, The Oval 17, 18, 19 June 1907; 147 & 105 –v– Middlesex, Lord's 20, 21, 22 June 1907.

Hayward holds the record for runs in a season for Surrey – 3,246 in 1906, and scored centuries against all 15 counties available to him at the time.

In early years a useful slow right-armed bowler he performed the 'double' in 1897 and altogether obtained 481 wickets during his career. He scored more runs between 1900 and 1910 than anyone: 25,957.

RECORD IN TEST CRICKET

Tests	Inns	n.o.	Runs	H.S.	Av'ge	100s	50s
35	60	2	1,999	137	34.47	3	12

Season	Matches	Inns	n.o.	Runs	H.S.	Av'ge	100s
1893	13	24	2	400	112	18.18	1
1894	26	37	4	884	142	26.79	2
1895	30	43	3	1,169	123	29.23	3
1895–6	4	6	0	277	122	46.17	1
1896	34	54	8	1,595	229*	34.67	5
1897	28	39	3	1,368	130	38.00	1
1897–8	12	21	3	695	96	38.61	–
1898	26	38	2	1,523	315*	42.31	3
1899	35	49	4	2,647	273	58.82	7
1900	38	57	7	2,693	193	53.86	10
1901	36	58	8	2,535	181	50.70	2
1901–2	11	19	1	701	174	38.94	1
1902	37	56	3	1,737	177	32.77	3
1903	38	64	3	2,177	156*	35.69	3
1903–4	11	17	0	785	157	46.18	2
1904	36	63	5	3,170	205	54.66	11
1905	34	64	6	2,592	129*	44.69	5
1906	36	61	8	3,518	219	66.38	13
1907	34	58	6	2,353	161	45.25	7
1908	37	52	1	2,337	175	45.82	5
1909	20	37	4	1,359	204*	41.18	3
1910	27	42	1	1,134	120	27.66	3
1911	30	51	6	2,149	202	47.76	5
1912	30	49	5	1,303	182	29.61	3
1913	23	41	2	1,326	146	34.00	3
1914	24	38	1	1,124	122	30.38	2
	710	1,138	96	43,551	315*	41.80	104

John Berry Hobbs

Born Cambridge 16.12.1882; Died Hove, Sussex 21.12.1963.
Knighted June 1953.

1st 100:   155 Surrey –v– Essex, The Oval 1905: Age 22 years, 140 days
           (this included reaching his century before lunch)

100th: 116 Surrey –v– Somerset, Bath 1923: Age 40 years, 143 days

CAREER RECORD AT TIME OF COMPLETING 100TH HUNDRED

821 Innings   34,929 Runs   45.96 Average

SOME STATISTICAL FEATS

HS 316* Surrey –v– Middlesex, Lord's 1926 remains highest –v– Middlesex in first-class cricket.

In 1925 scored 4 hundreds in successive innings, and 5 hundreds in 6 innings. He obtained thirteen hundreds before lunch on the first day of a match – a record, as is his total of 20 pre-lunch hundreds overall.

He obtained 2,000 runs in a season 17 times – a record. In 1909–10 he was the first batsman to score 1,000 runs in a South African season, and his 1,489 runs (av. 74.45) there in 1913–14 remained a South African record until beaten by D.C.S.Compton in 1948–9.

In 1925 he scored 16 centuries – a record until beaten by D.C.S.Compton in 1947.

His 43,554 runs (49.72) and 144 hundreds remain records for Surrey, while in 1925 he became the first Surrey player to score a century against all other 16 counties.

He was the first batsman to score 4,000 runs and 5,000 runs in Test cricket and when scoring 142 –v– Australia at Melbourne in 1928–9 he became the oldest ever Test century scorer at 46 years, 82 days. His 3,636 runs against Australia remains a record.

He scored 175 first-class centuries in England – a record.

Hobbs appeared in 598 first-class matches for Surrey – a record for the county. Hobbs scored 26,441 (58.63) after his 40th birthday. This beat the 22,141 scored by W.G.Grace and remains a record.

Statistical Appendix

RECORD IN TEST CRICKET

Tests	Inns	n.o.	Runs	H.S.	Av'ge	100s	50s
61	102	7	5,410	211	56.95	15	28

Season	Matches	Inns	n.o.	Runs	H.S.	Av'ge	100s
1905	30	54	3	1,317	155	25.82	2
1906	31	53	6	1,913	162*	40.70	4
1907	37	63	6	2,135	166*	37.46	4
1907–8	13	22	1	876	115	41.71	2
1908	36	53	2	1,904	161	37.33	6
1909	31	54	2	2,114	205	40.65	6
1909–10	11	18	1	1,124	187	66.12	3
1910	38	63	3	1,982	133	33.03	3
1911	36	60	3	2,376	154*	41.68	4
1911–12	11	18	1	943	187	55.47	3
1912	38	60	6	2,042	111	37.82	3
1913	32	57	5	2,605	184	50.10	9
1913–14	16	22	2	1,489	170	74.45	5
1914	29	48	2	2,697	226	58.63	11
1919	30	49	6	2,594	205*	60.33	8
1920	31	50	2	2,827	215	58.90	11
1920–1	12	19	1	924	131	51.33	4
1921	5	6	2	312	172*	78.00	1
1922	29	46	5	2,552	168	62.24	10
1923	34	59	4	2,087	136	37.95	5
1924	30	43	7	2,094	221	58.17	6
1924–5	10	17	1	865	154	54.06	3
1925	30	48	5	3,024	266*	70.32	16
1926	30	41	3	2,949	316*	77.61	10
1927	23	32	1	1,641	150	52.94	7
1928	28	38	7	2,542	200*	82.00	12
1928–9	11	18	1	962	142	56.58	2
1929	24	39	5	2,263	204	66.56	10
1930	30	43	2	2,103	146*	51.29	5
1931	31	49	6	2,418	153	56.23	10
1932	24	35	4	1,764	161*	56.90	5
1933	12	18	0	1,105	221	61.39	6
1934	12	18	1	624	116	36.71	1
	825	1,313	106	61,167	316*	50.68	197

Charles Philip Mead

Born Battersea, London 7.3.1887; Died Bournemouth 26.3.1958.

1st 100   109 Hampshire –v– Yorkshire, Southampton 1906: Age 23 years, 66 days

100th: 100* Hampshire –v– Northants., Kettering 1927: Age 40 years, 134 days, the first left-handed batsman to score 100 centuries

CAREER RECORD AT TIME OF COMPLETING 100TH HUNDRED

892 Innings   37,217 Runs   47.53 Average

SOME STATISTICAL FEATS

HS 280* Hants –v– Notts, Southampton 1921 – at the time the highest score against Notts in first-class cricket, beating the 250 scored by J.T.Tyldesley for Lancs in 1905. Amazingly it was again beaten on the very next day when C.G.Macartney scored 345 for the Australian tourists.

Mead scored 48,892 runs (av. 48.84) and 138 centuries for Hampshire – both records for the county, while his 46,268 Championship runs is a record for any county, as are his 48,892 runs in all county first-class matches.

Mead scored 1,000 runs in a season on 27 occasions, and in consecutive seasons. The latter was a record when Mead retired in 1936 but was beaten by F.E.Woolley in 1938.

Mead scored centuries against all other sixteen counties for Hampshire. His 2,843 runs in 1928, his 26 1,000 runs in a season, and 132 centuries in a career, are all records for the County Championship. Mead scored ten centuries –v– Yorkshire – a record.

Mead was involved in century stands for every wicket for Hampshire – a unique record.

RECORD IN TEST CRICKET

Tests	Inns	n.o.	Runs	H.S.	Av'ge	100s	50s
17	26	2	1,185	182*	49.38	4	3

SEASON-BY-SEASON: FIRST-CLASS MATCHES ONLY

Season	Matches	Inns	n.o.	Runs	H.S.	Av'ge	100s
1905	1	2	1	41	41*	–	–
1906	21	39	1	1,014	132	26.68	2
1907	25	46	1	1,190	102	26.44	1
1908	25	43	5	1,118	119*	29.42	2
1909	24	41	2	1,459	114	37.41	1
1910	27	48	3	1,416	111	31.47	1
1911	29	52	5	2,562	223	54.51	9
1911–12	13	18	2	533	98	33.31	–
1912	34	52	14	1,933	160*	50.87	7
1913	32	60	8	2,627	171*	50.52	9
1913–14	16	19	0	745	145	39.21	3
1914	31	53	5	2,476	213	51.58	7
1919	23	38	7	1,720	207	55.48	3
1920	26	44	6	1,887	178*	49.66	6
1921	33	52	6	3,179	280*	69.11	10
1922	32	50	10	2,391	235	59.78	8
1922–3	14	21	2	695	181	36.58	1
1923	32	52	8	2,604	222	59.18	7
1924	29	45	6	1,644	154	42.15	3
1925	29	45	4	1,942	213*	47.37	4
1926	29	45	8	2,326	177*	62.87	10
1927	28	41	9	2,385	200*	74.53	8
1927–8	3	5	1	418	151	104.50	3
1928	30	50	10	3,027	180	75.68	13
1928–9	10	14	3	460	106	41.82	1
1929	21	38	7	1,733	233	55.90	5
1930	29	49	5	1,305	143	29.66	1
1931	29	46	9	1,596	169*	43.14	3
1932	27	45	5	1,210	121	30.25	3
1933	27	44	6	2,576	227	67.79	10
1934	29	46	8	2,011	198	52.92	6
1935	30	55	12	1,650	151*	38.37	4
1936	26	42	6	1,190	126	33.06	2
	814	1,340	185	55,063	280*	47.67	153

Elias Henry Hendren

Born Chiswick, London 5.2.1889; Died Tooting Bec, London 4.10.1962.

1st 100:   134* Middlesex –v– Sussex, Lord's 1911: Age 22 years, 121 days

100th: 100 MCC –v– Victoria, Melbourne 1928–9: Age 39 years, 272 days

CAREER RECORD AT TIME OF COMPLETING 100TH HUNDRED

740 Innings   32,946 Runs   51.64 Average

SOME STATISTICAL FEATS

HS 301* Middlesex –v– Worcs, Dudley 1933. At the time this was the best ever score for Middlesex in first-class cricket, not beaten until J.D.B.Robertson scored 331* against Worcs in 1949.

The first batsman to score his 100th century outside England; unique until Bradman in 1947–8. 2,000 runs in 15 seasons puts him second to J.B.Hobbs. 40,302 runs (49.81) and 119 centuries both records for Middlesex.

Scored centuries against every other first-class county.

Made four first-class double centuries in the West Indies in 1929/30 – a record still, but equalled by G.M.Turner in 1971–2.

Scored 630 runs (205*, 254*, 171) before being dismissed in West Indies 1929/30. This remained a record until V.M.Merchant scored 634 runs before dismissal in India in 1941–2.

He scored 1,765 runs (av. 135.77) in West Indies in 1929–30. This remains a record for cricket in the West Indies. His six centuries also established a record jointly with A. Sandham on the same tour, which still stands.

In 1933 scored five centuries in six consecutive innings: 111, 101, 101, 12, 105, 154.

RECORD IN TEST CRICKET

Tests	Inns	n.o.	Runs	H.S.	Av'ge	100s	50s
51	83	9	3,525	205*	47.64	7	21

SEASON-BY-SEASON: FIRST-CLASS MATCHES ONLY

Season	Matches	Inns	n.o.	Runs	H.S.	Av'ge	100s
1907	1	–	–	–	–	–	–
1908	8	13	1	112	35	9.33	–
1909	22	37	1	698	75	19.39	–
1910	21	33	1	777	91	24.28	–
1911	23	36	4	1,030	134*	32.19	1
1912	25	40	6	975	97	28.68	–
1913	22	36	3	1,076	123	32.61	2
1914	22	30	4	968	133*	37.23	3
1919	23	34	7	1,655	214	61.30	5
1920	30	47	6	2,520	232	61.46	6
1920–1	12	20	1	1,178	271	62.00	3
1921	30	53	5	2,013	113	41.93	7
1922	27	38	7	2,072	277*	66.84	7
1923	31	51	12	3,010	200*	77.18	13
1924	35	48	11	2,100	142	56.76	5
1924–5	14	22	3	1,233	168	64.90	4
1925	33	50	6	2,601	240	59.11	8
1926	36	53	11	2,643	213	62.93	9
1927	35	43	5	2,784	201*	73.26	13
1928	35	54	7	3,311	209*	70.45	13
1928–9	12	17	1	1,033	169	64.56	3
1929	37	63	9	2,213	156	40.98	5
1929–30	11	18	5	1,765	254	135.77	6
1930	30	47	4	1,920	138	44.65	5
1930–1	14	18	1	914	170	53.77	1
1931	33	54	9	2,548	232	56.62	7
1932	30	47	7	2,041	194*	51.03	5
1933	36	65	9	3,186	301*	56.89	11
1934	33	55	6	2,213	135	45.16	7
1934–5	11	18	1	673	148	39.59	2
1935	30	50	7	1,867	195	43.42	5
1936	35	58	2	2,654	202	47.39	9
1937	33	50	4	1,809	187	39.33	5
1938	1	2	0	19	19	9.50	–
	831	1,300	166	57,611	301*	50.80	170

Frank Edward Woolley

Born Tonbridge, Kent 27.5.1887; Died Halifax, Nova Scotia, Canada 18.10.1978.

1st 100: 116 Kent –v– Hampshire, Tonbridge 1906: Age 19 years, 23 days

100th: 176 Kent –v– Middlesex, Lord's 1929: Age 42 years, 94 days

CAREER RECORD AT TIME OF COMPLETING 100TH HUNDRED

1,031 Innings   39,967 Runs   41.42 Average

SOME STATISTICAL FEATS

HS 305* MCC –v– Tasmania, Hobart 1911/12. 300* reached in 205 minutes, the fastest first-class triple century until D.C.S.Compton's 300 in 1948–9. It remains the highest first-class score *in* Tasmania and was the highest *against* Tasmania until W.H.Ponsford's 429 for Victoria at Melbourne in 1922–3. It was the first triple century for any touring side in Australia.

1,000 Runs in a season 28 times in succession – a record. *Total* of 28 times equals the record of W.G.Grace.

Career total of 47,868 runs (av. 41.77) and 122 centuries both records for Kent, as is season's total of 2,894 (59.06) in 1928.

Scored century for Kent against all other counties.

26,273 first-class runs after the age of 40 second only to J.B.Hobbs.

As all-rounder, performed double of 2,000 runs and 100 wickets on four occasions – a record, and performed eight 'ordinary' doubles, which is a record for a batsman with over 100 centuries. Woolley played 764 games for Kent – a record.

Woolley played for England in 52 consecutive Test matches – a record only equalled by P.B.H.May.

RECORD IN TEST CRICKET

Tests	Innings	n.o.	Runs	H.S.	Av'ge	100s	50s
64	98	7	3,283	154	36.08	5	23

231

SEASON-BY-SEASON: FIRST CLASS MATCHES ONLY

Season	Matches	Inns	n.o.	Runs	H.S.	Av'ge	100s
1906	16	26	1	779	116	31.16	1
1907	27	43	1	1,128	99	26.86	–
1908	30	46	3	1,286	152	29.91	2
1909	32	39	0	1,270	185	32.56	2
1909/10	12	19	1	343	69	19.06	–
1910	31	47	2	1,101	120	24.47	3
1911	30	47	2	1,700	148*	37.78	6
1911/12	14	18	4	781	305*	55.79	2
1912	35	49	5	1,827	117	41.52	2
1913	29	45	6	1,760	224*	45.13	4
1913/14	18	23	1	595	116	27.05	1
1914	31	52	2	2,272	160*	45.44	6
1919	20	27	1	1,082	164	41.62	3
1920	31	50	3	1,924	158	40.94	5
1920–1	13	20	2	619	138	34.39	1
1921	31	50	1	2,101	174	42.88	6
1922	33	47	3	2,022	188	45.96	5
1922–3	12	19	1	551	115*	30.61	1
1923	33	56	5	2,091	270	41.00	5
1924	34	49	2	2,344	202	49.87	8
1924–5	10	17	0	737	149	43.35	2
1925	29	43	4	2,190	215	56.15	5
1926	32	50	3	2,183	217	46.45	6
1927	31	41	2	1,804	187	46.26	5
1928	36	59	4	3,352	198	60.95	12
1929	35	55	5	2,804	176	56.08	11
1929/30	12	18	1	780	219	45.88	3
1930	29	50	5	2,023	120	44.96	5
1931	34	51	4	2,301	224	48.96	5
1932	35	52	2	1,827	146	36.54	1
1933	28	48	1	1,633	198	34.75	5
1934	33	56	1	2,643	176	48.06	10
1935	32	56	0	2,339	229	41.77	6
1936	32	58	3	1,532	101	27.86	1
1937	29	52	0	1,645	193	31.64	3
1938	29	52	3	1,590	162	32.45	2
	978	1,530	84	58,959	305*	40.77	145

Herbert Sutcliffe

Born Summerbridge, Yorkshire 25.11.1894; Died Gargrave, Yorkshire 22.1.1978.

1st 100:   145 Yorkshire –v– Northants, Northampton 1919: Age 24 years, 240 days

100th: 132 Yorkshire –v– Gloucs, Bradford 1932: Age 37 years, 226 days

CAREER RECORD AT TIME OF COMPLETING 100TH HUNDRED

700 Innings   33,350 Runs   54.70 Average

SOME STATISTICAL FEATS

HS 313 Yorkshire –v– Essex, Leyton 1932: The first triple century against Essex. Added 555 for first wicket with P.Holmes. This remains the best stand for any wicket in first-class cricket in England, and remained the best first-wicket stand in all first-class cricket until 1976–7, when Waheed Mirza and Mansoor Akhtar added 561 for Karachi Whites –v– Qetta at Karachi. When performed it was the best stand for any wicket in all first-class cricket, being beaten in 1945–6 when F.M.M.Worrell and C.L.Walcott added 574 for an unbeaten 4th-wicket stand for Barbados –v– Trinidad at Port-of-Spain.

Altogether Sutcliffe was involved in six first-wicket stands of 300 or more, and four with P.Holmes – both records.

Sutcliffe scored 1,839 runs in 1919; this remains the highest number of runs by a batsman in his debut season.

Sutcliffe went on to complete 1,000 runs every season from 1919 to 1939 inclusive and was the only player to achieve this feat for the 21 seasons between the wars, while his 21 1,000 runs, and his 112 centuries are both records for Yorkshire, in a career, and his 2,883 runs (av. 80.08) for Yorkshire in 1932 is a record for a season.

He scored centuries for Yorkshire against the 16 other first-class counties.

In Tests he reached 1,000 runs in only 12 innings while his Test career average of 60.73 is the highest for an England batsman.

Tests	Inns	n.o.	Runs	H.S.	Av'ge	100s	50s
54	84	9	4,555	194	60.73	16	23

SEASON-BY-SEASON: FIRST-CLASS MATCHES ONLY

Season	Matches	Inns	n.o.	Runs	H.S.	Av'ge	100s
1919	31	45	4	1,839	174	44.85	5
1920	30	45	3	1,393	131	33.17	4
1921	29	43	2	1,235	97	30.12	–
1922	34	48	5	2,020	232	46.98	4
1923	38	60	6	2,220	139	41.11	3
1924	36	52	8	2,142	255*	48.68	6
1924–5	12	18	0	1,250	188	69.44	5
1925	36	51	8	2,308	235	53.67	7
1926	35	47	9	2,528	200	66.53	8
1927	35	49	6	2,414	227	56.14	6
1927–8	14	23	3	1,030	102	51.50	2
1928	34	44	5	3,002	228	76.97	13
1928–9	11	16	0	852	135	53.25	2
1929	31	46	4	2,189	150	52.12	9
1930	29	44	8	2,312	173	64.22	6
1931	34	42	11	3,006	230	96.97	13
1932	35	52	7	3,336	313	74.13	14
1932–3	16	22	1	1,345	194	64.05	5
1933	35	52	5	2,211	205	47.04	7
1934	31	44	3	2,023	203	49.34	4
1935	36	54	3	2,494	212	48.90	8
1935–6	3	4	0	81	42	20.25	–
1936	35	53	7	1,532	202	33.30	3
1937	33	54	5	2,162	189	44.12	4
1938	32	50	7	1,790	142	41.63	5
1939	21	29	3	1,416	234*	54.46	6
1945	1	1	0	8	8	–	–
	747	1,088	123	50,138	313	51.96	149

George Ernest Tyldesley

Born Worsley, Lancashire 5.2.1889; Died Rhos-on-Sea, Denbigh 5.5.1962.

Brother of John Thomas Tyldesley (1873–1930), Lancashire & England batsman.

1st 100:   107 Lancashire –v– Sussex, Old Trafford 1912: Age 23 years, 99 days

100th: 122 Lancashire –v– Northants, Peterborough 1934: Age 45 years, 152 days

CAREER RECORD AT TIME OF COMPLETION OF 100TH HUNDRED

919 Innings   37,105 Runs   45.25 Average

SOME STATISTICAL FEATS

In 1926 scored 4 hundreds in four innings, 5 in 6, 6 in 7, 7 in 9 and 8 in 12. He also scored 10 consecutive fifties, a record still, though equalled by D.G.Bradman in 1947–8. Tyldesley's full sequence was: 144, 69, 144*, 226, 51, 131, 131, 106, 126, 81, 44, 139.

HS 256* Lancashire –v– Warwickshire, Old Trafford 1930.

Tyldesley scored 34,222 runs (av. 45.20) for Lancashire – a record for the county. He also holds the Lancashire record for centuries in a career (90).

Tyldesley scored centuries against every county except his own. He never obtained a century in Australia.

RECORD IN TEST CRICKET

Tests	Inns	n.o.	Runs	H.S.	Av'ge	100s	50s
14	20	2	990	122	55.00	3	6

Although known in the cricket world as 'Ernest', in legal documents such as marriage and death certificates, and his own will, he was 'George Ernest Tyldesley'.

SEASON-BY-SEASON: FIRST-CLASS MATCHES ONLY

Season	Matches	Inns	n.o.	Runs	H.S.	Av'ge	100s
1909	5	8	1	120	61	17.14	–
1910	18	20	1	302	66	15.89	–
1911	13	20	0	500	74	25.00	–
1912	19	23	1	561	107	25.50	1
1913	26	46	3	1,316	123	30.61	3
1914	27	44	2	1,325	156	31.55	1
1919	24	40	3	1,635	174*	44.19	3
1920	29	43	4	1,604	244	41.13	3
1921	29	46	8	1,880	165	49.47	5
1922	35	57	5	2,168	178	41.69	4
1923	39	60	6	2,040	236	37.78	4
1924	34	48	6	1,824	148*	43.43	4
1924–5	11	19	2	965	174	56.76	2
1925	16	24	3	1,010	114	48.10	3
1926	35	51	7	2,826	226	64.23	10
1926–7	2	3	0	258	118	86.00	2
1927	33	39	4	1,756	165	50.17	7
1927–8	14	21	2	1,130	161	59.47	4
1928	35	48	10	3,024	242	79.58	10
1928–9	12	16	2	509	81	36.36	–
1929	27	39	4	1,575	187	45.00	4
1930	32	47	8	1,904	256*	48.82	7
1931	27	43	4	1,516	144	38.87	4
1932	31	48	7	2,420	225*	59.02	8
1933	29	40	3	1,531	159*	41.38	4
1934	33	51	8	2,487	239	57.84	8
1935	11	15	1	654	137	46.71	1
1936	2	2	1	34	22	–	–
	648	961	106	38,874	256*	45.47	102

Walter Reginald Hammond

Born Dover, Kent 19.6.1903; Died Durban, South Africa 2.7.1965.
1st 100:   110 Gloucs –v– Surrey, Bristol 1923: Age 19 years, 324 days
100th: 116 Gloucs –v– Somerset, Bristol 1935: Age 31 years, 359
           days

CAREER RECORD AT TIME OF COMPLETION OF 100TH HUNDRED

680 Innings   32,081 Runs   52.94 Average

SOME STATISTICAL FEATS

HS 336* England –v– New Zealand, Auckland 1932–3. This was, at the time, the highest-ever Test score, and was beaten by L.Hutton in 1938. It remains the highest score by an English player touring abroad. Hammond reached 300* in 287 minutes. It remains the fastest triple century in Test cricket, while his 10 sixes are the most in a Test innings.

Hammond altogether scored four first-class triple centuries, a total exceeded only by D.G.Bradman. His three triple centuries in county cricket are a record.

Hammond's 302* -v- Glamorgan at Bristol in 1934, and his 302 against Glamorgan at Newport in 1939 are the only triple centuries against that county.

Hammond's 36 double centuries achieved by the 1946–7 season was a record beaten the very next year by D.G.Bradman in 1947–8.

Hammond scored a century in each innings of a match on seven occasions, a record beaten by Zaheer Abbas in 1982/3.

Hammond scored 1,000 runs on 28 May in 1927, a record beaten by one day by D.G.Bradman in 1938. Hammond's 1,042 runs in May 1927 remains a record however. Hammond's 1,281 runs in August 1936 also remains the record for that month.

In 1937 Hammond reached 3,000 runs on 20 August, to equal T.W.Hayward's 1906 record.

During 1945 and 1946 Hammond scored 6 hundreds in 7 consecutive innings: 121, 102, 132, 134, 59*, 143, 104.

Hammond's 2,860 runs (69.75) for Gloucs in 1933 is the county record, while his career records of 33,664 runs (57.05) and 113 centuries are also Gloucestershire records. He scored more runs in one single decade than anyone else: 31,165 in the 1930s.

Hammond scored centuries for Gloucs against every other county. His 22 Test hundreds are a record for an English batsman held jointly with M.C.Cowdrey and G.Boycott.

RECORD IN TEST CRICKET

Tests	Inns	n.o.	Runs	H.S.	Av'ge	100s	50s
85	140	16	7,249	336*	58.46	22	24

Season	Matches	Inns	n.o.	Runs	H.S.	Av'ge	100s
1920	3	4	1	27	18	9.00	–
1921	2	3	0	2	1	0.67	–
1922	5	9	0	88	32	9.78	–
1923	29	55	4	1,421	110	27.86	1
1924	27	45	4	1,239	174*	30.22	2
1925	33	58	5	1,818	250*	34.30	3
1925–6	10	18	3	732	238*	48.80	2
1926				Did not play			
1927	34	47	4	2,969	197	69.05	12
1927–8	14	21	2	908	166*	47.79	2
1928	35	48	5	2,825	244	65.70	9
1928–9	13	18	1	1,553	251	91.35	7
1929	28	47	9	2,456	238*	64.63	10
1930	27	44	6	2,032	211*	53.47	5
1930–1	13	19	2	1,045	136*	61.47	3
1931	32	49	7	1,781	168*	42.41	6
1932	30	49	4	2,528	264	56.18	8
1932–3	15	21	2	1,569	336*	82.58	5
1933	34	54	5	3,323	264	67.82	13
1934	23	35	4	2,366	302*	76.32	8
1934–5	10	17	3	789	281*	56.36	3
1935	35	58	5	2,616	252	49.36	7
1936	25	42	5	2,107	317	56.95	5
1936–7	14	23	2	1,242	231*	59.14	5
1937	33	55	5	3,252	217	65.04	13
1938	26	42	2	3,011	271	75.27	15
1938–9	15	18	1	1,025	181	60.29	4
1939	28	46	7	2,479	302	63.56	7
1942–3	1	2	0	78	60	39.00	–
1945	6	10	0	592	121	59.20	3
1946	19	26	5	1,783	214	84.91	7
1946–7	13	19	0	781	208	41.11	2
1950	1	2	1	107	92*	–	–
1951	1	1	0	7	7	–	–
	634	1,005	104	50,551	336*	56.11	167

Andrew Sandham

Born Streatham, London 6.7.1890; Died North London 20.4.1982.

1st 100: 196 Surrey –v– Sussex, The Oval 1913: Age 22 years, 359 days

100th: 103 Surrey –v– Hampshire, Basingstoke 1935: Age 44 years, 355 days

CAREER RECORD AT TIME OF COMPLETION OF 100TH HUNDRED

871 Innings   37,809 Runs   47.56 Average

SOME STATISTICAL FEATS

HS 325: England –v– West Indies, Kingston 1929–30: At the time was the highest score in all Test cricket and remains the best for England –v– West Indies. It is the best score for a Test No. 2 batsman, and the highest for a batsman in his final Test.

Sandham obtained 1,281 runs on this tour – second only to E.Hendren on the same tour for runs in a West Indian season. Sandham's six centuries on the tour makes him joint record-holder for centuries in a West Indian season with E.Hendren.

On tour in India in 1926–7 Sandham scored 1,756 in first-class matches (av. 62.71): this set a new record for an Indian season which stood until 1950–1 when F.M.M.Worrell, touring with the Commonwealth Team, scored 1,900 runs (av. 63.33).

Sandham also set a record in 1926–7 with his 7 first-class hundreds. It has since been equalled by the Nawab of Pataudi in 1964–5 and S.M.Gavaskar in 1978–9.

RECORD IN TEST CRICKET

Tests	Inns	n.o.	Runs	H.S.	Av'ge	100s	50s
14	23	0	879	325	38.22	2	3

SEASON-BY-SEASON: FIRST-CLASS MATCHES ONLY

Season	Matches	Inns	n.o.	Runs	H.S.	Av'ge	100s
1911	3	4	0	130	60	32.50	–
1912	2	1	1	23	23*	–	–
1913	9	16	3	439	196	33.77	1
1914	5	9	1	112	28	14.00	–
1919	20	30	4	840	175*	32.31	1
1920	27	45	2	1,694	167*	39.40	2
1921	30	48	5	2,117	292*	49.23	5
1922	28	45	5	1,875	195	46.88	5
1922–3	14	24	2	985	122	44.77	3
1923	32	52	6	1,894	200	41.17	4
1924	24	37	2	2,082	169	59.49	7
1924–5	12	19	0	866	137	45.58	3
1925	30	47	6	2,255	181	55.00	5
1926	31	44	2	1,905	183	45.36	4
1926–7	27	30	2	1,756	150	62.71	7
1927	33	46	6	2,315	230	57.88	7
1928	32	47	4	2,532	282*	58.88	8
1928–9	3	6	1	306	159	61.20	1
1929	31	52	2	2,565	187	51.30	6
1929–30	12	20	0	1,281	325	64.05	6
1930	35	50	4	2,295	204	49.89	6
1930–1	2	2	0	78	72	39.00	–
1931	32	50	8	2,209	175	52.60	9
1932	29	44	4	1,441	215	36.03	2
1933	24	35	4	1,034	169*	33.36	1
1934	28	46	0	1,635	219	35.54	5
1935	28	50	1	1,494	110	30.49	3
1936	28	47	1	1,559	173	33.89	3
1937	29	48	3	1,448	239	32.18	3
1937–8	3	6	0	119	51	19.83	–
	643	1,000	79	41,284	325	44.83	107

Donald George Bradman

Born Cootamundra, New South Wales 27.8.1908.

Knighted in 1949.

1st 100:   118 New South Wales –v– S Australia, Adelaide 1927: Age 19 years, 112 days (first-class debut)

100th: 172 Australian XI –v– Indians, Sydney 1947: Age 39 years, 80 days.

CAREER RECORD AT TIME OF COMPLETING 100TH HUNDRED

295 Innings   24,495 Runs   95.31 Average

SOME STATISTICAL FEATS

HS 452* New South Wales –v– Queensland, Sydney 1929–30: Remained highest score in all first-class cricket until Hanif Mohammed's 499 for Karachi –v– Bahawalpur, Karachi 1958–9. It is still the second highest score on record and the highest not out innings.

Bradman's final career average of 95.14 is by a long way the highest for anyone with any sort of career in first-class cricket. Similarly his Test average, 99.94, is by far the best ever.

Bradman's 334 for Australia –v– England at Leeds, 1930, was the highest Test score at the time, and it remains the highest for Australia in Tests. Bradman's six double centuries in 1930 was a record for an English season which still stands, and his career total of 37 double centuries is also a record.

Bradman was the first to average over 100 in an English season in 1938. His average that year of 115.67 is still the highest.

During 1938–9 Bradman scored hundreds in 6 consecutive innings, 8 in 11 consecutive innings; and in another run immediately afterwards, though overlapping, 8 in 12. Twice he obtained 4 successive hundreds, 7 times 3 in succession. Twice he scored 5 hundreds in 6 innings, 7 in 9 innings on 4 occasions, and 8 in 12 twice. In 1947–8 he equalled G.E.Tyldesley's record of 10 consecutive fifties; previous spells had seen him obtain 8 in succession and 7 in succession.

In 1929–30 he scored 455 runs in one match (3 & 452*, NSW –v–
Queensland) a total which remained a record until beaten by Hanif
Mohammed's 499. Bradman's 309 runs on 11 July 1930 during his
innings of 334 –v– England at Leeds is the most in a day's play in a Test.
His 334 is still the highest at Leeds in all first-class cricket. His 254 at
Lord's in the previous Test remains the highest in a Test there while his
299* –v– South Africa in 1930–1 remains the highest in a Test at
Adelaide.

Bradman obtained 1,000 runs in an Australian season 12 times –
I.M.Chappell is second on the list with 6.

In 1938 Bradman reached 1,000 runs in England on 27 May – the
earliest date ever.

Bradman's 5,028 runs and 19 centuries are both records for Australia
–v– England Tests, as is his total of 29 centuries in all Tests.

Partnerships: the 405 added by Bradman and S.G.Barnes for Australia
–v– England at Sydney in 1946–7 is still the record for the 5th wicket in
Test cricket, and Bradman also holds the Test record for the 2nd
wicket – 451 with W.H.Ponsford –v– England at The Oval 1934, and
the 6th wicket – 346 added with J.H.W.Fingleton –v– England at
Melbourne in 1936–7. Bradman also shares the Australian Test record
for the 2nd, 4th, 5th and 6th wickets.

The 'minor' records held by Bradman, and feats achieved by him are too
numerous to list here, all serve to confirm his standing as the best
batsman of all time.

RECORD IN TEST CRICKET

Tests	Inns	n.o.	Runs	H.S.	Av'ge	100s	50s
52	80	10	6996	334	99.94	29	13

SEASON-BY-SEASON: FIRST-CLASS MATCHES ONLY

Season	Matches	Inns	n.o.	Runs	H.S.	Av'ge	100s
1927–8	5	10	1	416	134*	46.22	2
1928–9	13	24	6	1,690	340*	93.89	7
1929–30	11	16	2	1,586	452*	113.29	5
1930	27	36	6	2,960	334	98.67	10
1930–1	12	18	0	1,422	258	79.00	5
1931–2	10	13	1	1,403	299*	116.92	7
1932–3	11	21	2	1,171	238	61.63	3
1933–4	7	11	2	1,192	253	132.44	5
1934	22	27	3	2,020	304	84.17	7
1935–6	8	9	0	1,173	369	130.33	4
1936–7	12	19	1	1,552	270	86.22	6
1937–8	12	18	2	1,437	246	89.81	7
1938	20	26	5	2,429	278	115.67	13
1938–9	7	7	1	919	225	153.17	6
1939–40	9	15	3	1,475	267	122.92	5
1940–1	2	4	0	18	12	4.50	–
1945–6	2	3	1	232	112	116.00	1
1946–7	9	14	1	1,032	234	79.39	4
1947–8	9	12	2	1,296	201	129.60	8
1948	23	31	4	2,428	187	89.93	11
1948–9	3	4	0	216	123	54.00	1
	234	338	43	28,067	452*	95.14	117

Leslie Ethelbert George Ames

Born Elham, Kent 3.12.1905.

The only wicket-keeper among makers of 100 centuries.

1st 100:   111 Kent –v– Hampshire, Southampton 1927: Age 21 years, 186 days

100th: 131 Kent –v– Middlesex, Canterbury 1950: Age 44 years, 251 days

CAREER RECORD AT TIME OF COMPLETING 100TH HUNDRED

915 Innings   36,340 Runs   44.05 Average

SOME STATISTICAL FEATS

HS 295 Kent –v– Gloucs, Folkestone 1933: This was the highest ever score by a regular wicket-keeper to that time (though Ames did not in fact 'keep' throughout the game). In 1945–6 C.L.Walcott scored 314* for Barbados –v– Trinidad at Port-of-Spain, and also kept wicket throughout the match. Ames's 295 was to that date the highest score for Kent but was beaten by W.H.Ashdown (332) in 1934.

Ames scored a century for Kent against every other first-class county – the first and only wicket-keeper to perform this feat.

Ames went from 25* to 148* before lunch on the third day, for England –v– South Africa at The Oval in 1935. The 123 added is the most scored before lunch by one player in any Test match.

The 246 added for the 8th wicket by Ames and G.O.Allen for England –v– New Zealand at Lord's, 1931, is still the best stand for that wicket in all Test cricket, and it remains the best at Lord's for all first-class cricket.

Ames twice won the Laurence Trophy awarded to the scorer of the fastest century of the season in the 1930s – the only player to win it more than once.

RECORD IN TEST CRICKET

Tests	Inns	n.o.	Runs	H.S.	Av'ge	100s	50s
47	72	12	2,434	149	40.57	8	7

Season	Matches	Inns	n.o.	Runs	H.S.	Av'ge	100s
1926	2	3	0	65	35	21.67	–
1927	30	41	5	1,211	111	33.64	1
1928	37	60	6	1,919	200	35.54	4
1928–9	8	8	3	295	100*	59.00	1
1929	34	53	3	1,795	145	35.90	5
1929–30	11	19	2	818	149	48.12	4
1930	33	54	5	1,434	121	29.27	1
1931	34	50	7	1,711	172	39.79	4
1932	35	50	7	2,482	180	57.72	9
1932–3	18	24	1	736	107	32.00	2
1933	36	57	5	3,058	295	58.81	9
1934	27	43	6	2,113	202*	57.11	5
1934–5	11	18	5	566	126	43.54	1
1935	31	54	5	1,730	148*	35.31	6
1936	9	16	0	717	145	44.81	3
1936–7	14	23	0	811	109	35.26	1
1937	30	52	4	2,347	201*	48.90	7
1938	16	27	1	1,116	170	42.92	2
1938–9	13	16	3	683	115	52.54	2
1939	25	46	6	1,846	201	46.15	5
1945	1	2	0	64	57	32.00	–
1946	25	40	3	1,336	114*	36.11	2
1947	22	42	7	2,272	212*	64.91	7
1948	26	45	2	1,943	212	45.19	7
1949	25	47	2	2,125	160	47.22	7
1950	22	39	4	1,422	131	40.63	5
1950–1	17	21	3	626	116*	34.78	2
1951	1	1	1	7	7*	–	–
	593	951	96	37,248	295	43.57	102

Leonard Hutton

Born Fulneck, Pudsey, Yorkshire 23.6.1916.

Knighted 1956.

1st 100:   196 Yorkshire –v– Worcs, Worcester 1934: Age 18 years, 3 days

100th: 100* Yorkshire –v– Surrey, The Oval 1951: Age 35 years, 23 days

CAREER RECORD AT TIME OF COMPLETING 100TH HUNDRED

619 Innings   30,647 Runs   56.23 Average

SOME STATISTICAL FEATS

HS 364 England –v– Australia, The Oval 1938: the highest score in all Test cricket until G.S.Sobers's 365* for West Indies –v– Pakistan, Kingston 1957–8. Still the second highest score in Test matches. Occupying 797 minutes it was the longest innings in all first-class cricket until Hanif's 337 for Pakistan –v– West Indies at Bridgetown 1957–8, which occupied 970 minutes. Hutton still stands second. During his innings Hutton saw 770 runs scored – another Test record. Finally his 364 is the best for a Test no. 1 batsman.

Hutton scored centuries for Yorkshire against every other county. Hutton's 1,294 runs (av. 92.43) in June 1949 is the highest in any month by one batsman.

In 1938 at the Oval Hutton shared in stands of 382, with M.Leyland for the 2nd wicket, and 225, with J.Hardstaff for the 6th wicket – the only time in Test cricket that one batsman has shared in stands of more than 300 and more than 200 in the same innings.

RECORD IN TEST CRICKET

Tests	Inns	n.o.	Runs	H.S.	Av'ge	100s	50s
79	138	15	6,971	364	56.68	19	33

SEASON-BY-SEASON: FIRST-CLASS MATCHES ONLY

Season	Matches	Inns	n.o.	Runs	H.S.	Av'ge	100s
1934	16	28	2	863	196	33.19	1
1935	17	23	3	577	131	28.85	1
1935–6	3	5	2	123	59	41.00	–
1936	34	49	6	1,282	163	29.81	1
1937	35	58	7	2,888	271*	56.63	10
1938	25	37	6	1,874	364	60.45	6
1938–9	14	19	1	1,168	202	64.89	5
1939	33	52	6	2,883	280*	62.67	12
1945	9	16	0	782	188	48.88	2
1946	24	38	6	1,552	183*	48.50	4
1946–7	14	21	3	1,267	151*	70.39	3
1947	26	44	4	2,585	270*	64.63	11
1947–8	5	10	1	578	138	64.22	2
1948	28	48	7	2,654	176*	64.73	10
1948–9	14	21	1	1,477	174	73.85	5
1949	33	56	6	3,429	269*	68.58	12
1950	25	40	3	2,128	202*	57.51	6
1950–1	15	25	4	1,382	156*	65.81	5
1951	31	47	8	2,145	194*	55.00	7
1952	28	45	3	2,567	189	61.12	11
1953	27	44	5	2,458	241	63.03	8
1953–4	8	12	2	780	205	78.00	2
1954	20	28	2	912	163	35.08	2
1954–5	15	25	2	1,059	145*	46.04	2
1955	11	19	1	537	194	29.83	1
1957	1	2	0	101	76	50.50	–
1960	2	2	0	89	89	44.50	–
	513	814	91	40,140	364	55.52	129

Denis Charles Scott Compton

Born Hendon, Middlesex 23.5.1918.

1st 100:   100* Middlesex –v– Northants, Northampton 1936: Age 18 years, 26 days

100th: 107 Middlesex –v– Northants, Lord's 1952: Age 34 years, 19 days

CAREER RECORD AT TIME OF COMPLETING 100TH HUNDRED

552 Innings   28,264 Runs   58.88 Average

SOME STATISTICAL FEATS

Compton's 3,816 Runs (av. 90.86) in 1947 is a record total of runs in first-class cricket in one season.

HS: 300: MCC –v– North-East Transvaal, Benoni 1948–9: This is the highest score for any tourist in South Africa. It was reached in 181 minutes – the fastest-ever triple century.

Compton's total of 1,781 runs (av. 84.81) was the highest for a South African season until J.R.Reid scored 1,915 for New Zealand in 1961–2. Compton's total of 8 centuries during the tour remains a record, though equalled by R.N.Harvey and A.R.Morris for the Australians in 1949–50.

Compton scored 18 centuries in the 1947 season in England, thus beating the previous record of 16 held by J.B.Hobbs since 1925. During this season Compton scored 1,187 runs off the South African tourists – a record.

Compton scored over 1,000 runs in his debut season – the youngest player to perform this feat.

In Tests Compton scored 2,205 against South Africa, more than any other batsman. He scored 102 –v– Australia at Trent Bridge in 1938 and at 20 years, 19 days, was England's youngest-ever Test century scorer. Compton's highest Test score was 278 –v– Pakistan at Trent Bridge in 1954. It was at the time the highest score in any Pakistani Test match. It remains the highest in a Test at Trent Bridge and the highest for an England –v– Pakistan Test match.

Compton added 370 for the 3rd wicket with W.J.Edrich for England
–v– South Africa at Lord's in 1947. This remains the best 3rd wicket
partnership in all Test cricket.

RECORD IN TEST CRICKET

Tests	Inns	n.o.	Runs	H.S.	Av'ge	100s	50s
78	131	15	5,807	278	50.06	17	28

SEASON-BY-SEASON: FIRST-CLASS MATCHES ONLY

Season	Matches	Inns	n.o.	Runs	H.S.	Av'ge	100s
1936	20	32	3	1,004	100*	34.62	1
1937	32	46	4	1,980	177	47.14	3
1938	28	47	6	1,868	180*	45.56	5
1939	31	50	6	2,468	214*	56.09	8
1944–5	10	13	2	990	249*	90.00	5
1945–6	3	4	0	316	124	79.00	2
1946	30	45	6	2,403	235	61.62	10
1946–7	19	31	4	1,660	163	61.48	5
1947	30	50	8	3,816	246	90.86	18
1948	29	47	7	2,451	252*	61.28	9
1948–9	17	26	5	1,781	300	84.81	8
1949	33	56	4	2,530	182	48.65	9
1950	14	23	2	957	144	45.57	2
1950–1	15	26	5	1,095	142	52.14	4
1951	25	40	6	2,193	172	64.50	8
1952	30	54	6	1,880	132	39.17	4
1953	26	47	5	1,659	143*	39.50	4
1953–4	10	14	1	630	133	48.46	1
1954	19	28	2	1,524	278	58.62	4
1954–5	11	16	2	799	182	57.07	3
1955	20	36	1	1,209	158	34.54	2
1956	13	21	1	705	110	35.25	2
1956–7	14	22	1	792	131	37.71	2
1957	24	45	0	1,554	143	34.53	3
1958	4	6	0	104	31	17.33	–
1959	1	2	0	107	71	53.50	–
1959–60	3	4	1	160	74*	53.33	–
1963	1	2	0	88	87	44.00	–
1964–4	2	4	0	146	103	36.50	1
1964	1	2	0	73	59	36.50	–
	515	839	88	38,942	300	51.85	123

Thomas William Graveney

Born Riding Mill, Northumberland 16.6.1927.

1st 100:   114 Gloucs –v– Combined Services, Gloucester 1948: Age 21 years, 72 days

100th: 132 Worcs –v– Northants, Worcester 1964: Age 37 years, 50 days

CAREER RECORD AT TIME OF COMPLETING 100TH HUNDRED

940 Innings   37,307 Runs   44.89 Average

SOME STATISTICAL FEATS

HS 258 England –v– West Indies, Trent Bridge 1957. This is still the highest score at Trent Bridge against West Indies for England.

Graveney scored 200 for Gloucs –v– Glamorgan at Newport in 1956 out of a Gloucs all out score of 298. This is the lowest innings total to include a double century in all first-class cricket.

Graveney scored 19,705 runs (av. 43.02) for Gloucs and 13,160 runs (av. 46.01) for Worcs; he is still the only batsman to score more than 10,000 runs for two counties.

Graveney was the first player to score 30,000 runs and the first to 100 centuries in purely post-war cricket.

In Test cricket Graveney's 943 runs –v– Pakistan is the most by an English batsman against that country.

RECORD IN TEST CRICKET

Tests	Inns	n.o.	Runs	H.S.	Av'ge	100s	50s
79	123	13	4,882	258	44.38	11	20

Statistical Appendix

Season	Matches	Inns	n.o.	Runs	H.S.	Av'ge	100s
1948	24	38	4	973	114	28.62	1
1949	31	55	1	1,784	159	33.04	4
1950	33	56	4	1,892	201	36.39	3
1951	29	50	3	2,291	201	48.75	8
1951–2	19	32	7	1,393	175	55.72	6
1952	29	50	7	2,066	171	48.05	6
1953	31	57	6	1,816	211	35.61	4
1953–4	8	14	3	617	231	56.09	1
1954	25	38	4	1,950	222	57.35	5
1954–5	15	22	3	855	134	45.00	4
1955	28	51	2	2,117	159	43.20	5
1955–6	4	6	0	373	154	62.17	2
1956	31	54	6	2,397	200	49.94	9
1956–7	5	9	1	613	153	76.63	2
1957	32	53	5	2,361	258	49.19	8
1958	28	47	6	1,459	156	35.59	2
1958–9	19	30	4	1,229	177*	47.27	2
1959	19	30	5	1,062	155*	42.48	1
1959–60	3	5	2	343	102	114.33	2
1960	31	54	6	1,625	142*	33.85	2
1960–1	4	7	0	177	105	25.29	1
1961	4	7	2	330	152*	66.00	2
1961–2	8	13	3	813	116*	81.30	2
1962	29	48	6	2,269	164*	54.02	9
1962–3	11	18	4	737	185	52.64	2
1963	28	50	7	1,492	100	34.70	1
1963–4	5	10	2	675	164	84.38	3
1964	30	51	7	2,385	164	54.21	5
1964–5	2	4	1	192	136	64.00	1
1965	28	45	9	1,768	126	49.11	4
1966	24	40	6	1,777	166	52.27	4
1966–7	1	2	0	41	31	20.50	–
1967	26	42	4	1,668	151	43.90	4
1967–8	11	17	2	389	118	25.93	1
1968	21	34	4	1,130	107*	37.67	1
1968–9	6	6	0	317	106	52.83	2
1969	21	33	7	963	110*	37.04	1
1969–70	2	2	1	15	15	–	–
1970	21	34	13	1,316	114	62.67	2
1970–1	4	7	1	102	56	17.00	–
1971–2	1	2	1	21	21*	–	–
	731	1,223	159	47,793	258	44.92	122

Michael Colin Cowdrey

Born Ootacamund, Malabar, India 24.12.1932.

1st 100:   143 Free Foresters –v– Oxford Univ, Oxford 1951: Age 18 years, 160 days

100th: 100* Kent –v– Surrey, Maidstone 1973: Age 40 years, 193 days

CAREER RECORD AT TIME OF COMPLETING 100TH HUNDRED

1,035 Innings   39,934 Runs   43.64 Average

SOME STATISTICAL FEATS

HS 307 MCC –v– South Australia, Adelaide 1962–3: at the time the highest score for any English touring team, and is still the highest score by any tourist in Australia.

Scored 1,000 runs in six overseas seasons – a record for an Englishman, while six tours of Australia also constitutes a record.

Added 411 for the 4th wicket with P.B.H.May for England –v– West Indies at Edgbaston 1957 – still a Test 4th-wicket record and the highest 4th-wicket partnership in any match at Edgbaston.

Total of 7,624 Runs in Test cricket was a record until beaten by G.S.Sobers, and an English record until overtaken by G.Boycott in 1981. Cowdrey's 114 Test appearances and 120 Test catches are also records, while his 22 Test centuries place him equal first among English batsmen along with W.R.Hammond and G.Boycott.

Cowdrey's 1,133 Test runs –v– New Zealand are a record and his 1,751 runs –v– West Indies place him second to G.Boycott among English batsmen.

Cowdrey became the first batsman ever to score centuries against every other Test-playing country; this was later equalled among English batsmen by K.Barrington and G.Boycott.

RECORD IN TEST CRICKET

Tests	Inns	n.o.	Runs	H.S.	Av'ge	100s	50s
114	188	15	7,624	182	44.07	22	38

Season	Matches	Inns.	n.o.	Runs	H.S.	Av'ge	100s
1950	4	77	0	104	27	14.85	–
1951	20	36	0	1,189	143	33.03	2
1952	25	45	3	1,391	101	33.12	1
1953	28	50	6	1,917	154	43.57	4
1954	27	47	3	1,577	140	35.84	2
1954–5	17	31	1	1,019	110	33.97	3
1955	14	25	4	1,038	139	49.43	4
1955–6	4	8	0	271	50	33.88	–
1956	28	45	4	1,569	204*	38.27	3
1956–7	18	27	1	1,035	173	39.81	2
1957	27	43	6	1,917	165	51.81	5
1958	28	41	4	1,437	139	38.84	3
1958–9	20	31	5	1,209	117	46.50	4
1959	26	44	4	2,008	250	50.20	6
1959–60	11	18	2	1,014	173	63.38	5
1960	23	37	1	1,218	155	33.83	3
1961	19	34	1	1,730	156	52.42	7
1961–2	2	4	1	146	83	48.67	–
1962	24	38	3	1,839	182	52.54	6
1962–3	16	29	5	1,380	307	57.50	3
1963	9	17	3	429	107*	30.64	1
1963–4	4	5	2	315	151	105.00	2
1964	23	37	5	1,763	117	55.09	4
1964–5	5	10	2	300	95	37.50	–
1965	27	43	10	2,093	196*	63.42	5
1965–6	16	26	6	1,076	108	53.80	2
1966	25	40	6	1,081	100*	31.79	1
1967	27	38	5	1,281	150	38.82	3
1967–8	9	15	1	871	148	62.21	4
1968	20	28	2	1,093	129	42.04	5
1968–9	7	8	1	228	100	32.57	1
1969	5	5	1	29	14	7.25	–
1969–70	4	6	1	239	83	47.80	–
1970	21	35	6	1,254	126	43.24	3
1970–1	11	18	1	511	101	30.06	1
1971	10	16	1	655	132	43.67	1
1972	19	33	8	1,080	107	43.20	2
1973	21	33	8	1,183	123*	47.32	2
1973–4	1	2	1	102	88	–	–
1974	21	30	3	1,027	122	38.04	5
1974–5	7	12	1	284	78	25.82	–

1975	18	31	6	777	151*	31.08	2
1976	1	2	0	40	25	20.00	–
	692	1,130	134	42,719	307	42.89	107

Geoffrey Boycott

Born Fitzwilliam, near Pontefract, Yorkshire 21.10.1940.

1st 100:   145 Yorkshire –v– Lancashire, Bramall Lane, Sheffield 1963:
Age 22 years, 224 days

100th: 191 England –v– Australia, Leeds 1977: Age 36 years, 294
days

CAREER RECORD AT TIME OF COMPLETING 100TH HUNDRED

645 Innings   31,318 Runs   57.36 Average

SOME STATISTICAL FEATS

HS 261* MCC –v– Presidents XI, Bridgetown, Barbados 1973–4.

He has scored at least one century and more than 1000 runs for
Yorkshire against every other first-class county – the only Yorkshire
player to perform this feat. In 1985 Boycott completed 100 centuries for
Yorkshire alone; Sutcliffe is the only other Yorkshire player to have
achieved this total.

Boycott is the only player to average over 100 in an English season on
two occasions. In 1971 he averaged 100.12 for 2,503 runs, and in 1979
his average for 1,538 runs was 102.53.

In Test cricket Boycott has scored more runs – 8,114 – for England than
any other batsman. Boycott has also played more Test innings – 193 –
than any other English batsman and his 64 fifties are also the best for
England. His 2,205 runs against the West Indies are the most by an
English batsman. Boycott's 22 Test hundreds put him level with
W.R.Hammond and M.C.Cowdrey among English batsmen.

When Boycott scored 107 and 80* for England –v– Australia at Trent
Bridge in 1977 he became the first English player to bat on all five days of
a Test. When scoring 99 and 112 –v– West Indies at Port-of-Spain in
1973–4 he became the first batsman in Test cricket to score 99 and a
century in the same match.

RECORD IN TEST CRICKET

Tests	Inns	n.o.	Runs	H.S.	Av'ge	100s	50s
108	193	23	8,114	246*	47.73	22	42

SEASON-BY-SEASON: FIRST-CLASS MATCHES ONLY

Season	Matches	Inns	n.o.	Runs	H.S.	Av'ge	100s
1962	5	9	2	150	47	21.43	–
1963	28	43	7	1,628	165*	45.22	3
1964	27	44	4	2,110	177	52.75	6
1964–5	15	25	5	1,135	193*	56.75	4
1965	26	44	3	1,447	95	35.29	–
1965–6	13	21	2	784	156	41.26	1
1966	28	50	3	1,854	164	39.45	6
1967	24	40	4	1,910	246*	53.06	4
1967–8	11	16	2	1,154	243	82.43	4
1968	20	30	7	1,487	180*	64.65	7
1969	23	39	6	1,283	128	38.88	3
1969–70	1	2	0	7	7	3.50	–
1970	25	42	5	2,051	260*	55.43	4
1970–1	12	22	6	1,535	173	95.94	6
1971	21	30	5	2,503	233	100.12	13
1971–2	1	2	0	148	107	74.00	1
1972	13	22	5	1,230	204*	72.35	6
1973	18	30	6	1,527	141*	63.62	5
1973–4	10	16	3	960	261*	73.85	3
1974	21	36	6	1,783	160*	59.43	6
1975	19	34	8	1,915	201*	73.65	6
1976	12	24	5	1,288	207*	67.79	5
1977	20	30	5	1,701	191	68.04	7
1977–8	13	20	3	867	123*	51.00	3
1978	16	25	1	1,233	131	51.38	6
1978–9	12	23	3	533	90*	26.65	–
1979	15	20	5	1,538	175*	102.53	6
1979–80	8	15	4	599	110	54.45	2
1980	17	28	4	1,264	154*	52.67	3
1980–1	9	17	2	818	104*	54.53	1
1981	16	28	2	1,009	137	38.81	3
1981–2	12	21	5	905	105	56.56	2
1982	21	37	6	1,913	159	61.71	6
1983	23	40	5	1,941	214*	55.45	7
1984	20	35	10	1,567	153*	62.68	4
1985	21	34	12	1,657	184*	75.31	6
	596	994	161	47,434	261*	56.94	149

John Hugh Edrich

Born Blofield, Norfolk 21.6.1937.
Cousin of W.J.Edrich, Middlesex and England batsman.

1st 100: 112 Surrey –v– Notts, Trent Bridge 1959: Age 21 years, 329 days

100th: 101* Surrey –v– Derbyshire, The Oval 1977: Age 40 years, 21 days

CAREER RECORD AT TIME OF COMPLETING 100TH HUNDRED

945 Innings   38,783 Runs   45.84 Average

SOME STATISTICAL FEATS

HS 310* England –v– New Zealand, Leeds 1965: still the highest score for England in any Test at Leeds, the highest score against New Zealand in England and the highest Test score for England since the Second World War. It is also the highest score for England by a left-handed batsman. 238 of his runs came in boundaries – the highest number in any Test innings, while the 57 times the ball went to the boundary is another Test record.

Scored nine consecutive fifties during the 1965 season – the best run in England since G.E.Tyldesley's ten in 1926. The innings were: 139, 121*, 205*, 55, 96, 188, 92, 105, 310*.

With 5,138 runs Edrich is the highest scoring English left-hander in Tests after D.I.Gower.

RECORD IN TEST CRICKET

Tests	Inns	n.o.	Runs	H.S.	Av'ge	100s	50s
77	127	9	5,138	310*	43.54	12	24

SEASON-BY-SEASON: FIRST-CLASS MATCHES ONLY

Season	Matches	Inns	n.o.	Runs	H.S.	Av'ge	100s
1956	3	6	0	34	14	5.67	–
1957	1	2	0	7	7	3.50	–
1958	1	1	1	24	24*	–	–
1959	24	45	11	1,799	126	52.91	7
1959–60	2	4	0	189	151	47.25	1
1960	30	52	3	1,887	154	38.51	5
1961	31	58	0	1,928	129	33.24	5
1962	30	55	7	2,482	216	51.71	7
1962–3	5	10	0	425	136	42.50	1
1963	31	55	7	1,921	125	40.02	2
1963–4	6	8	1	386	150	55.14	1
1964	26	45	3	1,727	124	41.12	2
1965	28	44	7	2,319	310*	62.68	8
1965–6	16	25	1	1,060	133	44.17	3
1966	28	49	3	1,978	137	43.00	3
1967	31	47	5	2,077	226*	49.45	5
1967–8	10	17	1	739	146	46.19	1
1968	27	50	5	2,009	164	44.64	5
1968–9	6	8	1	377	177	53.86	1
1969	22	39	7	2,238	181	69.94	8
1970	21	37	3	1,586	143	46.65	5
1970–1	14	25	5	1,136	130	56.80	3
1971	24	44	1	2,031	195*	47.23	6
1972	18	33	3	1,305	168	43.50	4
1972–3	2	4	0	72	32	18.00	–
1973	20	34	4	1,039	109	34.63	2
1973–4	6	10	1	441	170	49.00	2
1974	16	23	2	1,126	152*	53.62	3
1974–5	13	19	4	576	70	38.40	–
1975	20	38	5	1,569	175	47.55	4
1976	19	37	4	1,526	179	46.24	5
1977	15	26	4	1,044	140	47.46	3
1978	18	29	5	733	114	30.54	1
	564	979	104	39,790	310*	45.47	103

Glenn Maitland Turner

Born Dunedin, New Zealand 26.5.1947.

The first New Zealander to complete one hundred hundreds.

1st 100:   106* Worcs –v– Middlesex, Worcester 1968: Age 21 years, 84
            days

100th: 311* Worcs –v– Warwickshire, Worcester 1982: Age 35
            years, 3 days

CAREER RECORD AT TIME OF COMPLETING 100TH HUNDRED

779 Innings   33,426 Runs   49.23 Average

SOME STATISTICAL FEATS

HS 311* Worcs –v– Warwickshire at Worcester 1982. The highest score
for a batsman to reach 100 hundreds with, and the only time the 100th
hundred has been reached before lunch on the first day of a match. This
was the best score by a New Zealander outside New Zealand, the best
score for Worcestershire in a first-class match.

Turner became, in 1979, the first batsman to score hundreds against all
17 first-class counties, the one against Worcs being scored for New
Zealand.

When scoring 141* out of 169 for Worcs –v– Glamorgan at Swansea in
1977 this was 83.4% of the total score – a record for monopolising an
innings.

Turner scored 1,244 runs (av. 77.75) in New Zealand alone in 1975–6, a
record for a New Zealand season. His 1,214 runs in the West Indies in
1971–2 are the highest for a New Zealander in the West Indies while his
four double centuries on that tour equalled the record of Hendren in
1929–30.

In Test cricket Turner's 855 runs –v– West Indies are a record for New
Zealand while his 7 Test centuries put him joint top with B.E.Congdon
among New Zealand players.

The 387 added for the first wicket by Turner and T.W.Jarvis –v– West
Indies at Georgetown in 1971–2 is the best partnership for New Zealand

262

for any wicket, and the best first wicket partnership in any Test involving the West Indies, home or away, for or against.

RECORD IN TEST CRICKET

Tests	Inns	n.o.	Runs	H.S.	Av'ge	100s	50s
41	73	6	2,991	259	44.64	7	14

Season	Matches	Inns	n.o.	Runs	H.S.	Av'ge	100s
1964–5	6	10	1	126	28	14.00	–
1965–6	6	11	4	330	95	47.14	–
1966–7	6	11	1	224	64	22.40	–
1967	2	3	1	23	14	11.50	–
1968	25	44	3	1,182	106*	28.83	1
1968–9	10	16	1	708	167	47.20	2
1969	23	41	7	1,146	124	33.71	1
1969–70	15	28	2	823	110	31.65	1
1970	25	46	7	2,379	154*	61.00	10
1970–1	9	17	1	525	76	32.81	–
1971	19	31	4	1,126	179	41.70	2
1971–2	17	27	5	1,708	259	77.64	5
1972	21	38	4	1,764	170	51.88	7
1972–3	11	17	1	787	132	49.19	2
1973	26	44	8	2,416	153*	67.11	9
1973–4	10	17	2	714	110*	47.60	3
1974	20	31	9	1,332	202*	60.55	3
1974–5	9	17	1	874	186*	54.63	4
1975	17	29	5	1,362	214*	56.75	3
1975–6	16	30	5	1,563	177*	62.52	5
1976	20	37	2	1,752	169	50.06	4
1976–7	16	29	2	1,173	177*	43.44	2
1977	22	38	5	1,380	153	41.82	3
1978	22	38	7	1,711	202*	55.19	6
1979	18	31	2	1,669	150*	57.55	8
1979–80	7	13	0	327	136	25.15	1
1980	21	35	4	1,817	228*	58.61	7
1981	24	42	4	2,101	168	55.29	9
1982	9	16	3	1,171	311*	90.08	5
1982–3	3	5	0	133	55	26.60	–
	455	792	101	34,346	311*	49.71	103

Syed Zaheer Abbas

Born Sialkot, Pakistan 24.7.1947.

1st 100: 197 Karachi –v– East Pakistan, Karachi 1968–9: Age 21 years, 127 days

100th: 215 Pakistan –v– India, Rawalpindi 1982–3: Age 35 years, 140 days

SOME STATISTICAL FEATS

HS 274 Pakistan –v– England, Edgbaston 1971: Still the best score for Pakistan in a Test match in England and the best by any team against England at Edgbaston.

Zaheer has scored two separate hundreds in one match on eight occasions, and thus holds the record for first-class cricket. W.R.Hammond lies second with seven. Zaheer has performed this feat in the County Championship on six occasions; this too is a record, J.B.Hobbs being second with five.

Four times has Zaheer scored a double century and a single century in the same match. Only M.R.Hallam (Leics), who performed the feat twice, has done it more than once.

In 1976 scored 216* and 156* for Gloucs –v– Surrey. His match aggregate of 372 is the highest in England by a batsman without being dismissed.

His 583 runs for Pakistan in the three match series with India in 1978/79 is the highest ever aggregate for a Test series of only three matches.

Zaheer's career record of 31,005 runs is the highest total by an Asian; Mushtaq Mohammed lies second with 30,777. Only R.E.Marshall (35,725) and G.M.Turner (34,213) among non-Englishmen have scored more first-class runs.

Zaheer reached 100 hundreds in 658 innings. Only D.G.Bradman (295), D.C.S.Compton (552), L.Hutton (619) and G.Boycott (645) have taken fewer innings. Zaheer's career record at the time of completing 100th 100: 658 innings: 80 n.o. 30,890 runs: 53.44 average.

STATISTICAL APPENDIX

RECORD IN TEST CRICKET

Tests	Inns	n.o.	Runs	H.S.	Av'ge	100s	50s
53	89	6	3,638	274	43.83	9	14

SEASON-BY-SEASON: FIRST-CLASS MATCHES ONLY

Season	Matches	Inns	n.o.	Runs	H.S.	Av'ge	100s
1965–6	1	2	1	23	19*	–	–
1967–8	2	2	0	48	31	24.00	–
1968–9	6	7	1	409	197	68.17	1
1969–70	13	21	4	939	136*	55.24	3
1970–1	8	11	1	962	202	96.20	5
1971	19	31	4	1,508	274	55.85	4
1971–2	11	19	0	709	112	37.32	2
1972	8	14	0	353	72	25.21	–
1972–3	19	33	5	1,227	170	43.82	5
1973	22	36	6	1,064	153*	35.47	2
1973–4	13	24	5	1,597	174	84.05	5
1974	21	30	4	1,182	240	45.46	5
1974–5	11	21	0	808	157	38.48	2
1975	16	31	1	1,426	123	47.53	2
1975–6	13	23	1	1,026	170	46.64	2
1976	21	39	5	2,554	230*	75.12	11
1976–7	16	29	1	850	101	30.36	1
1977	20	36	6	1,584	205*	52.80	5
1978	22	35	1	1,535	213	45.15	6
1978–9	12	20	2	1,231	235*	68.39	4
1979	17	30	2	1,304	151*	46.57	3
1979–80	15	26	3	935	170	40.65	3
1980	20	35	1	1,296	173	38.12	2
1980–1	12	22	10	1,123	154*	93.58	5
1981	21	36	10	2,306	215*	88.69	10
1981–2	8	10	1	595	134	66.11	2
1982	16	25	4	1,475	162*	70.24	5
1982–3	13	15	1	1,371	215	97.93	7
1983	12	19	0	867	116	45.63	3
1983–4	14	23	4	799	85	42.05	–
1984	14	28	4	738	157*	30.75	1
1984–5	8	12	1	403	168	36.64	1
1985	1	1	0	38	38	–	–
1985–6	2	1	0	4	4	4	–
–	447	747	89	43,289	274	52.11	107

Dennis Leslie Amiss

Born Harborne, Birmingham 7.4.1943.

1st 100:   114 Warwickshire v Oxford University, Edgbaston 1964:
           Age 21 years, 86 days

100th: 101* Warwickshire v Lancashire, Edgbaston 1986: Age 43
           years, 113 days

CAREER RECORD AT TIME OF COMPLETING 100TH HUNDRED

1,081 Innings   41,866 Runs   43.61 Average

SOME STATISTICAL FEATS

HS 262* England –v– West Indies, Kingston 1973–74. This is the highest second innings score for England overseas. Only P.B.H.May (285* –v– West Indies at Edgbaston, 1957) exceeds the score for the second innings of any England Test match, anywhere.

Has scored 76 centuries for Warwickshire in first-class cricket, which is a record for the county, while his total of 33,589 runs for Warwickshire (as at 29.7.86) is beaten only by W.G.Quaife, who scored 33,842.

Amiss has more than 1,000 runs and at least one century for Warwickshire against every other county in first-class matches. No other Warwickshire player has achieved this feat. Amiss also holds the unique record of having scored a century against all the teams outside touring teams to have played against Warwickshire in first-class matches during his career. These teams are Oxford and Cambridge University, Scotland and MCC.

When Amiss made his Test debut, against West Indies at The Oval in 1966, he had yet to score a County Championship century. M.C. Cowdrey and E.R.Dexter were also chosen by England for their batting before their maiden championship hundreds.

Amiss scored 1,379 runs in Tests during 1974. He was the third English batsman to achieve 1,000 Test runs in a year, after D.C.S.Compton and K.F.Barrington, and his total remains a record for England.

Eight of Amiss's 11 Test centuries were of more than 150 runs.

STATISTICAL APPENDIX

RECORD IN TEST CRICKET

Tests	Inns	n.o.	Runs	H.S.	Av'ge	100s	50s
50	88	10	3,612	262*	46.30	11	11

SEASON-BY-SEASON: FIRST-CLASS MATCHES ONLY

Season	Matches	Inns	n.o.	Runs	H.S.	Av'ge	100s
1960	7	9	3	135	43*	22.50	–
1961	4	7	0	106	41	15.14	–
1962	9	15	1	352	62	25.14	–
1963	9	17	1	312	58	19.50	–
1964	8	16	3	307	114	23.62	1
1965	32	53	2	1,433	86	28.10	–
1966	29	52	5	1,765	160*	37.55	2
1966–7	7	11	2	575	131	63.89	2
1967	26	43	9	1,850	176*	54.41	5
1967–8	4	8	1	271	109	38.72	1
1968	30	46	4	1,222	128	29.09	2
1969	30	51	3	1,539	120	32.06	1
1970	27	48	10	1,757	110	46.24	2
1970–1	1	2	0	36	34	18.00	–
1971	25	37	3	1,294	124	38.06	2
1972	18	29	7	1,219	192	55.41	5
1972–3	12	23	4	861	158	45.32	2
1973	23	39	9	1,634	146*	54.47	3
1973–4	9	16	1	1,120	262*	74.67	5
1974	18	31	3	1,510	195	53.93	5
1974–5	15	23	2	983	164*	46.81	3
1975	19	37	2	1,564	158*	44.69	4
1976	21	38	6	2,110	203	65.94	8
1976–7	12	20	1	868	179	45.68	2
1977	19	34	5	1,513	162*	52.17	6
1978	23	41	3	2,030	162	53.42	7
1979	22	37	3	1,672	232*	49.18	6
1980	23	42	2	1,686	117*	42.15	1
1981	22	41	0	1,722	145	42.00	6
1981–2	4	7	2	308	73*	61.60	–
1982	21	38	1	1,404	156	37.95	1
1983	26	43	4	1,721	164	44.13	3
1984	26	50	10	2,239	122	55.98	6
1985	26	44	5	1,555	140	39.87	5
1986	18	33	4	1,193	110	41.13	4
	625	1,081	121	41,866	262*	43.61	100

BATSMEN WHO SCORED MORE THAN 80 CENTURIES

J.W.Hearne	96
C.B.Fry	94
I.V.A.Richards	91
W.J.Edrich	86
G.S.Sobers	86
J.T.Tyldesley	86
P.B.H.May	85
R.E.S.Wyatt	85
J.Hardstaff, Jnr	83
R.B.Kanhai	83
A.I.Kallicharran	82
M.Leyland	80
B.A.Richards	80

Index

Abel, R. 15, 29, 221
Abid Ali 202
Adcock, N.A.T. 133, 149, 156, 157
Alcock, C.W. 22
Allen, D.A. 147–8
Allen, G.O. 35, 40, 41, 47, 67–8, 74,
   77–8, 80, 91, 101, 109, 115, 117,
   140, 145, 246
Ames, L.E.G. 33, 34, 40, 58, 62, 63,
   64, 65, 66, 80, 86, 91, 97, 99, 101,
   109, 111, 113–20, 154, 215,
   246–7
Amiss, D.L. 3, 149, 156, 160, 171,
   172, 179, 181, 190, 197–210, 215,
   268–70
Andrews, W.H.R. 112
Arlott, John 37, 38,
Armstrong, W.W. 64, 107
Arnold, G.G. 186
Ashdown, W.H. 113, 246
Asif Iqbal 161
Astill, W.E. 34
Atkinson, C.R.M. 182

Bailey, T.E. 129, 146, 157, 211
Bannister, Jack 198
Bannister, Roger 161
Barber, R.W. 179, 180
Barlow, E.J. 182
Barnes, S.F. 15, 61, 244
Barrington, K.F. 98, 159, 166, 182,
   199, 200, 255, 268

Bedser, A.V. 45, 67, 83, 87, 98, 101,
   105, 106, 109, 111, 125, 128, 139,
   149, 169
Beldam, G.W. 49
Benaud, R.B. 129, 145, 151, 155
Bishen Bedi 194, 202
Blythe, C. 21, 22, 59, 60, 62
Booth, Major 25, 122
Bosanquet, B.J.T. 10, 30
Botham, I.T. 14, 58, 67, 77, 161, 183,
   184
Bowes, W.E. 28, 33, 36, 41–3, 54, 57,
   58, 63–4, 68, 73, 74, 80, 91, 102,
   104, 109, 121, 122, 123, 129
Bowley, F.L. 21
Boycott, G. 1, 2, 48, 55, 75, 122, 129,
   142, 150, 162–74, 175, 180, 181,
   182, 183, 187, 192, 193, 194, 197,
   202, 203, 205, 208, 215, 239, 255,
   258–9, 265
Bradman, Sir D.G. 1, 2, 3, 5, 7, 8, 14,
   27, 28, 29, 30, 32, 47, 48, 62, 70,
   78, 84, 85, 86, 87, 97, 100–12,
   117, 118, 121, 123, 124, 125, 137,
   140, 144, 153, 161, 194, 215, 236,
   238, 243–5, 265
Braund, L.C. 10
Brearley, J.M. 163, 170, 171, 173,
   192
Brearley, W. 21
Briggs, J. 16
Brown, A.S. 151

Brown, D.J. 149, 178, 180, 182, 185, 192, 198, 204, 206, 207
Brown, F.R. 33, 36, 38, 50, 54, 64, 83, 89, 126, 127, 137, 139, 145, 146, 154, 157
Brown, J.T. 24

Cardus, Sir Neville 48, 57, 68, 88
Cartwright, T.W. 156
Chandra 202
Chapman, A.P.F. 85, 100, 101, 113
Chappell, G.S. 6, 97, 153
Chappell, I.M. 160, 187, 191, 244
Chester, F. 64, 67
Chipperfield, A.G. 82
Close, D.B. 121, 158, 165, 166, 169, 172, 181, 202, 205
Coldwell, L.J. 150
Collinge, R.O. 179
Compton, D.C.S. 1, 3, 5, 14, 21, 27, 29, 48, 53, 54, 55, 79, 86, 93, 109, 111, 114, 116, 124, 125, 129, 130, 132–41, 145, 204, 215, 221, 224, 231, 250–2, 265, 268
Congdon, B.E. 262
Constable, B.D. 176
Constantine, Sir L.N. 2, 36, 50, 53, 91, 118
Cook, C. ('Sam') 92
Cornwallis, Capt. Hon. W.S. 62
Cotter, A.E. 45
Cowdrey, M.C. 1, 2, 6, 8, 75, 88, 121, 124, 140, 143, 146, 151, 153–61, 166, 179, 199, 215, 239, 255–7, 258, 268
Crapp, J.F. 144
Cresswell, J. 20
Cricketer 64
Croft, C.E.H. 45, 195
Croome, A.C.M. 13

Dalmeny, Lord 29, 30
Daniel, W.W. 181
Denness, M.H. 149, 159, 169, 180
Dennett, G.E. 84

Denton, D. 4, 21
Dexter, E.R. 65, 88, 103, 143, 155, 158, 268
Dipper, A.E. 78, 80
D'Oliveira, B.L. 147, 148, 158, 166, 185
Douglas J.W.H.T. 72, 91
Drake, A. 25
Ducat, A. 78
Duckworth, G. 81, 86
Duleepsinjhi, K.S. 101

Edrich, J.H. 75, 98, 159, 160, 166, 171, 173, 175–82, 205, 215, 260–1
Edrich, W.J. 5, 53, 54, 88, 109, 114, 124, 125, 128, 136, 138, 139, 176, 221, 251, 260, 271
Elliot, C.S. 82–3
Emburey, J.E. 192
Emmett, G.M. 89, 144
Emmett, T. 10, 12
Evans, A.J. 78
Evans, T.G. 65, 114, 116, 117, 119, 128, 130, 132, 140, 146, 156

Fairfax, A.G. 58
Farnes, K. 68, 91, 138
Faulkner, G.A. 24
Fender, P.G.H. 22, 25, 35–6, 43–4, 45, 65, 99
Ferguson, W.H. 36
Fielder, A. 22
Fingleton, J.H. 101, 107, 108, 244
Flavell, J.A. 150
Fleetwood-Smith, L. O'B. 80, 124
Fletcher, K.W.R 149
Foster, F.R. 62
Foster, R.E. 29, 30
Freeman, A.P. 22, 40, 113, 114, 117, 118, 135
Freeman, G. 10
Frindall, W. 54
Frith, D. 64–5
Fry, C.B. 3, 4, 6, 11, 29, 31, 78, 221

Gatting, M. 200
Gavaskar, S.M. 6, 153, 171, 187, 194, 241
Geary, G. 102, 118
Gibbs, L.R. 148, 199
Giffen, G. 10
Gifford, N. 148, 150, 164, 178, 182, 188, 189
Gilligan, A.E.R. 96
Goddard, T.L. 88, 138
Goddard, T.W. 34, 69, 87, 92, 115, 133, 135
Gooch, G.A. 170, 173
Gover, A.R. 34, 35, 41, 52, 53, 64, 67, 72–3, 98, 101, 116, 140, 157
Gower, D.I. 151, 260
Grace, E.M. 13, 19
Grace, G.F. 19
Grace, W.G. 1, 2, 3, 4, 7, 8, 9–19, 20, 21, 24, 25, 27, 28, 29, 30, 39, 48, 55, 67, 75, 84, 93, 94, 97, 100, 102, 103, 113, 146, 153, 215, 216–20, 224, 231
Graveney, D.A. 195
Graveney, T.W. 115, 128, 129, 133, 142–52, 159, 166, 183, 185, 192, 215, 253–4
Gregory, J.M. 42, 59, 78
Gregory, R.J. 44
Greig, A.W. 160, 205
Griffith, C, 148, 149, 180, 199
Grimmett, C.V. 34, 42, 80, 101, 118
Gunn, G. 4, 50
Gunn, J. 21

Hadlee, R.J. 184, 192
Haig, N.E. 2, 64
Hall, W.W. 148, 149, 154, 180, 199, 200
Hallam, M.R. 265
Hammond, W.R. 1, 2, 3, 7, 8, 9, 27, 29, 39, 40, 47, 48, 61, 67, 69, 75, 78, 79, 82–92, 101, 103, 105, 111, 113, 114, 117, 118, 119, 121, 122, 123, 127, 140, 143, 144, 146, 175, 183, 193, 215–17, 221, 238–40, 255, 258, 265
Hampshire, J.H. 149, 164, 168
Hanif Mohammad 6, 243, 244, 248
Hardinge, H.T.W. 78, 113
Hardstaff, J. Jnr 48, 53, 89, 91, 101, 124, 131, 135, 140, 248, 271
Hardstaff, J. Snr 96–7
Harris, Lord 4, 75, 84, 85
Harvey, R.N. 5, 6, 110, 139, 250
Hassett, A.L. 6, 8
Hawke, Lord 23, 27, 42, 73
Hayes, E.G. 21
Hayes, Frank 203
Hayward, D. 20, 26
Hayward, T.W. 20–6, 28, 29, 30, 38, 39, 61, 75, 95, 97, 121, 151, 177, 215, 221–3, 238
Hazare, V.S. 6, 8
Hazell, H.L. 90
Headley, G.A. 5, 70, 185
Hearne, J.T. 48
Hearne, J.W. 49, 51, 271
Heine, P.S. 133, 149
Hendren, E.H. 7, 27, 39, 40, 42, 47–56, 57, 58, 59, 67, 70, 71, 96, 97, 134, 135, 215, 229–30, 241
Higgs, K. 204
Hirst, G.H. 10, 25, 121
Hitch, J.W. 77
Hobbs, Sir J.B. 1, 2, 3, 4, 7, 8, 9, 14, 20, 22, 23, 24, 25, 26, 27–38, 39, 40, 45, 47, 52–3, 55, 67, 68, 69, 71, 76, 79, 84, 91, 93, 94, 95, 96, 97, 98, 99, 100, 102, 103, 110, 111, 121, 138, 140, 175, 176, 177, 183, 194, 215, 221, 224–6, 229, 231, 250, 265
Holding, M.A. 45, 170, 181, 195, 204, 205
Holmes, P. 70, 73, 75, 94, 130, 171, 233
Hookes, D.W. 221
Hopwood, J.L. 76, 80, 81
Hornby, A.N. 16

Howell, M. 65
Huish, F.E. 59
Hulme, J. 52
Hutton, Sir L. 3, 4, 5, 7, 9, 28, 32, 48,
  71, 75, 80, 88, 93, 105, 111, 114,
  121–31, 132, 143, 145, 148, 151,
  154, 155, 160, 165, 215, 238,
  248–9
Hylton, L.G. 118

Ibadulla, K. 184, 189
Ikin, J.T. 104
Illingworth, R. 121, 127, 131, 154,
  158, 161, 164, 168, 169, 172, 173,
  174, 180, 202
Imran Khan 45, 138

Jackman, R.D. 178, 179, 181–2
Jackson, 'Foghorn' 10
Jackson, Hon. F.S. 3, 18
Jackson, H.L. 127, 142, 177
Jameson, John 200, 201, 203
Jardine, D.R. 36, 38, 50, 63, 101
Jarvis, T.W. 262
Jenkins, R.O. 126, 139
Jessop, G.L. 10, 28
Johnston, W.A. 7, 145
Jones, E. 10
Jupp, V.W.C. 42, 69

Kallicharran, Alvin 197, 200, 206
Kanhai, R.B. 3, 5, 6, 197, 200, 201,
  211
Kapil Dev 193
Kelleway, C. 68, 107
Kennedy, A.S. 45
Kilner, R. 25, 73
Knight, D.J. 50, 95, 96
Knott, A.P.E. 117, 120, 149, 159,
  162, 172, 178, 187, 197, 203, 204,
  208
Knox, N.A. 15, 21
Kortright, C.J. 21

Laker, J.C. 34, 101, 105, 106, 115,

127, 142, 146, 153, 154, 157, 162,
  169, 171
Lambert, W. 217
Langridge, James 133
Langridge, John 37–8, 133
Larter, J.D.F. 150
Larwood, H. 36, 51, 53, 91, 95, 103,
  104, 115 '
Lawrence, J. 164
Lee, H.W. 49
Leveson-Gower, H.D.G. 15, 18, 31
Levett, W.H.V. 62, 117
Lewis, Tony 202
Leyland, M. 41, 57, 63, 115, 118,
  123, 248, 271
Lillee, D.K. 3, 14, 45, 154, 159, 160,
  171, 177, 181, 203, 204, 208
Lilley, A.A. 21
Lindwall, R.R. 7, 22, 122, 125, 128,
  130, 133, 136, 137, 145, 149
Lloyd, C.H. 5, 170, 171
Lock, G.A.R. 127, 137, 157
Lockwood, W.H. 10
Lohmann, G.A. 10
Lord, Gordon 209
Luckhurst, B.W. 160, 180
Lyon, B.H. 44

Macartney, C.G. 5, 106, 189, 227
Macaulay, G.G. 33, 34, 36, 72
MacDonald, E.A. 42, 49, 59, 77, 84,
  85, 91, 96
MacGregor, G. 49
MacLaren, A.C. 6, 25, 29, 81, 217
McCabe, S.J. 109, 111, 117, 118, 140
McCormick, E.L. 88
Madan Lal 193
Mailey, A.A. 34, 69
Makepeace, H. 77
Mansoor Akhtar 233
Marsh, Rodney 204
Marshall, R.E. 265
Marriott, C.S. 113
Martindale, E.A. 36, 53, 118
Matthews, A.D.G. 35

May, P.B.H. 3, 124, 140, 142, 143, 145, 146, 148, 154, 155, 156, 157, 158, 159, 161, 204, 231, 255, 268, 271

Mead, C.P. 1, 8, 27, 39–46, 57, 61, 62, 63, 96, 215, 227–8

Mercer, J. 32, 37, 62, 95

Merchant, V.M. 229

Merritt, W.E. 115

Miller, K.R. 7, 87, 125, 128, 130, 133, 136, 149, 158

Milton, C.A. 92, 143

Mitchell, A. 122, 135

Mitchell, T.B. 51

Mohsin Khan 193

Morris, A.R. 250

Mortimore, J.B. 147–8

Mosey, Don 165, 173

Moss, Alan 165

Motz, R.C. 179, 184

Murray, Derryck 201

Murray, J.T. 113, 156

Mushtaq Mohammad 265

Newman, J.A. 43

Nicholls, M.S. 91

Noble, M.A. 10, 122

Nupen, E.P. 79

O'Keefe, Kerry 208

O'Reilly, W.J. 53, 63, 68, 69, 87, 89, 118, 123, 124, 131, 158

Oakman, A.S.M. 146

Oldfield, W.A. 118

Oldroyd, E. 122

Ormrod, A.J. 188–9, 190

Oslear, D. 173

Packer, K. 3, 195, 197, 206, 207

Parfitt, P.H. 149

Parker, C.W.L. 33, 34, 35, 69, 83, 88–9, 91, 115, 119

Parker, J.F. 106

Parkin, C.H. 34, 40, 77, 84

Parks, J.M. 146, 199

Pawley, Tom 60

Peach, H.A. 52

Peate, E. 10

Peebles, I.A.R. 48, 51, 101, 111

Peel, R. 10, 123

Perks, R.T.D. 137

Pollard, R. 110

Pollock, P.M. 177

Pollock, R.G. 6

Ponsford, W.H. 6, 231, 244

Porritt, A. (W.G.'s 'Ghost') 17

Pugh, C.T.M. 147

Pullar, G. 156

Quaife, W.G. 268

Rait-Kerr, Col. R.S. 136

Ramadhin, K.T. 159

Randall, D.W. 170

Ranjitsinhji, K.S. 3, 8, 10, 20

Read, H.D. 36

Reid, J.R. 250

Rhodes, W. 4, 10, 19, 21, 25, 30, 42, 50, 54–5, 83, 84, 102, 152

Richards, B.A. 271

Richards, C.J. 114

Richards, I.V.A. 3, 171, 183, 271

Richardson, A.J. 34

Richardson, T. 10, 29, 49

Richardson, V.Y. 58, 103

Roberts, A.M.E. 45, 181, 205

Robertson, J.D. 133, 229

Robertson-Glasgow, R.C. 81, 94

Robins, R.W.V. 42, 51, 80, 101, 135, 136, 140

Robinson, E. 73

Root, C.F. 102

Russell, E. 199

Ryan, M. 133

Sandham, A. 6, 7, 38, 39, 75, 93–9, 101, 176, 177, 182, 215, 229, 241–2

Schwarz, R.O. 24, 30

Sellers, A.B. 134, 169
Shaw, A. 10
Shaw, J.H. 11
Shepherd, D.J. 142, 146
Sheppard, Rev. D.S. 128
Shrewsbury, A. 1, 121
Simpson, R.B. 5
Sims, J.M. 55–6, 119
Sinfield, R.A. 33, 45, 69, 88, 89, 94, 109, 111, 115
Small, Joe 53
Smith, Alan 201, 208–9
Smith, E.J. ('Tiger') 198
Smith, M.J.K. 149, 153, 154, 155, 157, 172, 182, 198, 199, 201, 202, 207
Snow, J.A. 158, 205
Sobers, Sir G.S. 3, 5, 6, 8, 57, 149, 153, 158, 199, 248, 255, 271
Solkar, E.D. 169
Spofforth, F.R. 10
Spooner, R.H. 10
Sportsman 18
Squires, H.S. 93
Statham, J.B. 127, 142
Steel, A.G. 1
Stevens, G.T.S. 38
Stewart, M.J. 179
Strudwick, H. 35
Surridge, W.S. 98
Sutcliffe, H. 1, 6, 8, 28, 33, 34, 38, 39, 48, 67–74, 79, 91, 94, 96, 103, 111, 114, 121, 122, 123, 130, 131, 136, 173, 175, 215, 233–5, 258

Tarrant, 'Tear 'Em' 10
Tate, M.W. 37, 46, 68, 83, 95, 100, 107, 140
Tattersall, R. 142
Tayfield, H.J. 138, 157
Taylor, B.R. 179
Taylor, Lynton 207
Taylor, R.W. 114
Tennyson, Hon. L.H. 43
Thompson, Roley 198

Thomson, J.R. 45, 154, 177, 203, 208
Titmus, F.J. 135, 139, 151, 157, 159, 161, 164, 175, 182
Trueman, F.S. 122, 154, 177
Trumper, V.T. 6, 10, 55, 76, 102, 125, 136
Tunnicliffe, J. 83, 84, 86, 122
Turnbull, M.J. 32
Turner, G.M. 1, 2, 3, 5, 75, 183–92, 215, 229, 262–4, 265
Tyldesley, G.E. 75–81, 221, 236–7, 243, 260
Tyldesley, J.T. 3, 4, 7, 21, 29, 60–1, 75–6, 215, 227, 236, 271
Tyldesley, R.K. 77, 84, 101
Tyson, F.H. 128, 177

Underwood, D.L. 182, 185, 186, 194, 204, 207, 208

Valentine, B.H. 113, 119
Venkat 202
Verity, H. 43–4, 58, 74, 110, 111, 118, 123, 138
Vigar, F.H. 102
Voce, W. 36, 67, 103, 105
Vogler, A.E.E. 24, 30

Waheed Mirza 233
Wait, O.J. 130
Wakeley, B.J. 103
Walcott, C.L. 5, 233, 246
Walker, M.H.N. 170, 208
Walsh, J.E. 136
Walters, K.D. 156
Wardle, J.H. 121, 126, 127, 130, 138
Warner, Sir P.F. 29, 49, 71, 85, 103
Warr, J.J. 119
Washbrook, C. 87, 124, 125
Weekes, E.D. 5, 6
Weighall, G.J.V. 41, 42, 116
Wells, B.D. ('Bomber') 140
White, G.C. 24
White, J.C. 53
Whitehouse, John 200, 201

Wickham, Preb. A.P. 12
Wilkinson, C.T.A. 25
Willis, R.G.D. 160, 164, 173, 182, 187, 189, 195, 208
Wisden Cricketers Almanack 1, 3, 4, 19, 20, 48, 95, 216
Wood, A. 123
Wood, B. 74, 164
Woodfull, W.M. 6, 110, 118
Woods, S.M.J. 12–13
Wooller, W. 146
Woolley, F.E. 1, 3, 4, 8, 22, 27, 39, 40, 41, 42, 47, 57–66, 67, 76, 79, 101, 111, 113, 114, 116, 119, 140, 142, 151, 153, 215, 217, 227, 231–2

Worrell, Sir F.M. 5, 6, 233, 241
Wright, D.V.P. 65, 66, 83, 87, 105, 111, 114, 116, 118, 133, 138, 145, 154, 160
Wyatt, R.E.S. 35, 40, 44, 51, 58, 63, 64, 65, 68, 69, 80, 91, 101, 118, 271

Yardley, N.W.D. 68, 72, 91, 105, 111, 114, 124, 126, 129
Young, J.A. 119

Zaheer Abbas 5, 170, 171, 193–6, 215, 238, 265–7